Personnel Management for the Single European Market

Personnel Management for the
Single European Market

Mark Pinder

Pitman

Pitman Publishing
128 Long Acre, London WC2E 9AN

A division of Longman Group UK Limited

First published in Great Britain in 1990

© Mark Pinder 1990

British Library Cataloguing in Publication Data

Pinder, Mark
  Personnel management for the Single European Market.
  1. European Community Countries. Personnel management
  I. Title
  658.30094

ISBN 0 273 03230 5

All rights reserved; no part of this publication may be reproduced,
stored in a retrieval system, or transmitted in any form or by any other
means, electronic, mechanical, photocopying, recording, or otherwise
without either the prior written permission of the Publishers or a
licence permitting restricted copying in the United Kingdom issued by the
Copyright Licensing Agency, 33-34 Alfred Place, London WC1E 7DP. This
book may not be lent, resold, hired out or otherwise disposed of by way
of trade in any form of binding or cover other than that in which it is
published, without the prior consent of the publishers.

Typeset in Great Britain
Printed in Great Britain by The Bath Press, Avon

Contents

Introduction

The advent of the Single European Market must surely be one of the most widely publicised happenings of the 1990s. Hardly a day goes by without reference in the press to the latest European Community developments, be they the process of debate and legislation in Brussels, the speeches of our own political leaders or newly publicised reports and views as to what the real effects are going to be. A great boost to the publicity process in this country has been the Department of Trade and Industry's 'Europe Open for Business' campaign which, in addition to setting out pretty clearly the British Government's standpoint, has raised awareness so much amongst the business community and the public at large.

But – what is the true nature of the process of change that is taking place? How many of us have a *real* understanding of the issues and likely outcomes, both generally and in the field of our own specialism? The problem is that unlike many other processes of change, there is no definitive agenda for managers in responding to the challenges set by the Single Market Programme. The issues to be faced by individual companies will vary greatly according to such factors as size, product type, competitor strength; the key question of where to position oneself in the wider market being particularly dependent on a wide range of variables. Is this perhaps because it is so difficult to hit upon the correct response that, despite the plethora of information on the subject, so little appears to be happening. Survey after survey has revealed that, while awareness among managers of the Single Market is high, a very small proportion is actually doing anything about it.

Taking the broadest possible perspective, the Single Market presents all of us with threats and opportunities. This is clearly foreseen by Michael Heseltine, the most pro-European of leading Conservative politicians, in his book *The Challenge of Europe: Can Britain Win?*: He writes:

'There are many unanswered questions but they do not obscure the opportunities for Britain in a single European market, nor the uncomfortable fact that opportunities confer no rights. The new openings presented by 1992 will find many British companies ready to seize the advantages of a dramatically expanded home market of more than 320 million consumers. But for some companies, some industrial sectors, even whole regions, the change will present overwhelming problems. There will be both winners and losers.'

The key message coming from this statement is that it is those who seize the opportunities who will be the 'winners', those who remain passive the 'losers'. No-one would pretend that the issues raised by the Single Market Programme are anything but complex. But it is those companies which are prepared to do the necessary groundwork now that will succeed in the long run. Starting from the broad, strategic perspective, they will be able to analyse the mass of information being generated and distil from this their own particular responses and action plans as their sphere of operation becomes inexorably more and more competitive.

As it is for companies, so it will be for personnel professionals. It is easy enough to sit back and take the view that the Single Market is of more relevance to those concerned with sales and marketing, distribution or manufacturing. But if personnel management is to consolidate the more dynamic, results-oriented role it has developed during the 1980s, it must look just as closely at the problems and issues raised. It must contribute to the full to the complex process of business management, involving as it does the development of corporate strategies that are fully appropriate to the needs of the organisation, and take account of all the variables.

The main objective of this book is first to identify and then to analyse the set of variables arising from the Single Market Programme that are of relevance to the personnel manager. From this, it will examine the potential change in human resources policy and practice throughout the 1990s, with particular emphasis on how Europeanisation will both accelerate existing processes of change, and create change in new areas and directions. I am fully aware that this is a complex task. I use the term 'variable' advisedly, as even as the Programme approaches its 'target' date of 31 December 1992, there are few known facts about the shape of things to come. But for personnel professionals as for other business managers, it *is* possible now to identify many of the potential impacts, the threats and opportunities, and the issues that will be of importance to us as we carry out our work throughout this decade.

I have tried as far as possible to retain a practical rather than a theoretical perspective in writing this book. Thus, I consider in detail the issues that are happening now, the declared intentions of politicians in Brussels and at Westminster, and above all the real responses of Personnel

Managers to changes perceived to be taking place. I also put into a European context some of the other major issues to be faced up to during the 1990s, such as the great change to the shape of the working population caused by demographic trends. But equally, I am trying to project forward, to offer a realistic and comprehensive view of what may happen in the future if particular initiatives are brought to fruition. In this the book is more challenging; my aim is not to prove a point so much as to provoke a response in the interests of ensuring that factors which may prove to be of great relevance are not overlooked. I ask not therefore that you agree with all my conclusions, but that you seriously consider the issues raised in terms of your own particular response to the challenge set by the Single Market.

In terms of structure the book falls into four distinct sections, each of which interlocks with the others, and which taken as a whole examine the issues raised in a logical sequence.

Part One takes a global view of the Single European Market, examining its origins and the declared objectives of the European Commission in bringing it to fruition. Most important, the details of the Single Market Programme are considered in the context of what their likely impacts will be. My aim here is to look at the issues from a business management prospective, as it is within this framework that personnel managers must operate effectively and make their contribution to the success of the organisation.

This section of the book also examines in some detail the political response within the UK to the broad initiatives being taken by the Commissioners in Brussels. The political debate is seen as key to the direction taken in the long term. In particular, I use the so-called 'Social Agenda' – a major set of initiatives of immense significance to employment and employee relations within the European Community – as the focus for this examination. This is appropriate as the Social Agenda has been one of the main causes of friction between Brussels and Westminster, and is of particular relevance to personnel professionals.

Part Two looks in detail at the challenges for the Personnel Manager that will arise during the 1990s, stemming directly from the process of Europeanisation or being accelerated by it. These challenges are seen as broadly of three types, which are reflected by the three chapters in this section of the book.

In the first, the Social Agenda is examined more closely for its actual content. Many individual initiatives are contained within it, of greater or lesser relevance to Personnel Managers and with greater or lesser chances of success; starting from a global perspective, those initiatives that are seen as of greatest potential importance are picked out and subjected to more detailed consideration.

In the second, the likely impacts arising from the changing business environment of the Single Market are carefully examined. Though in many cases less easy to define than proposed employment legislation, they may nevertheless be of greater significance as they stem directly from changes to employee and management attitudes, the nature of the workplace and most importantly the threats and opportunities to business in the wider market that need to be addressed by Personnel Managers.

In the third, the threats caused by demographic change to the working population across Europe are considered. While the general issue is of great concern to employers throughout the Community the specific differences between the UK and the rest of Europe create a particular challenge.

Part Three describes the ways in which the Personnel Manager can meet the challenges set. At one level, the response must be strategic; a company's personnel strategy must support and underpin its business strategy, and key decisions must therefore be taken which will influence the direction of the business in the European Market. Other major factors may include planning for and coping with changed operational circumstances, deciding on a centralised or decentralised management structure, and a mergers and acquisitions strategy.

At a second level the response must be operational. Individual chapters making up this section of the book will review these looking in particular at recruitment and resourcing, training and development, remuneration issues and employee communication and involvement.

Part Four of the book will link the three previous sections by the use of case studies. In illustrating different responses to the challenge of the Single Market it will also demonstrate how individual Personnel Managers and human resources professionals can adopt an approach that is, at the same time, both strategic and practical.

In the first chapter of this section the case studies presented are taken from the IT industry sector. For various reasons this sector is one of the most advanced in developing pan-European thinking, having adopted a

European market perspective long before the Single Market Programme was put in motion.

The second chapter will illustrate the responses of Personnel Managers in companies that, broadly speaking, come from the service sector. Very different in terms of the nature of the services offered, as well as in structure and size, these responses make an interesting contrast.

The third chapter will illustrate that, for companies that operate in what can be loosely defined as the manufacturing sector, there are particularly complex challenges and issues to be faced. This is true for companies that have been in international business for many years, as well as those going into Europe for the first time.

In coming full circle from a description of broad issues to illustrations of how these are actually being addressed I hope to present a comprehensive overview of the impact the Single Market will have on employment affairs within the UK. This book is intended to be a practical guide for personnel professionals who will inevitably encounter many of the issues raised during the 1990s.

Part one
The Single European Market in context

1 The development of the Single European Market

The words 'nineteen ninety-two' have become so much of a totem in the last two years that it is ironic that the date itself of 31 December, 1992 – that fixed for the completion of the Single Market Programme – is actually of relatively low importance to the progress of events as they unfold. This is not to say that their significance as a target, both symbolic and actual, should be underestimated: the appointed date, and particularly the nearness of it, has served wonderfully to concentrate the minds of legislators and businessmen alike. As it is put succinctly by the European Commission itself in publicising the Programme it has taken up with such determination, '1992 . . . is just around the corner! '

However, it should be realised that the creation of the pan-European free market is a *process* rather than an event, and will therefore gather momentum both in the months leading up to 1992 and in the months and years thereafter. It does not matter that the legislative programme is unlikely to be completed by the deadline set; the ongoing process is one that will be determined as much by the efforts of individual people and businesses as by the legislative framework being debated and passed, item by item, by the European Commission, Council and Parliament in Brussels. This, of course, is one of the most challenging aspects of the Single Market Programme – the process is one that we can all influence, as we plan our business strategies for the 1990s and carry them forward to implementation.

I make no apologies for beginning this book on human resources issues with a chapter that aims to take a wider perspective, and therefore mentions 'human resources' hardly at all. Personnel management is part of the complex process of business management; it cannot take place in a vacuum and must both underpin and be complementary to the corporate strategy of the organisation. A fundamental theme running through the book will be that personnel professionals need to be able to adopt a genuinely strategic approach if important issues such as staff cultural values, employment laws and norms and the many human inputs to cost-effective, forward-looking business planning are to be taken into account. To do this they must have in-depth understanding of the major trends, impacts and changes that affect employment, of which the Single Market Programme will certainly be one of the most significant throughout this decade.

This chapter, therefore, sets out to explain as fully and clearly as possible what the overall impacts of the Single Market Programme are likely to be. The purposes behind legislation, as well as the legislative processes themselves, will be explained. The key components of the Social Charter, within which most of the issues concerning employment and personnel management are addressed will also be given consideration. I shall begin, however, by putting the Programme in the context of the development of the European Community itself, exploring in particular the dynamic tensions that have so galvanised and transformed the Commission towards achieving its purpose.

The Single Market Programme in context

'But, by choosing a large, frontier-free market by 1992 as its goal, the European Community has undoubtedly hit upon the venture most likely to rekindle a forlornly guttering flame.' These words, taken from the European Commission's publicity booklet for the Single Market Programme, *Deadline 92*, are typical of much of the fine rhetoric being used to sell the economic vision of Jacques Delors to citizens and businesses of the Community throughout Europe. Other phrases are indeed stirring:

'The European Community is at long last . . . becoming a source of hope';

'The steps taken towards the 1992 deadline are irreversible';

'The countries of Europe are staking their survival in a world race against the clock'.

The blueprint for a frontier-free Europe is described as a 'revolution within a revolution', to some perhaps striking uncomfortable parallels with the Revolution that took place in France almost exactly 200 years ago!

There is, however, a considerable amount of substance behind the rhetoric, and a considerable message to be put across. By 'revolution within a revolution', the Commission is anxious to convey the view that, first, economic progress can only come about if there is a considerable degree of political harmony between the Member States; and second, that the institutions of the Community themselves must act in concert and with a strong sense of purpose if the goal is to be achieved. A clear comparison is therefore made between the politically fragmented Western Europe that existed for centuries until the recent past, and the ineffectiveness of the 'strange tribe – the Eurocrats' that presided over Community affairs in Brussels throughout the later 1960s and 1970s.

The extent to which the present Commission is prepared to be openly critical of its predecessors of even as recently as seven years ago is somewhat surprising, but does emphasise the degree of resurgence in its thinking that has taken place. Again, a few phrases from *Deadline 92* illustrate this best:

'Europe . . . was light years away from the cares and concerns of ordinary people';

'distressing spectacle of disarray';

'Yesterday The Twelve were manifestly apathetic, unassertive and disunited players in a card game in which the pack was being dramatically redealt on a world scale'.

These are strong words indeed in condemnation of what other commentators, more detached from Brussels, have no more strongly described as 'Eurosclerosis' or 'Euro-pessimism'! The Commission's overview of both its own history and its mission for the future do, however, give us an insight into the perceived importance of the Single Market Programme in the context of Europe's role on the world economic stage.

The Single Market's past

The principle of an internal European market is not new; it was fundamental to the signing of the Treaty of Rome in 1957 by which the six original member states established the European Economic Community, soon to be known as the Common Market. It was recognised by the Six that, only by the creation of a major tariff-free area in Western Europe could an economic entity to rival the considerable power of principal competitors such as the USA and Japan come to exist.

The creation of the European Economic Community in 1958 did not, by its own admission, cause much of a stir. Although its initial target of abolishing all tariffs and quotas between the Member States within 12 years was achieved, from this achievement on all efforts to further advance the enterprise – such as initiatives on joint foreign policy, and economic and monetary co-operation – failed to reach fruition. Although the Community grew considerably in size with the addition over time of further Member States including Britain and Ireland, it failed to develop its thinking as a cohesive entity in the way that had originally been envisaged.

Indeed, a combination of the removal of tariffs itself and the world recession of the 1970s created a situation in which Member States were encouraged to erect non-tariff barriers to trade. Never more than capable of protecting narrow, short-term interests, these took the form of, for example, discrimination in public procurement policies, elaborate customs procedures and protective national standards. Summit meetings degenerated into acrimonious bickering concerning such issues as Britain's subscription payments and details of the now discredited Common Agricultural Policy. The international trade situation perhaps most clearly puts in context why the present European Commission is prepared to be so openly scornful of its predecessors. In the 20 years from 1965 to 1985, the ability of European companies to compete was sharply eroded by comparison with those in Japan and the USA, where vast and co-ordinated domestic markets contrasted with the fragmented national ones within the Community. During this period not only did exports to non-EC countries steadily decrease but the Member States lost share in their own domestic market to a significant degree.

It was not until January 1985, on the appointment of a former French Finance Minister, Jacques Delors, to the presidency of the Commission, that the turning point came. Delors saw quite clearly not only that drastic change was necessary if the Community was to establish itself as a genuine trade rival to Japan and the United States, but also that the time was right to begin such change. Ironically, the creation of the Single Market was only Delors' fourth choice as a possible road to recovery. The first three choices – respectively the creation of a federal European government involving transfer of power from member states to the European Parliament; extending the European monetary system to create a common currency; and closer collaboration on defence – failed, however, to gain sufficient acceptance among the Member States to be regarded as realistic options. The fourth option – the proposal to create a truly free and open market by the removal of all non-tariff barriers – met however with almost universal acceptance.

Why was this? Part of the answer lies, of course, in the desire to reverse the recent histories of the Member States and of the Community itself, histories of economic slump, internal disharmony and the erosion of world markets. Part, also, lies in the desire to re-establish first principles, as laid down in the Treaty of Rome almost 30 years earlier, but this time as a bigger and more purposeful entity with an absolute commitment to the goal. More fundamentally, however, must be the simple desire to boost competitiveness. As Mrs Thatcher said in her September 1988 speech in Bruges:

'By getting rid of barriers, by making it possible for companies to operate on a Europe-wide scale, we can best compete with the USA, Japan and the other new economic powers emerging in Asia and elsewhere.'

In retrospect, it seems almost amazing that the goal was not agreed sooner or that it could have been regarded initially by Jacques Delors as only the fourth option towards recovery. Certainly, it has been adopted by almost all parties – businesses, workers' representatives and opposition parties as well as governments, with an enthusiasm that Delors could not possibly have envisaged at the beginning of 1985.

The commitment of the Member States to the implementation of the Single Market Programme was formally confirmed in the Single European Act which came into operation on 1 July 1987. This defined the internal market as 'an area without frontiers in which the free movement of goods, persons, services and capital is ensured in accordance with the provisions of the Treaty (of Rome)'. Whether the parties to the agreement realised at the time the colossal nature of the process they had enacted into being remains open to conjecture; certainly, in view of the lengthy list of measures identified as necessary to achieve the completion of the internal market, the deadline of 31 December 1992, proclaimed by the Milan European Council in mid-1985, appears in retrospect to have been extremely ambitious.

It was the British Vice-President of the Commission, Lord Cockfield, acting as Commissioner in charge of the internal market portfolio, who in 1985 had produced the Commission's White Paper to the Milan Council listing the 300 measures that would have to be drafted, agreed and passed in order to meet the objective. This document has been recognised as extremely shrewdly drafted, as well as all-embracing; on one hand sufficiently detailed to galvanise the legislative machine in Brussels into prompt and sustained action, yet maintaining a sufficiently broad perspective in order to be seen to meet even-handedly the diverse interests of individual Member States or industry sectors, thus minimising potential areas of opposition. A key measure contained in the Single European Act to facilitate the progress of the individual resolutions (reduced from 300 to 276) through the Council was the introduction of 'qualified majority voting' rather than a requirement for unanimity on the majority of them. This reduced considerably the extent to which representatives from individual Member States could block legislation and is a measure of the extent to which the Member States have been prepared to compromise their individual sovereignties in the interest of progress.

In order to understand this better and before moving on to consider in detail the particular areas of importance contained in the 1992 programme, it is necessary to explain – albeit briefly – the primary institutions of the European Community and how they work together in progressing legislation.

The institutions of the European Community

Article 189 of the Treaty of Rome states that 'in order to carry out their task, the Council of Ministers and the Commission shall . . . make Regulations, issue Directives, make Recommendations and deliver Opinions'. Each of these instruments has a different legal effect; the majority of items within the Single Market Programme will, however, be issued as *Directives*. This means that the piece of legislation in question is binding within each Member State and must be incorporated into national law by a date specified by the Commission, but the methods of implementation are left to the national governments themselves. A complainant who believes an EC Directive has not been properly implemented or complied with by the state of which he is a national may ultimately take the case to the European Court of Justice for a ruling, as has already happened in the employment field in relation to equal pay and freedom of movement of workers.

The three institutions that play the major role in debating and progressing Single Market Programme Directives are, respectively, the *Commission*, the *Council*, and the *Assembly* (or European Parliament).

The European Commission

This is composed of 17 Members appointed by agreement between the member governments for a four-year term, each taking specific responsibility for some aspect of Community affairs in addition to collective responsibility for overall policy. Each of the larger Community states – Britain, France, Germany, Italy and Spain – appoints two members, while the other states appoint one each. Members are required throughout their term of office to be independent of their own governments (indeed, several of them are appointed from opposition parties of the Member States, for example the British Commissioner Bruce Millan from the Labour Party).

Under the terms of the Treaty of Rome the Commission has a number of responsibilities, which may be summarised as follows:

- Acting as custodian of the Treaty itself, that is ensuring that Member States meet their Community policy obligations consistently and in accordance with the established rules. Infringement of Directives has proved to be a fairly common practice, and although in many cases this is due more to differences in interpretation rather than deliberate attempts at evasion, the Commission is taking an increasingly tough stance where it is perceived that the internal market programme may be threatened.

- Initiating Community policy, and ensuring its consistency as a whole. The best example of this is Lord Cockfield's White Paper on the Single Market Programme itself which, as already described, was a comprehensive and detailed document aimed at establishing the framework for the completion of the internal market.

- Executing Community policy, following its progress through the Council of Ministers and European Parliament. In addition to the issuing of decisions and enacting of regulations this role also includes the administration of safeguard clauses enabling Treaty requirements to be waived in certain cases, and the administration of Community Funds. By far the most significant of these tasks in the context of the Single Market Programme is the implementation of legislation, described in more detail below as the role of the European Council is explained.

The European Council

The Council is made up of representatives of the governments of the 12 Member States. It is not a 'standing' body but varies in composition according to the subject under debate – the Foreign Minister would be regarded as the main representative from each Member State but would be accompanied by other ministers for debates on specialised subjects. Presidency of the Council rotates on a six-monthly basis between the member governments.

The interface between the Council and the Commission can be seen to be key in that the Commission represents the interest of the Community, the Council that of the individual member governments. Key issues to this interface are:

- The Council can only operate if it receives proposals on areas of policy from the Commission.
- Following submission of a proposal, dialogue takes place between the two bodies, one representing the Community point of view, the other individual national points of view.
- The Council is empowered to reach decisions on proposals by a system of voting which according to the nature of the proposal itself may be either on the basis of unanimity or qualified majority decision. Where majority voting applies, the votes are apportioned on the following basis: Britain, France, Germany and Italy ten votes each; Spain eight; Greece, Portugal, Belgium and the Netherlands five each; Ireland and Denmark three each; Luxembourg two. A 'qualified majority' is defined as a minimum of 54 votes out of the total of 76.

The principle of qualified majority voting was, as already indicated, introduced with the Single European Act for the majority of measures contained within the Single Market Programme. The intention was to speed up the passage of legislation, which previously could only be passed by unanimous agreement, and was therefore vulnerable to indefinite blocking by individual Member States. In the words of Emile Noel, Secretary-General to the Commission for almost 30 years, 'The increasingly obvious danger of the institution's work being paralysed by an abuse of the unanimity role has . . . led to increased use of majority voting for Council decisions, even on very important matters. This has substantially extended the Council's scope for taking majority decisions, particularly as regards the internal market'. In a number of major areas, however, relating to tax and fiscal provisions, the free movement of people and certain employment rights, a unanimous decision by Council members is still required.

The European Parliament

The European Parliament or Assembly is not a 'Parliament' in the sense of the British parliamentary system; nor does it have the same functions or purposes. It was first elected in 1979 and is re-elected at five-yearly intervals, the latest election having therefore been in 1989. Key features of its structure are:

- the parliamentary seats are apportioned to member states according to their size, the largest (including Britain, France and West Germany) currently holding 81 seats each and the smallest (Luxembourg) holding six seats out of the current total of 518;
- voting within 11 states is on a proportional representation basis, only Britain using single-ballot majority voting;
- there are no national factions within it but rather Community-wide political groupings, from the Group of the European Right at one extreme to the Communist and Allies Group at the other.

The Parliament is, as Emile Noel puts it, 'a fully integrated Community institution . . . the fact that the Commission is answerable to Parliament, and Parliament alone, guarantees its independence; . . . Parliament thus keeps constant watch on the Commission's doings making sure that it faithfully represents the Community interest, ready at any time to call it to order if it gives the impression of yielding to the lobbying of governments'. In fact, the election procedure itself guarantees in large measure the Parliament's independence from Member States; being separate from national general elections it is perfectly possible for the representatives from a Member State to be of a different political balance than the national parliament, as is indeed the case with the British representatives following the European Elections in 1989.

The executive role of the Parliament was strengthened considerably by the Single European Act, but still remains essentially that of a multi-party advisory body, whose purpose is to debate draft legislation presented to it in Committee, and refer it back to the Commission with or without amendment. In practice, a large amount of the executive power of both the Commission and the Parliament is passed over to Committees – a fact which engenders some of the severest criticism of it, the legislative process being described variously as unnecessarily time-consuming, undemocratic, and out of touch with the views of national parliaments which therefore have no real means of effecting influence.

The ways in which the institutions of the European Community interact and do or do not represent the views of Member States or the best interests of the Community at large are, and will probably always be, the subject of vigorous argument. The Single European Act has put them 'under the microscope' to a degree that was unknown before, and perhaps ultimately their success or failure will be judged by the extent of success or failure achieved by the Act itself. This was stated clearly in a letter to the *Times* of 23 June 1989, by John Coleman, Editor of *New European*:

'The solution, . . . is to restrict the Commission in Brussels rigidly to its original remit the creation of a genuine Common Market, not closed in on itself but open to the world.'

Although the European Parliament is seen by many as a purely consultative body, there are others who argue that it has a key role in the application of European Community legislation in Britain, achievable through proper co-ordination between MPs and MEPs in the interests of their constituents. Only time will tell whether this co-ordination actually takes place and is effective in influencing the passage of legislation to standards that are acceptable both to the Commission and the individual member governments.

Details of the Single Market Programme

The broad brief of the Single Market Programme is to create freedom of movement within the Community of 'goods, persons, services and capital' in order to promote both trade with the rest of the world and ultra-Community trade. This section examines each of these four areas in turn, looking at existing barriers to free trade, the specific ways, and means that are proposed to reduce them as set out in Lord Cockfield's White Paper, and the likely extent to which the Commission will be successful in achieving its aims.

Movement of goods

There are a number of ways in which the free movement of goods between Member States is hampered by differing national regulations and standards. First, customs posts create physical barriers that in turn lead to higher costs; not only through delays created in clearing the posts themselves but the costs of meeting compliance with different countries' tax and transit regulations. Second, again related to transport, there are restrictions and quotas in force which limit the number of journeys foreign road hauliers can make within most countries. Third, there is a multitude of differing product standards between Member States, particularly in the food and drink sector, ostensibly for purposes of consumer protection but in many cases, in fact, to protect domestic suppliers. Fourth, there are major differences between the Member States' treatment of indirect taxation, particularly VAT differences but also relating to excise duty. This again distorts competition and creates complexities and costs at customs barriers – both to suppliers of goods passing through and to the States themselves through the need to enforce checks and collect duties.

The additional costs arising from the imposition of these barriers are both direct (e.g. the actual cost in terms of time and labour to clear customs barriers) and indirect (the imposition of unnecessary national product standards leading to reduced competition and the need to target several national rather than one common market). They are obviously extremely difficult to estimate but it is clear that they run to many billions of ECUs (the ECU, the standardised unit of European Commerce, representing approximately £0.65 sterling).

Customs

Turning first to customs control, the Commission's declared aim is, quite simply, to abolish internal controls within the Community entirely. This would be undertaken by a gradual process, starting with the easing of formalities including harmonising and reducing the amount of paperwork, collecting VAT at destination rather than country of origin, and introducing the concept of a common border post rather than the current two that have to be passed when crossing a national frontier. This seems an achievable objective; indeed much progress has already been made with the introduction of the Single Administrative Document and the transfer of controls on some products to point of departure rather than border post. However, the complete elimination of border controls appears more problematic, and the Commission has not as yet come up with detailed measures to overcome the drawbacks. These include the need to maintain security checks and to maintain a means of checking and collecting indirect taxation.

Road transport

Regarding road transport, the Commission aims to phase out the imposition of national quotas on foreign-based hauliers by 1 January 1993. Directives to harmonise in such areas as vehicle weights and dimensions and driver hours have also been proposed and in some cases already adopted. Although these measures have been resisted by some Member States (e.g. West Germany) it seems likely that the road haulage sector is one that will benefit greatly throughout the 1990s from the Commission's programme of change.

Product standards

Harmonisation of product standards within the European Community is a major area of the Programme but an extremely complex one because of the huge range of products across all sectors that need to be considered. It is likely therefore that overall progress will be slow and will take place on something of a 'piecemeal' basis. The Commission's aim is to establish the principle of mutual recognition of the standards that apply in other Member States, underpinned by the development of specific European minimum standards to ensure free circulation and use of products throughout the Community. A new European Organisation for Testing and Certification is being established to speed up the process of pan-European product standards and remove the necessity for testing and checking procedures to be carried out on the same product in different countries.

Interestingly, differences in product standards were probably as instrumental as anything else for the coming about of the Single Market Programme in the first place. The *creme de cassis* test case – in which the West German ban on importation of the French drink of that name, on the grounds that it failed to meet the parochial and self-serving definitions of a liqueur, was overturned by the European Court of Justice – was a particularly important landmark, and it has since been followed by a similar ruling overturning the German ban on imported beers that contain additives. The food and drinks sector, as well as toys and motor vehicles, are the likeliest candidates for early completion of the complex testing and certification processes necessary to draw up minimum standards.

Indirect taxation

In the field of indirect taxation, major differences exist between Member States concerning both VAT rates and excise duties. These create unfair competition and considerable complexities at border controls linked both to tax evasion and duty collection. On VAT the Commission proposes to create a two-band system (a standard rate of 14 per cent to 20 per cent and a reduced rate of four per cent to nine per cent) leaving Member States free to choose the rate on a specific product within the band – though the Commission itself would specify the band into which each product would be placed. On excise duty it is proposed to harmonise rates on alcoholic drinks, tobacco and mineral oils. Overall, these measures only go part way to total harmonisation in all areas and on all commodities, which is seen as too disruptive and controversial to be a practical option.

Movement of persons

The Commission has two broad aims to facilitate freedom of movement of individual citizens within the European Community. These are, first, the easing of formalities required in crossing customs and border posts; and second, the mutual acceptance of professional qualifications between Member States in order to allow equal access to employment.

Although the Commission has declared an ultimate intention to do away with all entry and exit controls between Member States, underpinned only by spot checks and the common EC Passport system, the individual Member States themselves have voiced considerable concerns regarding security and the control of illegal movement of arms and drugs. Proposals concerning the mutual recognition of professional qualifications have been much better received; these are considered in detail in conjunction with other measures concerning employment in Chapter Four.

Provision of services

The three major business sectors in which the Commission seeks to create major changes are, respectively, financial services, public procurement and air transport.

Financial services

The financial services sector is hugely important to the Community's economy, providing work for one in every 30 employees and representing a major share of total earnings. Although the transfer of money across frontiers obviously presents no physical problems, a plethora of national regulations ensures that the provision of services is tightly confined within frontiers. These regulations create both taxation differences and technical restrictions, in many cases precluding the marketing of products across national boundaries. The Commission's aim therefore is to deregulate as far as possible, allowing financial institutions to establish themselves in any Member State and offer a full range of services throughout the Community.

In this area again the overall strategy is to harmonise controls as far as possible, by the installation of a system in which financial institutions will be supervised by national authorities according to mutually recognised standards and underpinned by minimum European regulatory standards. A number of Directives have been tabled, covering banking activities, consumer credit, insurance services and the creation of an integrated European securities market. The implications of these are far-reaching and it is likely that many of them will be resisted; in the longer term, however, companies offering financial services may well find themselves faced with a wall of EC legislation which, effectively, forces them to price down those services to the European 'common denominator'. This should be good news for the consumer, although the effects will be felt more in some countries than others. A particular worry for British companies is that the toughest regulatory system is in Britain whereas elsewhere in Europe the authorities are not so thorough. European 'minimum regulatory standards' could therefore open the door to overseas companies selling inferior products to British investors.

Given that differences in national taste and habit will make it difficult for foreign financial institutions to put together products or services which will suit each Member State, many European companies are positioning themselves to best face the changes by considering joint ventures with counterparts in other Member States. In the financial services sector generally, the likelihood of increased merger and acquisitions activity is probably higher than anywhere else, and all the evidence suggests that British companies are taking a lead in this. A number have already been very acquisitive in Europe. Takeovers in EC countries rose from 44 in 1985 to 252 in 1988, with a doubling of the acquisition of European assets by the companies to £2.6 billion in 1988. France was the most popular target accounting for £1.1 billion of this total, followed by the Netherlands (£466 million), West Germany (£380 million) and Spain (£201 million).

Public procurement

Public procurement represents a huge market within the EC, particularly in the area of telecommunications, energy, water supply, transport and defence. At present the scope for cross-border competition is, however, severely limited by a number of restrictive government practices such as the inclusion in contracts of standards biased towards the domestic supplier and the widespread failure to publish invitations to tender. The Commission's main strategy is to apply a 'policing' Directive, first ensuring that government and local authority contracts cannot contain discriminatory clauses and second allowing unfairly excluded companies to apply to national courts for redress. Although this is a highly contentious and politically sensitive area, the Commission is showing determination in laying down the necessary measures to scrutinise current practices and allow increased cross-border tendering.

Air travel

The relative costs of air travel within Europe are notoriously high compared with costs from Europe to other destinations, or with those of equivalent journeys in North America. This is largely due to restrictive arrangements between governments and operators designed to protect relatively small national airlines from competition, and particularly to exclude the much bigger American operators from the European market. Competition between European airlines, as much as EC proposals to liberalise fare promotions and route capacity restrictions, may lead to increased merger activity and a gradual reduction in both costs and fare prices.

Movement of capital

This is something of a 'grey area' within the Single Market Programme, recognised as of considerable significance to other aspects of it – in particular financial services provision – but itself subject to destabilisation as different elements of the Programme are progressed at different rates. Restrictions on capital movements are most prevalent in the relatively underdeveloped Member States such as Greece and Portugal, but it is precisely these countries that will need most time to introduce changes.

Proposals to integrate them into the EMS and harmonise tax on company and individual capital may therefore be a long time in coming.

Overall effects of the Programme

In summary, what are the major effects of the Single Market Programme likely to be, and what should companies do in order to meet the challenges presented – the threats and the opportunities?

Overall, there are likely to be four general effects:

- **Increased competition**, with greater opportunities throughout Europe as well as stiffer competition in domestic markets; arising largely from the removal of narrow, national product and service standards and their replacement by common European standards in a wide variety of business sectors.

- **New markets**, as previously closed areas, such as large public procurement contracts, are opened up to wider competition. The deregulating of customs and border controls and harmonisation of indirect taxation will also be of major significance in this respect.

- **Reduced costs**, as wider sources of suppliers, fewer modifications to basic models and easier access to distribution channels are exploited. It is likely that ultimately economies of scale will be created as, in each product area, a smaller number of producers are able to manufacture and market to common specifications across the Community.

- **Increased European merger, acquisition and joint venture activity**, as companies ensure that they are well positioned to succeed in the single market. This is likely to take place across industry and business sectors, the financial services sector being perhaps the most likely to benefit from such activity in the short term.

Companies of whatever size and business sector will have to consider very carefully the nature of their operation if they are to make the most of the opportunities that will become available. Individual issues that will need to be addressed will vary considerably but may include:

- analysis of current and projected markets;
- the extent of competition, both domestically and abroad;
- the adaptability of the product or service;
- sales and distribution outlets;

- the extent of any existing protective measures that are advantageous to the product or service being offered to the home market, and the likelihood of these being removed by the Single Market Programme;
- similarly the likelihood of existing or potential foreign competitors having their domestic trade advantages eroded by the Programme.

Finally, what will the effect of the Single Market Programme be on trade with the rest of the world? The Americans and Japanese are highly fearful that a 'Fortress Europe' will be created, putting up trade barriers to counteract the considerable advantages currently held by Japan and the United States which give them such a large slice of world trade. The Community, naturally enough, does not see things that way; the European Council has declared: 'the Single Market will be of benefit to Community and non-Community countries alike by ensuring continuing economic growth. The internal market will not close in on itself. 1992 Europe will be a partner not a ''Fortress Europe''. The internal market will be a decisive factor contributing to greater liberalisation of trade on . . . principles of reciprocal and mutually advantageous arrangements'. However, the major industrial nations remain highly sceptical of these declared principles. A persistent problem remains that extra-Community trade has been largely considered to be the responsibility of individual Member States rather than a Community-wide issue, and as a result, a number of ominous measures suggested by politicians representing narrow trade interests have served to undermine the official view. For example, in November 1988 a vice-president of the Commission proposed that Japan pay retroactive compensation to European exporters for having kept them out of its market for years; in similar vein, France has maintained a dogged fight to restrict imports of Japanese cars made in Britain. The biggest scare to date occurred in December 1988, when a trade war threatened to break out between Europe and America over the EC ban on £150 million worth of American hormone-fed meat imports. Though a crisis was averted, this could have led to the US imposing tariffs or official quotas on a wide range of European imports. After a period of equanimity during 1989, the US view appears to be hardening once again, the recent adoption of Community regulations on cars, computer chips and television broadcasting being seen in particular as putting up trade barriers.

The Community has taken a more concerted approach with regard to the European Free Trade Association (Austria, Finland, Iceland, Norway, Sweden and Switzerland) which is collectively its biggest trading partner and with whom a number of agreements concerning technical issues as well as trade itself have been reached. These agreements are being followed up with negotiations to create a common economic zone with the EFTA countries, which will effectively extend the freedom of movement of goods, services, capital and people into and out of the Community. The EFTA countries will have to accept EC rules, but will be empowered to help influence future Community law, without taking part in final decisions. In due course these measures may be extended to the new democracies developing in Eastern Europe; it is encouraging that the calls of many leading politicians to turn declared statements into action and extend a genuine free trade approach towards other world markets are being heeded by the Commission. This momentum must be maintained both if the EC is to assert itself as a purposeful, competitive entity in the world trade market, and if it is to avoid the generation of 'tit for tat' protectionism which could be so damaging to growth as it seeks to range itself alongside Japan and the United States.

The social dimension to the Single Market Programme

In September 1988 the EC Commission published a document entitled *The Social Dimension of the Internal Market*. Consultative rather than directive, it nevertheless drew together many strands of enacted and proposed community legislation, some of them going back to first principles established under the Treaty of Rome, into a cogent and realistic statement of intent. The proposals contained in it have, however, become one of the most contentious areas of debate, with pressure for and against coming from all sides. Why is this? – and what exactly is the 'Social Agenda' all about?

The answers to these questions may be found by referring back to Lord Cockfield's White Paper which set the Single Market Programme in motion. Although, as already described, the White Paper was extremely wide-ranging in its scope and content, it did not specifically address the social – and, in particular, the employment – issues arising from the creation of the single market. In retrospect this can be seen to have been a major oversight. The economic and social issues are inextricably linked, for example higher employment costs in wages or sick pay, or individual national legislation necessitating the provision of higher environmental standards in the workplace, would add significantly to the costs faced by an employer in competition with rival employers in other Member States with lower norms or standards.

Harmonisation

The Social Dimension Document can be seen, therefore, as a measure to redress this balance – not just for the sake of the social issues themselves, but in the interests of the Programme as a whole. It has split political opinion within Europe down the middle, the UK and Denmark in particular taking a deregulationist approach with all other Member States broadly in support of the Commission's view that harmonisation across the Community – a 'level playing field' – regarding social and employment affairs is required.

The principle of harmonisation is, as has already been seen from the description of the main areas of legislation contained in the Single Market Programme earlier in this chapter, fundamental to the success of the Programme itself. The breaking down of trade barriers can only be achieved if it is underpinned by the establishment of *European minimum standards* – entailing the harmonisation of national legislation at a common level, in order to ensure fair competition. As a result harmonisation also becomes necessary in other fields than those directly concerned with trade – the environment, for example, where without it lower pollution controls in one country could put its industries at an unfair advantage (and, following from this, could encourage new industries to relocate there, thus creating even more pollution). It is argued that it is logical, therefore, that harmonisation should also take place in the field of employment and social legislation. The time-limit in which this can reasonably be expected to occur, and the extent to which it can take place, is extremely difficult to judge – given that in translation to formal Directives individual measures would be subject to the process of unanimity voting within the Council in order to be accepted as law.

The Commission's social policy

The European Commission defines its social policy as emphasising 'the prime importance, for economic and social cohesion, of improving living and working conditions and promoting a high level of employment . . . greater freedom for people to move from one member country to another, creating the conditions for successful adaptation to the changes which increasing European integration will inevitably entail, and intensifying dialogue between the social partners'. It can be seen from this that its scope goes well beyond purely employment-related issues, though these form the core of it; its development since the Treaty of Rome can be described as one of steady and sustained refinement from first principles. These principles, as outlined in the Articles of the Treaty, included:

- Equal treatment for men and women, in particular regarding equal pay for work of equal value. 'Pay', as defined within the Treaty, includes indirect as well as direct remuneration in cash or kind (Article 119).

- The free movement of workers throughout the Community, outlawing discrimination based on nationality regarding selection for employment, remuneration and terms and conditions of work (Article 48).

- The social security of migrants, by the provision of benefits to migrant workers and their families based on accrued service across the Community (Article 51).

- Closer co-operation between Member States in a wide variety of areas mainly concerning employment law and practice, including vocational training, occupational hygiene, rights of association and collective bargaining (Article 118).

- Measures to encourage improvements in the working environment, particularly regarding health and safety (Article 118a).

- A commitment to develop dialogue between the two sides of industry (Article 118b).

- The creation of a Social Fund to reimburse Member States in part for the costs of retraining and resettling the unemployed.

In the early years of the Community, these principles remained dormant as little more than statements of intent, and it was not until the 1970s that they were lifted out of the overall framework for economic integration and formed into a coherent policy for social affairs standing as a separate programme in its own right. However, in 1974 a social action programme was approved by resolution which identified the action required in three broad areas; full and improved employment, improved living and working conditions and the participation of workers in company affairs. Considerably more purposeful than previous efforts, progress was however severely hampered by economic slump and the growing diversity of living standards between the Member States.

The Social Dimension Document

It is perhaps because the social action programme had been removed from the Community's economic objectives in the 1970s that the Single Market Programme did not initially address the issues it contained; however, there is no doubt that the Programme, together with the gradual improvement in living standards during the last decade gave it the required impetus to propel it to its next development, the Social Dimension Document of September 1988. This analysed social affairs with reference to the needs and aims of a wider market, including issues raised by such details as the harmonisation of technical standards and company laws, and the adaptation of the labour market to these. It was further updated in May 1989 and further in September 1989 by the publication of a 'non-binding Community Charter of Fundamental Social Rights', which has added greater detail to the list of measures the Commission seeks to implement in parallel with those contained in the Single European Act.

In the words of Mark Hall of Warwick University's Industrial Relations Research Unit, writing in *Personnel Management* magazine:

the final version of the Social Charter 'takes the form of a declaration to be adopted by the European Council setting out essential rights or minimum standards in respect of a number of aspects of industrial relations practice and working conditions. . . . Its rationale (is) that, in the context of the increased competition and economic restructuring associated with the completion of the internal market, there should be a range of basic employment rights which should not be undercut by competitive pressures'.

The Charter comprises 12 sets of fundamental social rights:

- The **right to freedom of movement**, covering measures to promote labour mobility including rights of residence, recognition of academic and professional qualifications and co-operation between national labour markets. More controversially equal treatment throughout Europe in terms of social security and tax entitlements is proposed. This includes equal rights to wages and social security provisions for migrant workers.
- **Employment and remuneration** including the controversial issue of 'a decent minimum wage', as well as fostering the growth of flexible,

temporary and part-time working arrangements drawn up by individual employers, sectors and Member States. Measures proposed include equal treatment with full-time workers for such categories of staff, where appropriate translating this into Community Law.

- **Improvement of living and working conditions** including such contractual rights as minimum periods of paid annual leave and a maximum level of working hours.

- **Right to social protection**, in particular to a minimum income for the unemployed and those unable to claim unemployment benefit. An action programme for 'reinforcing economic and social cohesion' is proposed, including the provision of funds and resources to redevelop declining industries, combat long-term unemployment and develop employment demand generally.

- **Right to freedom of association and collective bargaining** including the right strike but also fostering dialogue between 'social partners' that is, employers and employees – at all levels. Looking at this in a positive way it is clear that the Commission believes that dialogue may take place to the benefit of the Community at large and that individual measures agreed between parties can, in some cases, be adopted generally to the common good.

- **Right to vocational training**: this is seen as assisting individual workers in making the transition to employment within the wider market. In particular, new technology training, language learning programmes and increased links between firms and training providers such as colleges and professional institutions is proposed.

- **Right to equal treatment for men and women** in all aspects of employment including pay, access to work, training and career opportunity.

- **Rights for workers** by the establishment of a standard form of work contract and revised company law procedures to provide increased information, consultation and involvement mechanisms.

- **Rights covering living and working conditions**, including implementation of a new action programme on health, safety and hygiene in the workplace, and the social (again particularly health and safety) issues arising from technical standardisation.

- **Protection of children and adolescents** coming into the labour market by the establishment of a minimum working age of 16, minimum wage and training rights.

- **Protection of the elderly** through the provision of adequate social security.
- **Rights for the disabled** including integration into working life.

It can be seen that these proposals bear close resemblance to the employment-related principles contained in the Treaty of Rome, as listed earlier. Although the Charter has no legal force in itself, the individual Member States were asked to approve the measures contained within it in the form of a 'solemn declaration' at the European Council, followed by an action programme to be drawn up by the Commission. This will be based on the principle of 'subsidiarity', by which implementation of specific measures to European minimum standards would be left to individual governments whenever possible.

The Charter may seem at first sight a curiously idealistic document, containing many vague areas and little-attuned to the realities of employment and industrial relations in this country. It is underpinned however, by a strong sense of commitment from within the Commission itself, not the least from its President, Jacques Delors, and by the considerable funding that individual governments have been persuaded to set aside towards more effective social and economic cohesion. At its base it remains firmly rooted to the principles behind the Single Market Programme, to 'liberate the forces of growth which are present in Europe, . . . accompanied by measures which are social in the widest sense'.

The programme of social legislation – which I shall examine in more detail in Chapter 4 – is likely however to be hampered by two factors which will make progress difficult:

- First, the passing of legislation will not in most cases make a visible or measurable difference to trade. In addition to the technical complexity of harmonisation across Europe in such areas as Social Security legislation and employer/employee contractual relations, individual states with low standards in a particular area will be reluctant to see legislation enacted which forces those standards upwards towards a common denominator, as whatever this does for intra-Community trade it will add to their national costs. For example, a national programme to improve health and safety measures to European common standards could be extremely costly to any nation below those standards.
- Second, most social legislation comes under the category of 'the free movement of persons and legislation affecting the rights and interests

of employers' and as such requires unanimous voting within the Council of Ministers under the terms of the Single European Act, in order to become statute. Many of the measures proposed are sufficiently controversial to make it extremely unlikely that unanimity will be achieved in the foreseeable future.

2 The UK perspective

There can be no doubt that, in terms of commitment at least, the UK has thrown itself wholeheartedly behind the Single Market Programme. This commitment has generated a significant awareness of many of the broader issues at stake; although it is doubtful whether this awareness has in turn generated a similar level of action to address them in detail. A much quoted CBI survey of companies with sales of over £20 million, carried out in 1989, revealed that 90 per cent were undertaking no market research in Europe, 93 per cent were undertaking no language training and 95 per cent had no sales agents within the EC.

Nevertheless, it is an impressive fact that almost every political party, and interest groups as diverse as the TUC on one hand, and the CBI and individual employers' representatives on the other, are supportive of the objectives of the Programme as a whole. The only notable exception is the Green Party, which, dedicated to the long-term goal of reducing man's impact on the world's natural resources, sees it as taking account only of economic and not ecological interests. Otherwise, economic interests are, indeed, the crux of the matter; the economic benefits of the free market are so obviously considerable that they simply cannot be ignored by those whose focus is the generation of wealth, be it to the benefit of businesses or individuals within society.

If the objectives themselves are subject to little disagreement, however, the means of attaining them are not, and have generated some of the most heated debates between groups within the UK representing different interests, and between UK politicians and the EC itself. To a large extent these have been exacerbated by the voting procedure within the EC Council – the introduction of qualified voting has meant that no individual Member State can block the passage of legislation unless it has some measure of support for its objection, while even on those measures where unanimity is required (such as most of the group of Directives and recommendations concerning employment that are covered by the Social Charter), changes to the balance of political power within Member States can mean the difference between a measure being accepted or rejected by the Council as European Law. This creates an extremely interesting situation for any government that is at variance with the majority over a specific issue, and one that is worth considering in some detail with reference to the Social Charter.

The UK's attitude

Is the UK alone, within the EC Council, in refusing to countenance the passing into law of those items within the Social Charter that would introduce, for example, worker participation or a 'decent minimum wage' (however loosely this is defined) as a statutory right? While our Conservative Government has been the only voice raised openly in the Council against such measures, it is arguable that other governments such as, for instance, Denmark's, that have so far maintained an uncommitted stance would, if put to the test, also back down from voting through the necessary legislation. However, this remains speculation and it is certainly highly probable that, should a Labour Government with its commitment to 'social Europe' come to power in the UK at the next General Election, even the most contentious items of the Social Charter would receive endorsement within the Council and be translated into formal Directives. The policies of our major political parties concerning the Charter, as well as the views of those groups across the spectrum of commerce and industry that support them, are therefore highly relevant to the direction of employment law throughout the next decade.

Broadly speaking, political views within the UK concerning the Single Market Programme are polarised towards one of two extremes. On the one hand is the deregulationist school of thought, characterised by the Conservatives and the CBI, who hold that legislation covering matters not *directly* related to free trade should not be the concern of the European Community but must be left to individual Member States to define within their own national boundaries. Most aspects of employment law are certainly held to be in this category. On the other hand is the view promoted by Jacques Delors and Vasso Papandreou, the current European Social Affairs Commissioner – and one vigorously espoused by the UK Labour Party and the Trade Union Movement – that employment legislation must be enforced to common standards throughout the Community in order both to ensure fair treatment of European workers and fair competition between European firms. The arguments for and against have raged so fiercely that they have spilled over into other, less contentious areas, and have unfortunately even damaged to a considerable extent the credibility of our present Government's standpoint towards the Community as a whole.

The deregulationist view

In the months prior to its considerable reverse at the June 1989 European Parliament Elections, the Conservative attitude towards the Commission was indeed frequently one of open criticism. In part, this can no doubt be attributed to the Government's unquestioned pride in its record of improving the economic competitiveness and prosperity at home, as evidenced by the growth in manufacturing productivity, income tax cuts and foreign investment growth; the Conservative Manifesto for Europe put across an almost xenophobic view:

'Over the last six years, we have created more new jobs than any of our European partners. Unemployment has fallen fast, and is now well below the European average. Output, investment and living standards are all at record levels.'

Many policies directly related to employment, and deliberately easing central controls and legislation, are described in the manifesto as central to the Government's success, in particular, the changes in trade union law: 'creating a new attitude of co-operation and enterprise in industry', and the ongoing and even more controversial programme of privatisation: '. . . has returned major undertakings – and well over half a million jobs – to the private sector, greatly boosting efficiency'.

The Government has also taken great pride in the fact that, despite the many and well-publicised clashes with the Commission throughout the last decade, it actually has an outstanding record concerning both the number of Single Market measures it has adopted, and in the high standards it has set in the interpretation and implementation of Directives. In 1988, for example, there were only two cases in which Britain breached Community rules compared with nine in West Germany and 28 in Italy. Regarding the Single Market Programme, the Conservative Manifesto declared:

'We believe that creating a single Community market will be good for Britain, good for Europe and good for the world. It will provide more opportunity for industry. More profits for the competitive. More investment and more jobs. More growth to improve services and cut taxes. Better quality, better value for money and more choice for consumers. Wider horizons for those with skills to market. Greater chances for those with good products to sell, from inside and outside the Community, from poor countries and rich alike.'

Conflicting views

Why, in the face of such a strident declaration of intent, have there been so many clashes with the Commission over individual details of the Programme and in particular over the Social Charter? There is certainly a belief within the Conservative Party that the goal-posts have been moved – that the Charter represents 'Socialism through the back door', an attempt by left-wing politicians operating in the European sphere to impose central controls that have nothing to do with the objectives originally intended by the signing of the Single European Act. It is the Government's view that social benefits will arise as a matter of course from the gains in growth, prosperity and employment that the free market economy will create, just as it perceives such benefits to have come from its domestic programme of deregulation since it took office in 1979.

The Social Charter and the government

Open conflict with the Commission has been damaging to the Conservatives at the European Elections and has created the opportunity at home for opponents – even from within the Conservative Party such as Edward Heath, still an influential figure in European affairs – to declare that they are out of step with the progress of European Community affairs altogether. However, it is arguable that with regard to the Social Charter the Conservative stance has been at least a partial success. In its current form, the Charter does two things: first, it draws together items of draft legislation from the Single European Act that relate directly or indirectly to employment; examples are directives to promote health and safety at work, and proposals contained in the Fifth Company Law Directive concerning compulsory worker participation. Second, it seeks to weld onto the Act a series of additional measures not specifically included in the original programme, such as the establishment of a fair wage, the right to strike and, potentially, European-standard contracts of employment. Within both categories there are measures that are highly controversial and fundamentally at odds with Conservative views on deregulation, decentralisation and the free market economy. However, it must be remembered that in its final form the Social Charter has been watered down considerably from earlier drafts, principally by the subordination of many of the original 'basic rights' to the national employment laws and practices of individual Member States. For example, any intention to create a European minimum wage has been removed, the Charter now declaring simply that 'all employment shall be fairly remunerated ... either by law or by collective agreement at national, regional, interoccupational, sectoral or company level or in accordance with national practices'. It is quite clear that, were it not for the strong UK Conservative Party lobbying that took place throughout 1988 and leading up to the European Council Meeting in Strasbourg in December 1989, the Charter would have carried much more weight and even the fundamental principle that voting within the Council on most employment-related Directives requires a unanimous rather than a qualified majority might have been attacked.

Following the 1989 European Parliamentary elections, the Conservative stance towards the Commission moderated to some extent, perhaps as much due to indications that the Commission was prepared to alter its views as much as to the party's poor showing at the polls. Prior to May 1989, the Social Charter was regarded by many Conservatives as a 'hidden agenda' kept largely secret within the minds of socialist-inclined bureaucrats at Brussels who were merely waiting for the most opportune moment to vote through a package of stringent employment and industrial relations laws across the Community. The published Charter, though containing many proposals that are indeed anathema to right-wing politicians, sets out fully and clearly its objectives in a form designed to encourage open debate. This may encourage right-wing politicians and industrialists in other European countries to declare their reservations as specific items are debated, so that the Conservatives need no longer regard themselves as the sole champions of free enterprise at Community level in the face of passivity among the other 11 Member States.

The outcome of the Strasbourg Council Meeting was that the European Social Charter was adopted, without a formal vote but with the UK Government's clear dissent, by the 11 other Member States. While the action programme to follow on from this is likely to lead to a number of measures covering UK employment affairs being proposed by the Commission, the silence in Westminster circles concerning this has been deafening. The reason for this has been most clearly articulated by Señor Enrique Baron, president of the European Parliament:

'The systematic references to national practices and the generalised referrals to the legislation of the Member States (in the Social Charter) seem to represent more a step backwards in the process of integration than a step forward in the widening of the Community's powers.'

What is sauce for the Westminster goose is most definitely not, in this context, sauce for the Brussels gander!

Implementation

The action programme to implement the proposals contained in the Charter has already begun, and is planned to be completed by 1 January 1993. Despite the UK Government's dissent, discussions have already taken place between Mrs Vasso Papandreou and Government ministers concerning those parts of the Commission's social action programme the Government is prepared to support. It is vital that Britain continues to take part in the process of debate if it is to make the most of the Single Market opportunities, a point that has been made consistently by Michael Heseltine in *The Challenge of Europe – Can Britain Win?* He writes:

'By treaty we are committed to the European Community, and in 1986, we gave a powerful new momentum to the business of making it work. That was our free choice, as it was for all of our European partners. Each of them will exploit the multiplying opportunities to the full. The rules to which we have all subscribed are scrupulously fair. The treaties allow each signatory the same opportunities; what they cannot do is prescribe the extent to which the member states separately or jointly, will exploit those opportunities. That is for us.'

If these views become more widely accepted by senior Conservative politicians, the possibility of give and take on both sides regarding the social agenda is substantially increased. While it remains unlikely that a Brussels-imposed, highly generalised Social Charter will ever be regarded as acceptable, Conservatives may be more inclined to think seriously about some of the individual measures proposed, thus meeting half-way the Commission's objectives concerning social issues.

The Social Charter and non-government organisations

What views have been expressed by the representatives of employers and business leaders within the UK? Not surprisingly, these have tended to follow the Conservative Party lead that social improvement should be left to follow on from the economic benefits to be derived from the Single

Market Programme. Peter Brighton, Director General of the EEF, for example, has stated:

'As employers, we are concerned particularly about the socio-employment initiatives and those who talk about using qualified majority voting to force them through. We, too, believe in greater social progress, but we believe that it will come from greater economic progress, not from prescription'.

The EEF view that social harmonisation as part of the Programme itself is an unrealistic, Utopian dream is highlighted by some of the specific issues of concern, which can be summarised as follows:

- first, that the Social Charter might introduce qualified majority voting on such issues as worker participation, leading to universal imposition of this and other measures within fixed European standards;
- that harmonisation of health and safety standards, leading to increased costs, would require a bureaucratic framework too rigid to be practical and hence could not be implemented;
- that pensions and retirement laws also cannot practically be harmonised across Member States;
- generally, that the economic differences between Member States are so great that poorer nations simply cannot afford to 'harmonise upwards' to higher common standards.

The CBI has devoted much effort to co-ordinating the views of industry in order to lobby politicians both in Westminster and in Brussels. While it accepts that the European challenge contains a social element, again the view is expressed that attempts to harmonise will be hampered by cultural as well as economic differences until the Single Market Programme is well and truly under way. Health and safety and worker participation again appear to be the main concerns – although employee involvement on a voluntary basis is regarded as a positive measure – as well as the differences in pay levels that continue to exist between equivalent companies in different Member States.

The British Institute of Management remains more non-committal, and has produced a number of discussion papers on the Single European Market, including one entitled, 'The European Employer'. This gives a balanced view on social affairs proposals, pointing out the implications of failure to harmonise social legislation as well as the problems inherent in it. Last year it produced the results of a survey of its 70,000 members which indicated that, while 75 per cent are prepared to accept some form of

European legislation, there is widespread opposition to rigidly enforced employment laws as 'inefficient and inflexible'.

The socialist view

Labour

Not surprisingly, the Labour Party has consistently supported the Social Agenda, both in itself and as a stick to beat the Tories with: 'For them, the future is in deregulation without social obligation'. They see the agenda as providing a mechanism for upwards harmonisation of employment rights, encompassing the full range of issues – training, industrial relations law, worker participation and information, equal rights for part-time workers, health and safety standards and 'a fair minimum wage'. Considerable dismay was expressed by Labour MPs at the 'watering down' of the Charter in its final form, particularly as so many items are now to be proposed as recommendations to the governments of individual Member States rather than legally binding directives.

The Labour Manifesto for Europe is unclear as to how far the Party would actually go towards implementation of the measures contained in the Social Charter, should it be in a position to be able to do so. It is quite clear, however, in stating that it regards the right of veto on employment issues that the Conservatives have been able to exercise within the Council as unacceptable:

'Mrs Thatcher has continually blocked any social legislation designed to improve our working lives. . . She has her veto and the Single European Act does not allow majority voting on taxes or social improvements.'

It also recognises fully the need to work closely with the Commission and other Member States in debating and agreeing the detail of potential future employment legislation – something that the Conservatives, at least to public appearances, have signally failed to do. The clearest indication of the Labour Party's commitment to the Social Charter to date has been its preparedness to abandon support for the closed shop, as this runs against Article II of the Charter which gives workers the right to join or not join a union. By ditching support for this long-cherished principle, Labour believes it may have a more effective voice in persuading the Government to introduce other elements of the Charter.

The Social and Liberal Democrats

The Social and Liberal Democrats largely echo the Labour Party in their view on the Social Agenda. Specifically, they target industrial democracy and employee participation, equal rights for part-time employees and common social welfare rights – encompassing health and safety and full transferability of pension and social benefits rights across frontiers – as top of their own agenda. They are also strongly committed to increasing opportunities for women and have proposed a Community 'Working Women's Charter' with the aim of ending all indirect discrimination by the provision of such measures as extended parental leave, the encouragement of workplace childcare facilities and training for women entering the labour market.

Trade Unions

The TUC, and individual trade unions represented by it, have been the most unequivocal group in expressing full support for the European Social Charter. A major boost to their campaign was given by Jacques Delors when, at the 1988 Conference, he outlined how union solidarity for the package of measures proposed could help gain maximum benefits for workers across Europe. Perhaps more than anything else, this served to drive the wedge between the UK Government and the Commission, that has subsequently been so harmful to the dialogue between them; however, given the direction that trade union and employment law has taken during the 1980s, it is hardly surprising that the TUC should look to Europe for support. Overall, the TUC's programme covers a number of areas: job and collective bargaining guarantees, rights to information and consultation on company plans being highest on the agenda. Equal opportunities for women have also featured prominently in debates, the strategy being to turn prospective labour shortages throughout the 1990s into better pay and conditions for women employees. Specifically, in this area the TUC would seek legislation concerning minimum standards for maternity and childcare provision, and rights for home and part-time workers. Most unions have accepted that the days of the closed shop are effectively numbered, the TUC General Secretary, Norman Willis, declaring: 'We can't now pick and choose which bits of the Social Charter we like'.

Regarding the key issue of worker participation, the TUC has surprisingly adopted a flexible view. While insisting that it strongly supports those proposals in the Social Charter that would introduce this measure, the General Secretary, Norman Willis, has declared that the Charter 'would not seek to impose one particular model of worker participation on all member states' and furthermore, that British trade unionism would not seek a confrontational approach: 'Most trade unionists in Britain, as elsewhere, want to work for a successful enterprise, co-operating with management in providing a better service and creating greater wealth'. Such statements may provide the key to future progress as, hopefully, we move into a phase in which more constructive debate on pan-European employment issues becomes possible.

Overall, the trade union perspective on the Single European Market is comprehensively summed up in the 'Ten-Point Strategy' published by the Manufacturing, Science and Finance Union early in 1988. The ten action points are:

- the establishment of European industry sector joint committees bringing together unions, principal employers and Commission representatives to consult on matters of mutual concern;
- language training and paid time off work for union nominees serving on such committees;
- the right to six-monthly consultation meetings between unions and individual employers;
- the statutory right to union consultation regarding proposed mergers and takeovers;
- common European legislation concerning trade union solidarity action;
- joint employer/union committees to develop action plans for vocational training, backed up by EC funding to facilitate retraining and redeployment of workers;
- consultation in the regulation of products and services (in the ten-point strategy this is specific to insurance and financial services);
- collective bargaining aimed at 'upwards harmonisation' of terms and conditions including a minimum wage, a 35-hour basic working week and the right of all workers to an occupational pension scheme;
- upwards harmonisation of health and safety standards, backed up by guaranteed union monitoring rights;
- measures to ensure some form of compliance with EC minimum standards in non-EC trading partners, in order to remove the possibility of 'social dumping', i.e. to prevent multinational companies diverting production and investment to countries with lower employment conditions and hence costs.

This extremely thoughtful document, while directly addressing many of the proposals contained within the Social Charter, takes a broader perspective and it can be seen that many of the individual clauses relate directly to the Single Market Programme itself. In particular, it represents a realistic approach to those employment issues raised by a free market economy, and a keenness to participate in the development of that economy. The individual clauses it contains are worthy of consideration by any group representing political or employers' interests that is keen to establish dialogue with a trade union counterpart.

The Social Charter – a way forward?

Most UK forecasters see little prospect of rapid advancement of the measures outlined in the Social Charter. The political issues are too complex, it is argued, for a sufficient level of agreement to be achieved; filling in the detail will prove to be a highly complex and time-consuming process, given the wide differences in economic and social living conditions between the Community's Member States. It is even doubted whether the Commission still has sufficient willpower to seek harmonisation across a multitude of diverse areas affecting employment conditions and worker mobility.

Against this, the real need for *a certain level* of harmonisation, of employment conditions, if the Single Market Programme is to achieve its fundamental objectives, cannot be denied. To the employer, a major benefit would be the levelling out of costs across Europe to provide a fairer basis of competition; to the employee would come the benefits of better conditions, increased training opportunity and access to a wider employment market – though not in the context of social dumping, involving countries with higher living and employment standards attracting large numbers of migrant EC citizens from poorer neighbours. It is also argued that, faced with a steeply declining labour force from the mid-1990s, an ageing population and the long-term prospect of economic recession, the need for a cohesive policy will become more and more urgent.

In a political as well as a practical sense, the period leading up to the end of 1992 would appear to be ideal for compromise on the Social Charter, leading to implementation – in part and over a lapsed period of time – of some of the measures it proposes. The 1989 Charter of

Fundamental Social Rights can be seen in retrospect to have provided a platform for open debate on many issues, and an opportunity for our present Government perhaps to lay the ghost of the previous era of confrontation. There are three sound reasons why this opportunity should be grasped:

- First, the Conservatives cannot afford to continue to be seen as the 'odd man out' on social agenda issues. No longer the majority UK group within the European Parliament, such a stance is likely to cause considerable damage to their political standing both in Britain and throughout the Community. Concern over this is nowhere more keenly felt than amongst Conservative MEPs. In an article in the *Times* of 14 September 1989 entitled 'An Isolated Patch of Blue', the leading MEP Lord Bethell expressed in almost plaintive terms their rejection by their natural political allies the Christian Democrats: 'It was therefore a great shock to us when their MEPs decided neither to accept us into their group as members, nor even to broaden co-operation with us. . . Mrs Thatcher's outright rejection of the Social Charter is seen by them as short-sighted, as is her view that the European Parliament is not a parliament at all and therefore does not need to be directly elected. They resent the vigour with which she, representing a country with decades of mediocre economic performance, chides countries like Germany for corporatism and lack of enterprise.'

- Second, it is already becoming clear that the Commission has begun to adopt a greater sense of urgency regarding the Social Charter. The Secretary-General of the EC's Economic and Social Committee, an assembly of 189 delegates representing employers, workers and other interest groups and appointed by the 12 governments made it clear before Strasbourg that while consensus was still regarded as essential, 11 of the 12 were prepared to accept the Charter in full and to implement an action programme to bring laws in different countries into line on all social issues. While discussions at Strasbourg were reported as being 'calm and procedural', 11 of the 12 did indeed vote the Charter through, and considerable pressure is likely to be brought to bear on the UK Government if it remains absolutely intransigent in its position.

- Third, they cannot count on remaining in Government indefinitely, and the possibility of political changes within Member States and hence within the Council of Ministers could drastically transform the situation. Although the requirement for unanimity Council voting on most employment-related measures is likely to remain, there is little doubt that a UK Labour Government would vigorously support the Social Charter, and that the stumbling block to consensus on its most far-reaching proposals would be removed. It is therefore in the Conservatives' interests to try and reach a compromise while they have the opportunity to do so.

Views and opinions on worker participation – a summary

I have already indicated the views and opinions being expressed by UK political parties and interest groups concerning worker participation – one of the most contentious issues within the social programme. A summary of these might serve to illustrate the change that is taking place and the possibilities that are emerging for increased dialogue on this and in other areas of the Charter.

There is little doubt that, on the worker participation issue, opinion within the UK and throughout Europe has in the past been totally polarised. German politicians on one hand, have pointed out how the model of industrial participation within their firms has kept their capitalist economy virtually strike-free and prosperous, and therefore must be implemented by law throughout Europe if the Single Market Programme is to be successful. On the other hand is the view taken by the British Government that legally enforced participation represents 'creeping continental Marxism' and would lead to an upsurge in political strife within British industry.

There are undoubtedly good reasons why rigidly enforced participation would not work within the UK or within certain other Member States, and furthermore the signs now seem to have been read by the Commission which moderated its stance considerably in the period of time leading up to the December 1989 Strasbourg Summit. Jacques Delors, in a speech in Bruges just prior to the Summit, was at pains to emphasise the principle of subsidiarity underlying the final version of the Charter, enabling 'the full respect of existing diversities' between the employment norms of different Member States. This principle is fully apparent in the clause concerning the 'Right of workers to information, consultation and participation':

'Information, consultation and participation for workers must be developed along appropriate lines and in such a way as to take account of the laws, collective agreements and practices in force in the Member States.'

This statement falls some way short of full-blown Marxist rhetoric! Within the UK, some more middle of the road proposals are being put forward by surprisingly diverse interest groups. For example, Michael Heseltine, in *The Challenge of Europe*, argues for a liberal approach in which companies would be free to choose whether or not to 'buy in' to higher level pan-European employment standards in order to obtain attendant rights facilitating the relocation of plants in Europe, 'where the efficiencies of production attracted them'. Ronald Butt, the political columnist of the *Times*, has written:

'She [Margaret Thatcher] is right to condemn a blanket Brussels-imposed social policy and any idea of a generalised social charter which the courts might have to interpret. But there is nevertheless a case for looking again at worker-management relationships in Britain.'

In a more recent article on the subject, Ronald Butt warns most strongly that to ignore the worker participation issue would be to opt out of governmental decision-making responsibility, leaving it entirely to the Brussels bureaucrats to lead the argument. Furthermore, it would be to miss a genuine opportunity. He writes:

'In particular it makes no sense for Tories to be contemptuous of the German system. For this could largely bypass the unions, setting up consultation within work places. It could assist what Britain needs, which is not blanket pay awards negotiated by national craft unions, but agreements on pay and conditions reached within each business in the light of local conditions and in acknowledgement of employers' and workers' shared interest in their businesses' prosperity.'

Even the British Institute of Management, which states that less than 18 per cent of its members support employee involvement proposals, has proposed that participation on a more informal basis could be included in EC legislation. While certainly not going far enough to satisfy the left-wing lobby at the Commission, these proposals include expanded employee share ownership to increase employee influence at board level, and quarterly financial review meetings between managers and employees to ensure two-way communication and attendant benefits in annual reports.

On the other side of the political spectrum, our trade unions are issuing signals that fall well short of 'marxist' confrontationism, as I have already illustrated earlier in this chapter. Indeed, while a substantial gap clearly remains between the views expressed by, respectively, employers and employees' representatives, they are certainly moving much closer together than has been the case in the past.

Overall, the debate concerning worker participation has moved forward to the extent that the opportunity to reach a consensus view is there to be grasped. It remains to be seen whether or not politicians in both Brussels and the UK can capitalise on this and can ultimately produce a set of proposals to resolve the issue to common satisfaction.

Worker participation is only one of the many measures concerning employment contained within the Social Charter, which I shall examine in detail in a practical rather than a political sense in the next chapter. Before doing so, however, it will be worthwhile to consider briefly those aspects of EC employment legislation that have already been adopted by the UK. This will not only illustrate the way in which Directives are translated into national law, but may also give some indication of the likely adoption of the proposed future directives and their impact within the UK.

The impact of EC employment legislation to date

Employment-related Directives approved by the Council of Ministers to date, and adopted within the UK, have been limited in number and confined to just four areas. These are:

- Collective redundancies (Directive approved February 1975), requiring prior notification and consultation when collective redundancies are proposed.
- Employee protection following insolvency (Directive approved October 1980), requiring the establishment of funds to meet contractual obligations, for example wages due during notice periods, holidays and retirement benefits providing claims made before insolvency.
- Transfer of undertakings (Directive approved February 1977), requiring consultation with employees to protect against dismissal, and safeguard employment rights.
- Equal treatment of men and women (several Directives from 1975 to 1978), covering discrimination in promotion, training and employment conditions, social security matters, and equal pay for work of equal value.

Collective redundancies

This Directive applies to organisations in the private sector only, where group redundancies over a 30-day period are to be effected. Where an employer is contemplating redundancies prior consultation with employees' representatives is required, in order to avoid or reduce the necessity for dismissals as far as possible. The notification requirement applies in the following circumstances:

- ten or more redundancies in an organisation employing 20 to 100 people;
- ten per cent or more in an organisation employing 100 to 300 people;
- 30 or more in an organisation employing more than 300 people.

The Directive has been implemented in the UK through the 1965 Redundancy Act, the 1975 Employment Protection Act and the 1978 Employment Protection Consolidation Act. It covers only a small part of UK law concerning redundancy, for example it does not touch on redundancy pay; it could also be argued that it does not go as far as UK law as framed in the Employment Protection Act. In particular, the latter specifies minimum periods for consultation that in some cases are longer than those intended by the Directive (e.g. 90 days when 100 or more staff are involved) irrespective of the size of the organisation, and requires employers to consult with a trade union even if only one person is to be made redundant from the bargaining unit for which it is recognised.

Although the Directive undoubtedly had an effect in the shaping of the relevant clauses within the Employment Protection Act, its impact overall has been limited. The penalties against an organisation for non-compliance are not great; a tribunal finding in favour of a complaint can make a protective award to those declared redundant limited to no more than the wages due during period of non-compliance (i.e. a maximum of 90 days where 100 or more employees are involved).

Employee protection following insolvency

The effect of this Directive on UK law has been nil because certain debts owed by the insolvent employer to the employee were, by 1980, already guaranteed by the state under the provisions of the Employment Protection Consolidation Act. Employees have the right to make a written request to the Secretary of State for a payment out of the Redundancy Fund to meet the following contractual pay items:

- eight weeks arrears of pay;
- statutory minimum notice;

- holiday pay up to six weeks in the prior 12 months;
- basic compensation in redundancy or unfair dismissal;
- maternity pay;
- return of certain fees by articled clerks or apprentices.

The definition of pay under the Act includes statutory sick pay, remuneration payable during suspension on medical grounds and under certain other circumstances.

Transfer of undertakings

This Directive is consolidated within the Transfer Regulations 1981, although the latter deals only with undertakings situated wholly or partly within the UK prior to transfer. Regulation 10 concerns the duty to inform and consult with recognised trade union representatives, dealing with this in two parts:

- First, general information concerning the transfer which may affect a group of employees must be given (arguably this could be interpreted to be all employees in all cases).
- Second, any specific information concerning measures to be taken which directly relate to a group of employees (e.g. redundancy) must be given 'long enough before a relevant transfer to enable consultations to take place'. Essentially, the new owner cannot use the merger or transfer as a means of justification for redundancy or changes to terms and conditions.

The nature of the circumstances in which transfers of undertaking take place will tend to water down the force of these regulations even though they are phrased in precise terms. For example, they only apply to *the fact* of a transfer, rather than one that is proposed; and the penalties for non-compliance may be reduced where there are 'special circumstances' which make compliance not reasonably practicable. In any case, the penalties are not great; they parallel those concerning collective redundancies under the Employment Protection Act when redundancies do indeed occur; the maximum compensation which can be awarded for failure to comply with the Regulations itself is two weeks' pay for each employee affected. Overall, the courts and tribunals have experienced considerable difficulty in interpreting the legislation, which has therefore had little impact on employment in the UK.

Equal treatment of men and women

Several of the Directives concerning equality of treatment are pre-dated within the UK by the Equal Pay Act 1970 and the Sex Discrimination Act 1975. The Sex Discrimination Act in particular covers a wide range of non-contractual benefits as well as procedures relating to recruitment, training, promotion and dismissal. The Equal Opportunities Commission has issued Codes of Practice with the aim of eliminating sex discrimination in employment practices throughout the UK.

The original Equal Pay Act deliberately excluded retirement ages and pensions provision, and until 1978 no EC legislation existed covering equality in social security benefits. However, in December 1978, the Directive on State Social Security Schemes was approved, prohibiting discrimination regarding access and entitlement to payment of *statutory* social security benefits received in respect of unemployment, sickness, disability, old age, industrial accidents and diseases. The main impact of this in the UK has been on retirement ages; the ruling of the Court of Justice in the case of *Helen Marshall* v. *Southampton Health Authority* forced the UK to introduce the 1986 Sex Discrimination Act allowing men and women to continue working until the same age. In this case the Court ruled that an age limit for the compulsory dismissal of workers relating to an employer's general policy concerning retirement fell within the term 'dismissal' of Article 119 of the Treaty of Rome and so 'a general policy concerning dismissal of a woman solely because she has attained the qualifying age for a state pension, which age is different under normal legislation for men and women' constituted discrimination on the grounds of sex contrary to equal treatment directives. Although the 1978 Directive applied only to state employees, the Government was quick to extend its effect to all employees within the UK in the Sex Discrimination Act. The Act, which came into effect on 7 November 1987, requires that employers do not discriminate between men and women as regards the normal retirement age that is set.

Although the pensions' provision is inextricably linked to retirement age, as yet there is no requirement that equal pension ages are applied. This is undoubtedly why, for the present, the many employers including the UK Government which continue to break the law by applying different retirement ages have therefore gone unchallenged. This is clearly, however, an equal treatment issue: taking, for example, a scheme in which men are retired at 65 and women at 60, a woman insisting on continuing to 65 would 'lose out' on five years pension qualification and conversely a man insisting on retiring at 60 would receive neither pay nor pension as of right for five years.

A number of recent developments seem certain to change all this. In 1989 the Equal Opportunities Commission announced its intent to take the Government to court to answer charges that it is guilty of sexual discrimination against men in the way it administers the old age pension. The EOC's argument is that this discrimination arises through men having to pay National Insurance for 44 years to quality for a full state pension, compared with only 39 years for women. The EOC clearly sees this issue as a half-way house to full equalisation of pension ages. Mr Alan Hart, Chief Executive of the EOC, has said as much in the following statement made in 1989:

'The decision to challenge the Government on this issue is an important step in our strategy to tackle the different state pension ages and the various inequalities surrounding them.'

The EOC's aim appears, however, to have been largely met as a result of an important ruling by the European Court of Justice in May 1990. In the Baker v. Guardian Royal Exchange Assurance Group case, any discrimination between men and women regarding retirement benefits – and therefore by definition retirement ages – was deemed to be in breach of Article 119 of the Treaty of Rome. UK employers that apply different retirement ages are consequently required to equalise them, at a cost to their pension funds estimated to be up to £2 billion per year. Application of the law may be delayed by arguments concerning the complex actuarial issues surrounding life expectancy, and by many companies' insistence that the Government acts first and equalises the state retirement age; however, the EOC will no doubt continue to press its claims hard.

It seems likely that in most cases retirement ages will ultimately be equalised upwards, towards the higher age limits that apply to men over women in the state and many other pension schemes.

Equal pay for equal value

In 1982 it was held by the European Court of Justice that the original Equal Pay Act did not comply in full with the Commission's Directive concerning equal pay for men and women. This led to the Equal Pay Amendment Act which came into force on 1 January 1984. It has been, to date, not only the most publicised but by far the most significant instance of European Community legislation having an impact on UK employment law.

The Directive requires member states to apply equality provisions to 'work for which equal value is attributed', covering 'all aspects and conditions of remuneration'. The European Court held that the UK was in breach of this because the Equal Pay Act stipulated that women were entitled to equal pay for work of equal value only if their employer had chosen to undertake job evaluation. It therefore became necessary for the Government to introduce regulations to enable female employees to have their jobs compared and evaluated with those of male employees (and vice versa), whether a formal job evaluation system applied or not.

The basis of comparison between jobs, therefore, now rests on the concept of 'like' work. Jobs can be 'like', and of the same value, if they are 'broadly similar' – to quote from the EOC guidebook on the subject, 'by a general consideration of the type of work involved and the skill and knowledge required to do them'. They do not have to have the same job title or contractual obligations, indeed even if graded the same under a formal job evaluation system this system itself must be free from sex bias. Furthermore, where a court deems that two diverse jobs carried out respectively by a man and woman are of equal value, the total conditions of employment package, not just basic pay, must also be equivalent.

In terms of actual cases brought to tribunals by women against their employers, the new legislation is having an increasing effect: the Department of Employment's official statistics have shown a dramatic rise in the number of cases from only 100 in 1984 to 517 in 1986/87. However, success rates are extremely low (only 44 in 1986/87 with a further 71 cases being settled by arbitration). This undoubtedly relates in part to the extreme complexity of the equal value procedure, as well as the difficulties of interpretation that courts face in specific cases. Much use has been made by employers of the 'genuine material factor' defence, which invalidates the equality clause if it can be shown that the contract variation is 'genuinely due to a material factor which is not the difference of sex'.

However, the impact of the legislation should not be judged just by the success and failure rate of cases to date. All evidence points to the conclusion that the Equal Pay Amendment is playing an increasing part in the defining of employment conditions and industrial relations. There are a number of reasons for this:

- First, a number of the most significant cases have taken a considerable length of time to progress through the legislative system, but the verdicts given at the highest level (the House of Lords) have been highly significant. In the case of *Hayward* v. *Camell Laird Shipbuilders*, not settled until May 1988, it was held by the Lords that if a woman can demonstrate that her job is of equal value to that of a male employee, she may insist that any specific term in her contract must be brought up to equivalent level. The *Pickstone* v. *Freemans* 1989 case removed the possibility of employers placing a 'token man' into a job also carried out by a group of women, in order to preclude the bringing of an equal value claim. The Lords' judgement in these and other test cases, has been widely criticised as inconsistent, which in itself illustrates the difficulties in interpretation of equal pay law that courts and tribunals face; however, there is no doubt that the two cases mentioned above have done much to raise awareness of the potential consequences of failure to comply.

- Second, the potential costs involved in cases where an employer is found to be in breach of law are extremely high. This is of course especially so where large numbers of women are employed in relatively low paid jobs. Linked into this is the use that unions and negotiating bodies are now making of the law in support of pay claims – on behalf of qualified and experienced nurses in the National Health Service, for example. The equal value law has certainly become a solid platform for employees' representatives to boost the pay of such categories of staff and trade unions are showing an increasing willingness to support equal pay claims as they progress through the courts.

- Third, employers across all sectors have been forced to look critically at their job evaluation and pay and conditions structures in order to ensure their validity in relation to the law. Although the Equal Opportunities Commission has held all along that employers with fair pay structures have nothing to fear, the subjectivity both of job evaluation systems and pay and benefits comparison makes it extremely difficult for companies to be certain they are acting completely in accordance with the Act.

This has been underlined by the ruling of the European Court of Justice in the Danfoss case in Denmark, where it was held that, even under an established pay and grading scheme, if it can be shown that the average pay of female employees within a grade is below that of male employees, the employer must be able to demonstrate that its pay practices are not discrimatory. This puts the existing onus on employers to justify their practices even more open to challenge, the 'genuine material difference' defence no longer being sufficient in many potential cases. Discrimination claims are likely to be upheld if, for example, differences are due to such factors as flexibility or training opportunity where women are frequently at a disadvantage due to family commitments.

Equal pay for work of equal value clearly demonstrates a number of points. It is the prime example to date of an EC directive in the field of employment law being interpreted by the UK in a way the Commission has found unsatisfactory. In being rectified within UK law it has become an issue of great significance that has had considerable impact on the treatment of staff by employers. The concept of equality it underpins is a simple one, but because of the judgemental nature of the issues involved it has been extremely difficult for courts and tribunals to reach verdicts. Where they have done so, however, the precedents created have enormous potential consequences for organisations in terms of equal opportunity policy and direct employment costs. Equal pay cannot be ignored; it remains a model for the kind of effect that future EC social policy directives may have within the UK in adoption as employment law.

Part two
The challenge for the personnel manager

3 Europe: the impact of the Commission's social policy

In this chapter I shall examine those social policy initiatives being taken by the European Commission that are of impact in the sphere of employment, using as a reference point the Commission's September 1988 working paper 'The Social Dimension of the Internal Market'. I have chosen this document rather than the 1989 Social Charter that emerged from it, as the Social Dimension Document goes into much greater detail on the Commission's specific proposals. Effectively, it is the 'White Paper' behind the Social Charter.

The chapter falls into two parts. In the first, I shall summarise the broad areas of policy outlined in the paper. In the second, I shall give a more detailed analysis of those that are of most direct relevance to Personnel Managers; the potential consequences will be set in the context of the likelihood of the Commission achieving its objective in each specific case.

The Social Dimension working paper

This document covers a huge amount of ground, and proposes different types of measure to address the issues raised. At one extreme, it seeks revision to existing regulations, and the preparation of new regulations and directives to the Council; at the other to instigate studies into specific problem areas, the monitoring of national policies and Community-wide trends, the preparation of reports, codes of practice and action programmes. Overall these measures are classified under five broad headings, as follows:

- Living and Working Conditions in the Enlarged Market.
- Economic and Social Cohesion.
- Priority Measures to Promote Employment and Training.
- Working Conditions and Work Organisation.
- Social Foundation.

Living and working conditions in the enlarged market

Freedom of movement

Freedom of movement is the major area of attention under this heading. Proposals include:

- A revision of the SEDOC regulation which promotes the provision of information throughout the Community on unfilled job vacancies and applications.
- A host of amendments to existing regulations concerning state social security provision for migrant workers and their families, mainly concerned with extending provision to the self- employed, unemployed and 'those who are not economically active' such as students. It should be noted that the Commission's intentions fall well short of attempting to harmonise benefits completely throughout the Community in such areas as unemployment and family benefits and accident at work compensation. Due to the many differences between Member States this is recognised as a complex and unrealistic task; however, the Commission's declared objective is to 'establish the principle of equivalence'.
- Measures to facilitate rights of residence administration and procedures.
- A review of the practices of certain member states of limiting access to employment in the public sector to nationals of their own country; under European law this can only take place where 'the safeguarding of the general interests of the state' are in question. The review will consider practices in public utilities, the health and education services and state departments.
- The framing of draft directives concerning recognition of vocational qualifications. These follow from the common position adopted by the Council of Ministers on this issue; there are two distinct areas. First, a directive concerning equivalence of higher-level educational qualifications requiring a minimum of three years' study, to enable professional workers to practice freely throughout the Community. Second, directives relating to specific vocational qualifications, mostly of a lower level, for which the much more detailed principle of mutual recognition will be required. This follows on from previously agreed directives which listed member states' diplomas in certain professions in order to obtain Community-wide recognition; to date most of these

specifically concern health service professions such as doctors, nurses and midwives. The process is complex and time-consuming as it involves more detailed consideration of the training and experience components of each diploma than is the case with equivalence, leading to agreed descriptions of professional activities and the drawing up of common standards of competence. Priority action has been given to job categories in the hotel and restaurant trade, car repairs, the construction industry, electrotechnology, agriculture, forestry and textiles.

Specific sectoral measures concerning the completion of the internal market

The second major area listed under freedom of movement is headed 'specific sectoral measures concerning the completion of the internal market' and rather surprisingly lists worker participation as a prime objective. The proposal therefore seeks Council affirmation for the much debated and amended Fifth Company Law Directive which, in its latest form, would require public companies employing more than 1,000 people to implement procedures for informing and consulting with employees.

Relations with non-Community countries

The third 'freedom of movement' area concerns relations with non-Community countries, in particular the setting up of systems for monitoring the immigration of non-Community nationals, and for communication and consulting with non-member countries regarding migration and social integration.

Economic and social cohesion

Unemployment

Unemployment has consistently been a major concern of the European Commission, and as will be seen, a large number of proposals contained in the Social Dimension Document relate to its alleviation by one method or another. The European Social Fund, providing a means for financing retraining and redeployment of workers is described in Article 123 of the Treaty of Rome:

'In order to improve employment opportunities for workers in the common market and to contribute thereby to raising the standard of living a European Social Fund is hereby established . . . it shall have the task of rendering the employment of workers easier and of increasing their geographical and occupational mobility within the Community.'

Its provisions included meeting 50 per cent of the cost of state-sponsored expenditure on the unemployment grants; it has been reformed several times in order to make it more specific to small and medium enterprises (SMEs) and to cover certain categories of workers felt to be at risk. The guidelines for 1989-91 are to give priority to vocational training in connection with new technology, the needs of skilled staff in SMEs, the long-term unemployed, the disabled, migrant workers and women in occupations in which they are under represented.

Population studies

These priorities are also apparent in other areas listed under the heading of 'Economic and Social Cohesion'. A group of initiatives not requiring endorsement by the Council seek to implement studies and reports into issues such as demographic trends, the ageing of the Community's population, and family policies. These will, no doubt, address some of the major areas of concern to the Commission which run as fundamental trends throughout the Social Dimension Document – the uneven distribution of population structures and unemployment patterns, long-term and rural unemployment and increased employment opportunities for women.

Disadvantaged population groups

A further area of concern is headed 'solidarity towards disadvantaged population groups'. This concentrates on the disabled, and seeks to build on already approved action programmes which would standardise policy towards the classification of disability, the employment of disabled workers and the development of rehabilitation, training and job placement programmes.

Priority measures to promote employment and training

This heading encompasses two subsections entitled, respectively, 'Promotion of Employment' and 'Education and Training'.

Promotion of employment

The Commission's broad concern about the effects on employment of the completion of the Single European Market is a theme that runs consistently throughout the Social Dimension Document. The statement is made early on that 'as part of the programme to complete the internal market, social policy must put into effect a wide-ranging package of distinctive measures'. A distinction is made between short and medium to long-term effects, particularly in relation to freedom of movement and job creation. In particular, reference is made to the Cecchini report which identifies an initially negative impact leading to some job losses, but which will be offset in the medium-term: 'In the medium-term there could be five million new jobs created in the Community, and there could be an increase in the Community growth rate of seven per cent, provided the Community implements simultaneously the economic support and structural policies liable to lead to the best possible use of the margins for manoeuvre created'.

Emphasis is therefore placed on the SEDOC system as already mentioned, and the related MISEP programme to disseminate and analyse information on special employment programmes in member states and publish this throughout the Community. An action programme on local job creation initiatives is also proposed, initiating from a resolution promoted by the UK Government and involving business as well as state support. A third area is an action programme of support for the long-term unemployed. This aims to develop a Community-wide approach to 'harness the most fruitful experience gained in each Member State', recognising that considerable demographic differences exist in different states and that changes to the Community's structural funds are needed to target the problem most effectively.

A large number of measures are proposed to promote the employment, work integration and fair treatment of women. Many of these will be consultative rather than directive. However, in two specific areas the Commission is anxious to see harmonisation of practices throughout the Community. The first of these concerns parental leave; although an original draft directive which would have given working parents at least three months' leave on the birth or adoption of a child has been withdrawn for the time being, a draft recommendation to the same effect is being promoted. The second concerns the burden of proof in the area of equal pay and equal treatment for women and men. Here a draft directive is proposed which would strengthen the law in favour of the claimant in sex discrimination cases by requiring the respondent to prove that discrimination had not taken place, rather than requiring the claimant to prove that it has. The directive also seeks to broaden the definition of indirect discrimination to include 'an apparently neutral provision, criterion or practice (which) disproportionately disadvantages the members of one sex, by reference in particular to marital or family status'. Both measures are supported by the Equal Opportunities Commission.

Other items proposed concerning women include programmes to encourage both occupational and physical mobility, and a code of practice on pregnancy and maternity protection.

Education and training

The Social Dimension Document declares that the achievement of the Single Market must go hand in hand with improved access to vocational training including training linked with work. It therefore specifies a large number of measures linked to education, the transition from education to employment, and training in the workplace. It also recognises the need to maintain a flexible Community workforce in order to respond to changing technological and industrial trends and ensure a constant supply of appropriately qualified workers.

In the field of primary and secondary education, the document proposes little more in the short term than to carry out studies into teaching standards throughout the Community, in order to raise standards towards those of the better Member States. In the tertiary education sector a more positive proposal is the ERASMUS programme, to encourage co-operation between universities in the different member states.

The programme has considerable funds at its disposal to provide financial support to students and lecturers to carry out studies in Community countries other than their own.

The document is also more positive in promoting measures that relate to the transition from education to employment. These include:

- **THE COMETT Programme** (Community Action for Education and Training for Technology) established in 1987, which promotes co-operation between universities and businesses by providing funding for training programmes on a 'joint venture' basis. The benefits are seen as two-way, providing Universities, their students and staff with the resources to carry out technological research, and businesses with the means to maintain their competitiveness by drawing on, and contributing to a highly trained and qualified pool of labour. The second phase of the programme will run from 1990 to 1993.

- **A vocational training programme** 'to prepare young people for working life': with the aim of supporting the individual programmes of Member States, setting up joint actions and youth initiatives wherever appropriate. This relates clearly to state-sponsored programmes of job preparation.
- **The 'YES for Europe' programme**, to encourage youth exchanges between the ages of 15 and 25. This clearly aims to encourage an infrastructure of short and medium-term exchange visits at non-governmental level. In particular, funding for young employers to gain work experience for periods of up to 18 months in establishments in other Community countries is proposed.

A number of measures are also proposed to provide increased training opportunity for those already in work. These are as follows:

- An action programme for the development and improvement of foreign language skills throughout the Community; related both to the teaching of languages in formal education and training for those in employment.
- The EUROTECNET programme to 'encourage vocational training in the new information technologies by identifying the most innovative experiments and setting up a system for exchanging information gained from such experiments'. Established in 1985, the second phase of the programme is about to begin by building on the successes of the first. The UK in particular, through the offices of the Training Agency, has contributed a number of demonstration projects and in return has received a considerable amount of information concerning other countries new technology training.
- An action programme on vocational training for adult employees, concentrating initially on the needs of those working within small and medium-sized firms and in less developed regions.
- A proposed directive on the right to special leave for purposes of vocational training. No details of this have yet emerged but, following the practice adopted in many other areas, the programme is likely to build on current practice in the Member States that already have formal schemes with a view to obtaining 'upwards harmonisation'.

Working conditions and work organisation

The two major areas covered under this heading are, respectively, health and safety at work; and 'work organisation and relations', concerned mainly with information and consultation procedures.

Health and safety at work

Legislation concerning health and safety has been a major area of activity for the Commission over many years, and one in which it has achieved much success in the adoption of Directives. This activity was intensified by the Single Market Programme, as it was recognised that the removal of barriers could, if uncontrolled, lead to a free market for unsafe products or the exploitation of low health and safety standards for competitive trade advantage. Most specific Directives adopted since 1987 have concerned the protection of workers against exposure to dangerous substances, and machine/workplace safety.

In June 1989 a 'Council Directive on the introduction of measures to encourage improvement in the safety and health of workers at work' was adopted, based on Article 118a of the Treaty of Rome. Known as the 'Framework Directive' this contains general principles only but obliges employers in all sectors to take measures to 'ensure the prevention of occupational risks, the protection of safety and health, the elimination of risk and accident factors, the information, consultation, balanced participation in accordance with national laws and/or practices and training of workers and their representatives' by compliance date of 31 December 1992. Within the UK, the Department of Employment considers that most of the specific measures proposed are already met by the 1974 Health and Safety at Work Act.

1992 has been designated the European Year of Safety, which has given further impetus to the programme of change already under way. It is envisaged that some 40 individual proposals for Community-wide legislation will be agreed by this year, mostly on the principle of gaining agreement to 'minimum acceptable standards' rather than upwards harmonisation – a recognition both that many states with generally good standards do not have detailed legislation and that for practical as well as political reasons the agreement of common highest standards would take many years and would be damaging to companies' profitability. The most immediate outcome from the 'Framework Directive' is the drafting of a set of five more specific Directives, covering general health and safety improvements and requirements, minimum requirements for machinery and equipment, protective equipment, visual display units and the handling of heavy loads. These will be underpinned in the future by further detailed directives covering sectors such as agriculture, fisheries and construction, and providing protection against exposure to further hazards including carcinogens, chemical and biological agents.

The Commission is also now beginning to show more interest in the area of occupational health service provision. Here again, many of the Member States have good general standards but little formal legislation; although the Social Dimension Document contains a number of indications of the Commission's intention to pursue a policy, the direction this will take is unclear. There is however a declaration that 'the starting point is still consultation with the social partners, taking into account the particular situation of small and medium-sized enterprises'.

Work organisation and relations

The proposals under this heading within the Social Dimension Document concern, respectively, a 'standard contract' for Community employees, contractual rights for part-time and temporary workers, and information and consultative rights of employees. They are among the most contentious, but also the vaguest in the Commission's thinking. Very closely bound up with the broad philosophical tenets of social policy, as such they have perhaps become somewhat diffused as the Commission attempts to moderate its stance and establish a wider appeal to political extremes across the Community.

The Social Dimension Document itself declares: 'the harmonisation of provisions regulating labour relations and conditions of work is a topic on which there are highly divergent opinions'. It attempts to bridge this ideological gap by stating that greater homogeneity not only maintains the rights and duties of employees, but also strengthens the trade position of the Community and can 'facilitate the mobility of productive capital and place firms completing with one another under more similar operating conditions'. However, there is clear recognition that the complex differences between the societies of Member States, their economic, labour market and labour relations situations, dilute the significance of harmonisation both from the employees' and employers' point of view. Other specific factors are identified:

- the quality of products and services offered by enterprises: the link between competitiveness and pay and conditions is not stated, but is strongly implied;
- productivity levels, which have a direct impact on labour costs; linked to operating efficiency, mechanisation and labour intensity.

The conclusion reached from this is that problems of unfair competition and social dumping are not, generally, likely to be significant in the open economies and democratic political environments that prevail throughout the Community. In a practical sense, the difficulties involved in extensive standardisation except in 'specific facets of the labour market', such as health and safety, are also outlined. These are:

- first, the ways in which enterprises' cultures and norms are closely linked to those of their home states;
- second, and by far the most important factor, upwards harmonisation could force some enterprises out of business and thus add to the community unemployment problem;
- third, over-restrictive legislation could reduce the level of dialogue (and hence, it is implied, labour relations) between employers' and employees' representatives.

The Commission's stance is, therefore, summed up in the following words:

'These arguments by no means imply abandoning all harmonisation in this area, apart from measures directly concerned with health and safety conditions. It means that it is essential to remain highly aware at all times of the balance between the costs of maintaining diversity and the costs of reducing it, and that full account must be taken of the fact that since the institutions are more dynamic in some Member States than in others, the impact of every measure taken could well vary too.'

Given this highly qualified standpoint on workers' rights, it is hardly surprising that the Commission's proposals to establish some form of standard contract to define formal employer/employee relationships has to some extent run out of steam. The declared position remains, however, that the Commission is 'considering proposing generally-applicable rules relating to the basic labour rights of workers'. The specific areas that are being considered within this are:

- the right to a written contract stating basic terms and conditions;
- equal treatment for men and women (including equal pay and maternity/pregnancy rights);
- the obligation 'to inform and consult workers in the case of important changes which may affect the firm'.

The second and third of these items, in particular, are worthy of more detailed consideration, which appears further on in this chapter.

Part-time contracts

The Commission has been engaged in consultation with COREPER (the Permanent Representatives Committee of the Council of Ministers) since 1983, but has so far failed to gain adoption of any directives. As currently drafted, proposals would establish equal contractual rights with full-time workers in a number of areas including wages and emoluments, health and safety, pension entitlement and time off work. The Commission is as concerned about the job creation possibilities inherent in a better matching between the demand of employees for more flexible working and employers' work capacity as it is about equal rights in themselves. Nevertheless, reaction from a number of member states, including the UK, to proposed directives continues to be hostile; the proposals are seen by many as a first step down the road towards standard terms and conditions throughout the Community.

Temporary contracts

The measures proposed here reflect those for part-time contract employees in many respects, including such items as equal rights to social security provisions and companies engaging agency supplied temporary workers would be liable for social security costs and pay in the event of agency default.

Information and consultation

The Social Dimension Document states:

'The Commission is convinced that the dialogue between labour and management has an absolutely essential role to play in building Europe.'

Proposals on this issue go back the 'Vredling Directive' of 1980, which would have required all groups or individual companies employing more than 1,000 workers to disclose to employee representatives a considerable amount of information concerning its activities. This information would have included details concerning company structures, the financial situation, the employment situation and probable trends concerning production, sales and development prospects. The Directive would also have required parent companies to establish formal consultation procedures to take place on any decision 'liable to have serious consequences for the interests of employees of its subsidiaries in the Community'.

The substantial criticisms of this proposal – not least from United States and Japanese companies which even threatened to divert corporate investment elsewhere should it be implemented – have led to a number of revisions from the original which show a greater sensitivity towards business concerns. Nevertheless, there is still a substantial political lobby that would seek the adoption of some modified form of the Directive, and the Commission itself continues to regard greater employee involvement in the decision-making process as essential to the Community's economic prosperity.

Social foundation

The Social Dimension Document is a declaration of the European Commission's commitment to a programme of change to run in parallel with, and be supportive of, the Single Market Programme. While it recognises that social change can only evolve over time, and must develop through dialogue between the social partners, it sees the date of 31 December 1992 as the deadline for establishment of a Community Social Foundation just as it is the 'deadline' – so called – for the Single Market Programme itself. In summary the Commission hopes to have reached agreement on as many as possible of its priority measures in the field of employment by this date.

The European Charter of Social Rights would be the instrument in which these agreed measures would be laid down. To quote the penultimate paragraph of the Social Dimension Document:

'Maximisation of gain by an active employment policy and by ongoing observation, means of ensuring freedom of movement in practice, the reinforcing of workers health and safety in the work environment, labour law, solidarity, social dialogue, all of which, in the eyes of the Commission, are the essential elements on which the Community social foundation is based, and which could be embodied in a European Charter of Social Rights, to be transmitted to the Council and European Parliament in due course.'

The social agenda – its potential for change in the UK

In the second part of this chapter I shall consider in more detail those aspects of the Commission's social policy that are of greatest potential impact on employment in the UK. I wish to examine both the chances of success of each measure of being adopted by the community and the likely effect on our domestic employment situation should they become adopted.

At the time of writing, the UK Government has expressed only qualified support for the 1989 Social Charter, declaring its intention to continue its resistance against many of the individual measures the Charter proposes. Just as significantly, a study carried out by Henley Management College has predicted, first, that UK companies will have to become much more aware of the speed and the scope of the processes of legislative and cultural change; and second, that there *will* be major impacts on employment practices arising from the Single Market Programme. To quote a CBI spokesman: '10,000 UK companies appear to be sleep-walking their way to 1992'.

Looking specifically at Commission-led rather than cultural aspects of the change process – which I shall consider in detail in the following chapter – the areas that I believe merit particular attention are as follows:

- Equivalence of Higher Education Level Professional Qualifications.
- Employee Involvement.
- Equal Treatment and Pay.
- Vocational Training and Cultural Exchange.
- Health and Safety at the Workplace.
- Part-time and Temporary Contractual Rights.
- Informing and Consulting with Employees.

Equivalence of Higher Education Level Professional Qualifications

The Commission's programme in this area has been developed rapidly: in December 1988 a directive was adopted by the Council of Ministers on a 'general system for recognition of higher education diplomas awarded on completion of professional education and training of at least three years' duration'. This sets out in detail the measures to be implemented to verify teaching standards, professional experience levels and certificates, the bodies to be responsible for monitoring in the member states, and the remedies for non-compliance. The directive includes a provision which enables Member States to require a migrant professional either to take a test or undergo a period of supervised practice if his qualifications are substantially different from those required for the same profession in the host country. In most cases the migrant can choose between the two, although the host country can stipulate one or the other where the profession requires a precise knowledge of national law, and involves advising on it as a constant and essential aspect of the professional activity.

The provisions of the directive must be implemented by Member States from January 1991, which is a measure of how generally well-received the Commission's proposals in this area have been. In the UK, the Training Agency will undertake the complex task of establishing and publishing the ground rules and monitoring compliance.

The directive will clearly act as a catalyst to the mobility of professional staff throughout the Community. From the point of view of the professionals themselves, they will be free to obtain work and to practice in any Member State they choose, without the need to requalify (in some cases a limited amount of 'topping up' of qualifications may be required, to compensate for significant differences in training or experience). From the point of view of companies which employ such professionals, they will be able, first, to open up their recruitment campaigns to encompass the pan-European employment market; and second, to offer their professional services on a European scale. Overall, the potential effects are therefore highly significant, and could increase considerably the competitiveness of professional service provision to the benefit of those who buy such services.

It should be remembered that the directive does not apply to vocational or any other form of qualification requiring less than three years' study. A second Diplomas Directive, however, was proposed in 1989, intended to complement the first Directive as described above. If adopted, this would require the mutual recognition of occupational diplomas and certificates gained after less than three years' study, enabling people holding such qualifications to practise their occupation in another Member State where entry is limited to those holding a relevant qualification. Again, there is provision for host countries to require migrants to undertake a period of supervised practice or aptitude tests to prove their professional competence.

Employee involvement

I have already discussed this issue in a political sense in the previous chapter, where I considered the extent to which the various interest groups, including the European Commission itself, have moved tentatively towards the middle ground. Although there are many political advantages to be gained from the establishment of a mutually acceptable position, in a practical sense it seems inevitable that delays will occur and that it may be some time before Britain's position as the 'odd man out' in the Council of Ministers is changed. Part of the delay may well stem from the Commission itself which, highly sensitive to the UK Government views in the past, has shelved debates on the subject in order not to embarrass Conservative MEPs.

Nevertheless, in the longer term solutions will have to be found to the impasse. The proposed Fifth Company Law Directive, which contains the clause introducing worker participation as part of the harmonisation process for the structure of limited liability companies in the Community, presents four options for worker participation:

- worker representatives elected as members of the supervisory board;
- worker representatives co-opted as members of the supervisory board;
- participation through a separate body representing the workers;
- participation through an equivalent system established by collective agreement.

The Commission has also suggested that the problems of harmonising company boards could be solved by not obliging a company to follow a specific EC regulation but by introducing the principle of mutual recognition in this sphere so that each Member State would recognise the validity of another Member State's company board structure. Dr Richard Brown, author of the British Institute of Management's discussion paper *The European Employer* see this route as the key to a rapid resolution of the problem:

'The most likely option will be a framework directive which sets out the aims of increasing employee participation, but will be much less prescriptive than the current drafts. Given the conviction of the European Commission, it looks politically inevitable that there will be some forms of European employee involvement legislation adopted before the end of 1992.'

It is difficult to predict the impact of legislation in this area on UK personnel practice without knowing precisely what form the legislation itself will take. It is clear however that the main concerns are in the sphere of collective bargaining and industrial relations.

As long ago as 1976, the Institute of Personnel Management published its response to the Commission's Green Paper, as it was then, on employee participation and company structure. The issues raised then are just as valid today: the main basis of the IPM's opposition to the proposals was that employee representation at main board level would severely jeopardise the British 'voluntarist' tradition of employment relations, in particular the possibility for meaningful bargaining at local level. This would create acute practical difficulties for companies of all sizes and structures, but especially those with decentralised organisation structures or operating in a multinational environment:

'One multinational enterprise, for example, has subsidiaries in 14 Western European countries in which ten different languages are spoken. The number of employees in individual countries ranges from 800 to 80,0000. In one country its subsidiaries negotiate with 18 different trade unions. Clearly there would be serious practical difficulties in establishing even a consultative body which would not be so large as to be functionally ineffective, and yet which could ensure reasonable representation of all the nationalities, companies and levels of employees concerned.'

Obviously, this is a response to the prospect of employee involvement in its most extreme, regulated form: a more diluted, less restrictive version of the original proposals may well now emerge enabling the maintenance of local bargaining initiatives and 'management's right to manage'.

The Institute of Personnel Management, never slow to identify an opportunity for the personnel profession, specifies two subsidiary impacts arising from employee involvement legislation:

- First, the need to provide training to employee representatives regarding company structures, norms, constraints and operating environments. This is seen as essential if success is to be made of participative arrangements.
- Second, an increased role for the Personnel Manager arising from the higher profile that will be given to companies' personnel policies. In

particular, it will be necessary for there to be personnel representation at board level, to counterbalance the power of employee representatives and confirm 'the importance attached to the personnel function in particular and good employee relations in general'.

Equal treatment and pay

Although a considerable amount of European law in this area has been adopted by the UK, its interpretation and the slow progress of actual cases through the courts means that in a number of areas its effects have not yet been fully felt. The Commission is well aware of this, and in its most recent booklet on the subject, 'Equal Opportunities for Women' declares its determination to see through its programme:

'We have seen how the Community has already adopted several legal measures to promote equal opportunities. It is still necessary to see that they are properly translated into national law, correctly interpreted and applied in practice, with individuals being able to have recourse to the law as intended.'

This is not just empty rhetoric, but is backed up by an action programme to build awareness amongst interest groups, lobby governments and compare and monitor the practices of individual Member States. Two examples of this programme are, first, Vasso Papandreou's keynote speech at the 1989 TUC Women's Conference at which, *inter alia*, she spoke of the need to harmonise childcare and maternity leave standards and push for increased opportunity for women to obtain vocational training; and second, the Commission's detailed criticism of the French Government's failure to implement fully the Equal Treatment Directive of 1976.

It is inevitable, therefore, that the combined pressure of the European Commission itself, the Equal Opportunities Commission and individual trade unions representing women members will ensure that the current Directives and amendments to them are progressed as far and as quickly as possible to the advantage of women employees in the UK.

The complex area of *pensions* is one in which the effects of successive stages of social security legislation are likely to be significant. Building on the 1978 Social Security Directive, a further Directive adopted in 1986 legislates against direct and indirect discrimination based on sex, in the application of both state and private sector occupational pension schemes. The Directive is due to be implemented by the end of 1992 and stipulates that:

- equal treatment must apply regarding pensionable age, although in occupational schemes this is deferred until the question of equalising retirement ages in the state scheme has been settled. As indicated in Chapter 3 this has not yet taken place within the UK; but in the wake of the *Barber* v. *GRE Assurance Group* case ruling seems sure to happen soon;

- equal treatment of 'survivors' pensions' must be implemented, in other words widows' and widowers' benefits must be equalised. The potential costs are considerable for those firms whose schemes provide no or reduced widower benefits.

The question of pension entitlements for part-time staff is another major issue where it seems increasingly likely that claims of indirect discrimination will be held by the courts to apply. In a significant case in West Germany (*Bilka-Kaufhaus* v. *Weber von Hartz*) the Court of Justice held that the exclusion of part- timers from an occupational pension scheme is indirectly discriminatory because it automatically excluded more women than men. Still to be tested within British courts, the implications are considerable for employers with large numbers of part-time female workers and where an occupational scheme does not extend to part-timers.

A further area where rights for part-timers is likely to lead to claims of indirect discrimination being brought before British courts concerns statutory sick pay provision. The Rinner-Kuhn case, a further West German dispute, is the test case here; it was held by the European Court of Justice that SSP could not be refused to a cleaner because she worked only eight hours a week. Furthermore it was held that denial of SSP to a part-timer constitutes indirect discrimination because, as is the case in most EC countries, the majority of part-time employees are female. This ruling seems certain to be tested in British Courts. Although the legal complications are considerable, the implications could ultimately reach as far as the UK government's treatment of part-time workers in the public sector, where discrimination relative to full-timers in a number of areas including redundancy payments and sick pay entitlement may be held to be in breach of Article 119 of the Treaty of Rome.

The Commission's proposal to shift the burden of proof in equal treatment cases onto the defender (employer) rather than the complainant (employee) is the second area concerning equal opportunity that could have a major impact. Although the draft directive has not yet been adopted and may well be vigorously opposed by the UK Government, it contains the statement: 'The complainant shall have the benefit of any doubt that remains' in any case brought before a court, which will undoubtedly cause a substantial shift to the balance of decisions in favour of complainants. This illustrates the extent to which the courts' interpretation of equal treatment legislation holds the key to the direction that legislation will take in the future and the consequences on employment.

Vocational training and cultural exchange

The Commission has, as I have already described, launched a number of schemes designed to encourage and improve vocational skills and the free flow of ideas and values between students, workers and researchers in different Member States. There is increasing evidence that these are having an impact within the UK as awareness of them grows. The ERASMUS programme, launched in 1987 with the primary objective of enabling higher education students to carry out part of their study at colleges in other Member States, is a clear demonstration of this. The UK is one of the leading users of the scheme, accounting for 22 per cent of exchanges and sending 2,500 students to European institutions during 1989/90 for periods of between three months and a year. Grants provided by the European Social Fund are administered by the UK ERASMUS Student Grants Council at the University of Kent, and a number of polytechnics and universities now have joint venture schemes with equivalents in other countries, predominantly for students engaged on business administration, technology and law courses. The improved technical and cultural skills that are being acquired by those who will be entering the employment market at professional and managerial level cannot fail to be of value to the organisations that employ them.

The COMETT Programme, providing grants to enable managers and professionals as well as students to undertake technological training in other Member States, has yet to have the impact of ERASMUS but it is not difficult to envisage this occurring in the near future. The advantages of participation are equally considerable; the potential benefits include the acquisition of skills in the most modern technologies, the personal experience of living and working in another Member State, and the establishment of international links between industry and educational institutions.

Regarding the provision of vocational training within individual Member States, the Commission has maintained a relatively distant approach. In part this is a recognition of the different emphases placed by different countries on training provisions, and the attendant difficulties in drawing up common standards. However, the dialogue between the Commission and the Training Agency is good, and has led to a number of Community-wide initiatives being applied vigorously within the UK. A good example is the EUROTECNET programme, as already described on page 57. More generally the current range of Training Agency-driven initiatives in the field of youth training, retraining and schemes for the unemployed closely reflect the Commission's views on common minimum standards. It is likely that in the future the Training Agency will continue to follow on from the Commission's leads in the field of vocational training.

In terms of European Social Fund sponsorship of UK training initiatives such as the Youth Training Scheme and Employment Training, Britain is the biggest beneficiary taking 18 per cent of the total available budget during 1989/90. A total of 2,128 individual projects will have received funding, spread widely throughout the country; the biggest slices of funds going, respectively, to Northern Ireland (£45m) the North West (£33.4m) and Scotland (£31.1m) with far less being available for schemes in more prosperous regions such as East Anglia (£0.4m) and the South West (£2.5m).

Health and safety at the workplace

It is important to note that Health and Safety Directives may be approved by the Council of Ministers on a majority rather than a unanimous basis, therefore individual member governments cannot exercise the right of veto on the process of legislation. Just as in the past, this will undoubtedly facilitate the passage of current draft and any future directives in translation into national law.

There is some recognition that the impact of current draft directives within the UK will be low because our standards of health and safety at work are generally high; the DTI declares proudly that 'we can fairly claim that almost all the major directives established up to the time qualified majority voting was introduced have been based on UK thinking and standards'. However, a number of responses to the proposals indicate that there are some areas of concern:

• A debate in Parliament towards the end of 1988 produced the all-party view that the minimum standards proposed in various areas by the specific Directives – concerning workplace safety, handling of heavy loads, personal protective equipment, and the use of machinery and VDUs – are insufficient. In particular, the Directives should seek to build up health and safety practice from these minimum standards towards the higher standards that prevail in the 'better' Member States.

- The CBI, on the other hand, has expressed concern that the proposals are over-complex and may therefore impose unrealistic burdens on companies in terms of compliance.

- Generally, there is a concern that the details of Directives may lead to additional costs. A good example of this has been identified in the Directive concerning VDUs, which specifies that employees involved in VDU work must be given eye-tests before taking up their jobs.

Calls from the lobbying groups to modify the legislation in order to make it more flexible may bring some change to the form of draft directives if echoed widely throughout the Community. This may not, however, be forthcoming and British companies should therefore prepare themselves for the burdens in terms of costs and compliance procedures that will arise from their passage into employment law.

Part-time and temporary contracts

The Commission's proposals concerning improved contractual rights for part-time, temporary and fixed-contract workers have consistently been vetoed by the UK and a small minority of other Member States. However, the Commission has maintained a keen interest to push through a directive of some form, supported by the views it has obtained from surveys of European companies and employees which have indicated an increasing willingness to consider flexible working patterns.

Indeed, it is the changing attitudes of business rather than the views of governments that may well hold the key in this area. As the supply of labour throughout Europe dwindles, there is increasing evidence that companies are needing to adopt a more imaginative approach towards staffing, and in particular are having to match more closely the requirements of existing and potential employees. This is likely to be of impact in two ways:

- First, greater flexibility in working time leading to an increase in part-time employment, job sharing, and, in some areas, home working. It is widely recognised that the supply of part-time labour will continue predominantly to be, as it has always been, female; recognition is therefore being given to the need to reconcile the conflicting demands of home and working activities in order to attract women into the workplace.

• Second, the terms and conditions for part-timers are likely to be enhanced considerably by companies in order to entice them into employment. Many companies may simply adopt the approach that terms and conditions should match those for full-time employees thus largely meeting the content of the Commission's Directive concerning part-time workers. Specifically, enhancement may take place in the following areas:
  – improved rates of pay, moving towards pro rata equivalence with full-time rates of workers carrying out identical jobs;
  – equal access to vocational training, promotion and social facilities;
  – 'pro rata' entitlement to holiday pay, redundancy and retirement benefits;
  – access to occupational pension schemes.

Although the above items are included in the Commission's draft directive on part-time working, nevertheless the lead is likely to come from employers on this issue, perhaps in the course of time increasing the pressure on the UK and other governments to agree to some form of Community-wide competition. As standards and norms improve in this country, neither the Government not the Commission will be content to see lower standards continuing elsewhere in countries such as Greece and Portugal, where the demographic pressures on employment are not so great; the former from the point of view of loss of competitive advantage, the latter from that of the likelihood of 'social dumping'!

A final point worthy of note is that the issue of part-time and temporary working is inextricably linked with that of equal treatment of women. Because of the high proportion of female part-time employees, a further pressure on equalisation of pay and benefits for part-timers may come via the equal pay route, particularly if the burden of proof in equal pay cases is shifted. I have already mentioned the case in West Germany where exclusion of a part-time female employee from an occupational pension scheme was held to be indirect discrimination. Any company employing large numbers of part-time women on lower rates of pay or conditions than equivalent full-timers could potentially be vulnerable to a similar charge.

Informing and consulting with employees

It is generally accepted that the 'Vredling Directive' in its original form is unlikely to make any progress at all at the European Council; even considerably amended, it is likely to move forward but slowly. However, it must be borne in mind that it is the British Government's voice in the Council that is raised loudest in opposition and that a change of Government could, potentially, drastically alter the situation.

The effect of the 'Vredling Directive' would be to formalise and increase the amount of information given to employees concerning the running of businesses and the potential impacts on the employment situation. Whether this would be a good or bad thing depends very much on one's point of view – the TUC is very much in favour, almost all interested employers and business representative groups are against, although recognising the necessity to maintain a voluntary approach to consultation. The view of the British Institute of Management, following the result of its questionnaire of members in 1984, is perhaps the most balanced:

'It was not too surprising to find that the majority of those to whom the Vredling Directive would apply . . . thought that implementing the information requirements on the subjects of structures, financial situation and the probable development of business would require either minor or no change at all in their present company practice, either on a company-wide level or at site level.'

While offering a fair critique of the substance of the directive itself, the BIM's summary does not however address the real concerns that must exist within companies of all size that their information and consultation procedures would be open to scrutiny and ultimately to challenge within the courts. As in the area of equal pay, the difficulties to be faced in interpretation of legislation renders the issue a hostage to fortune for companies, and one that would be left largely to the courts to decide in the final analysis.

4 Europe: the cultural impact

It has become a truism that the effects of change brought about by the Single European Market will affect different organisations in different ways. The strategy that will need to be adopted by a large multinational company already well-established in Europe, or an expanding company seeking to launch itself into a new market, will be different to that of a purely domestic company that intends to protect its existing customer base. Equally, the impacts will vary dependent on such factors as the industry or business sector in which the company operates, its size, structure and position in the market, and the maturity of that market. Whatever the specific circumstances, however, it is certain there will be significant challenges that will need to be met.

In the previous chapter, I described some of the main impacts stemming from the Commission's programme of social change that will be of importance to the Personnel Manager. These have, I believe, been underestimated by some commentators who have perhaps tended to regard them purely in the context of their progress through the Brussels legislative machine rather than in that of their relevance to changing employer and employee values. However, it is certainly true that their impact will be matched by that arising from the process of *cultural* change the Single Market Programme will bring about. This change will occur at market level, where companies rise to the opportunities and respond to the threats that the enlarged market will bring; but also at employee level, as managers and staff also begin to perceive the opportunities they have to develop careers, increase their marketability and, above all, play a larger part in the success of their employers' enterprises and of the European economy.

The European Commission is not blind to this; indeed it sees many of its 'social dimension' measures as no more than a means to the end of creating a pan-European business and management culture. A Commission spokesman, addressing a conference of personnel professionals in Brussels, has declared:

'The first thing I would say is that Europe after 1992 will be a more competitive place, so that it will be more important than ever for a company to make the most of its human resources . . . In the European Community we have a great diversity of cultures and traditions . . . Far from being a weakness, these cultural differences are a potential strength for the Community. Cultural differences give us all subtly different approaches to how we live and work, and subtly different approaches to business and management. Closer links with our counterparts in other member states will give us the opportunity to learn from each other and develop new and diverse techniques for management and business. This is a potentially powerful weapon for European industry as it competes in world markets.'

These statements are echoed in the report published last year by Henley Management Centre entitled 'The living market: the impact of 1992 on Europe at work'. This promotes the view that market forces will make it imperative for companies operating on a European scale to build their own cohesive cultures by establishing consistency and effectiveness across national boundaries; in doing so they face a delicate balancing act in reconciling a common corporate approach with sensitivity to different national employment norms. In some areas, the Commission's Social Agenda and these cultural/economic factors will combine to create powerful currents of change, for example regarding equal opportunity where the European women's lobby is forecasted to make rapid progress in standardising maternity and parental leave throughout the Community.

Personnel Managers and 1992

The extent to which UK companies, and their Personnel Managers in particular, are aware of the changes that will inevitably take place is, at present, unclear. Among others, the Henley Management Centre report takes a pessimistic view, declaring:

'If UK companies are not to find themselves at a competitive disadvantage after 1992, they will have to awaken to the speed and scope of these (i.e. employment related) changes and the importance of making their views known.'

On the other hand, as we move towards 1992 the indications are that the majority of companies in the UK have carried out some form of strategic review of their position relative to the Single Market, compared with much lower proportions in other European countries. One might be tempted, from these divergent views, to conclude that while the senior managements of companies are preparing themselves for 1992, Personnel Managers are not

– or at least are not inputting the consequences of European legislative and cultural change on employment at strategic level.

However, the variety of reports and surveys targeted specifically towards the personnel profession indicate that this is almost certainly not so. While it is undoubtedly true that the priority for most companies is to investigate the Single Market implications for sales and marketing and product/service ranges, the majority are also looking seriously at the human resources implications. It is clear from this that a number of specific areas of concern are emerging as of common interest; these are summarised as follows:

- managerial and staff mobility, and management development;
- executive pay and benefits;
- recruitment of professional/managerial staff in the wider market – a threat and an opportunity;
- vocational, cultural and language training.

Many of these areas are closely interlinked, and in some cases are given further impetus by the legislative and other initiatives being taken by the European Commission, as already described. However, I shall attempt in the rest of this chapter to separate them as far as possible in order to define clearly the major issues to be addressed by the Personnel Manager.

Managerial and staff mobility, and management development

Getting the right management for 1992 and thereafter is likely to be an issue of increasing concern for Personnel Managers. Three particular factors are of major significance:

- First, **the changing needs of companies**. As rival operations in different Member States eye each other more closely – in some cases seeking to improve their market position at the expense of such rivals, in others pooling their resources through joint venture, or mergers and acquisitions – they will undergo fundamental structural and cultural change, necessitating fresh attitudes at management level. They will therefore need either to 'buy in' the talents of new managers with the cross-cultural skills to create a competitive advantage, or to develop such skills within their existing cadre of managers. It seems likely that the service sector, including the providers of professional services such as legal and accountancy firms, marketing agencies and management consultancies as well as financial services organisations, may be the first to feel the impact of increased competition as clients look increasingly towards those who can provide a pan-European rather than just a domestic service. Wider skills will therefore be at a premium; an understanding of the professional practices and norms of other Member States, their markets and consumer preferences, the structures and strategies of their industries, their legal systems – can make a vital difference between winning or losing a contract, or establishing a viable market pitch.

- Second, **the attitudes of managers** themselves. As the overall business culture becomes more focused towards the Community as a whole, professional people with the will to succeed will come increasingly to regard themselves as truly 'international' – and will expect enhanced rewards as they acquire the skills to match. In a competitive employment market those companies that cannot offer good benefits including a progressive, pan-European career to the talented will be likely to lose staff to rivals with more attractive and lucrative career structures.

- Third, **the attitudes of those who will become the managers of the future**. I have already described the impact of the European Commission's social policy regarding equivalence of qualifications and, most particularly, vocational and cultural education schemes; these are creating considerable awareness and action among students, and among colleges and universities which are developing their own programmes for cultural exchange. It is among young people, the managers and professionals of the future, where the greatest expectations are likely to be created. With more time and inclination to learn about and adapt to the cultural differences, and fewer ties to restrict Community-wide career development, as students move into the employment market they too will expect employers to be able to offer them challenging and rewarding career paths across the whole of Europe.

In summary, as the decade progresses employers in all sectors of the economy will come increasingly under pressure to find, retain and develop the calibre of management and professional staff to give their operations a competitive edge.

The 'Euro-Executive'

What price, therefore, the Euro-Executive? A survey published by Saxton Bampfylde International, the London-based headhunters, entitled 'The Search for the Euro-Executive', indicates that he – or she – is a rare, exotic beast. Fluent in at least one other Community language, of greater importance is exposure to a diversity of cultures stemming both from family background – he or she is likely to have a mixed education, multi-cultural marriage and parents of different nationalities – and working experience. In terms of career, the Euro-executive will have graduated from an internationally-oriented business school, have gained line management experience in a foreign culture company, and have obtained experience through various career moves of different skills, roles and environments. The survey even extends to a commentary on clothes, job pressures and lifestyle. Readily adaptable to living and working in different European capitals, the Euro-manager is likely to be unobtrusively but expensively dressed, to enjoy eating well and above all to have the ability of assimilating rapidly the subtleties and values of different cultures. He or she must be capable of absorbing the pressures of a stressful lifestyle which will involve extensive travel and disruption to social life.

It is easy enough to dismiss analyses such as this one as shallow, and to fail to recognise that the effects of the Single Market will necessitate the development of a much more broad-based cadre of managers who are able to operate comfortably in a wider sphere. However, two important points should be borne in mind: first, the survey is a reflection of the views of its participants rather than the survey organisers themselves, and as such perhaps represents an ideal rather than a reality. Second, the most significant issue to emerge is, again, the need for cultural interchange and recognition that the European market is the 'home' market and not to be regarded as alien or fragmented.

Another leading management consultancy has identified four groups of employee who are most likely to regard themselves as mobile. These are:

- new graduates;
- younger managers, especially those with language skills;
- professionals and specialists with skills that are in demand across Europe;
- senior executives who are already 'bought in' to a mobility culture.

What is certain is that, whatever the level of such staff on the career ladder, they will be looking for benefits in return for the added value they can bring to their jobs. These benefits will be work-related (enhanced career and training opportunity, improved pay and benefits) but also lifestyle-related, stemming from the more interesting working and domestic environment that exposure to different cultures can bring.

Returning to the Saxton Bampfylde survey, this is perhaps most revealing in describing what the Euro-manager is not; it is the traditional style expatriate who is identified as the least likely to be able to adapt to the demands of a pan-European management culture. Cocooned within the environment of the corporate culture and by exposure to the closed expatriate community with its reliance on company-based facilities and support, the survey concludes that he simply will not be able to make the transition. Unfortunately, there is little evidence to suggest that the traditional expatriate package can be done away with entirely – the problems involved in transferring managers abroad, even to other countries within the European Community, are likely to remain considerable. They may be summarised as follows:

- **Domestic problems**: a whole host of issues is faced by any employee, even if personally willing to accept a relocation to a different country, in this respect. They may include spouse's career; the schooling of children who may be part-way through the UK education system and who are probably not fluent in a foreign language; the general disruption to the family of relocation and resettlement in a different cultural system; the specific problem of housing costs and norms within different countries.

- **Tax, social security and pension problems**: the many differences between provisions in different Member States, which are unlikely to be resolved in the medium-term future, act as a powerful brake on an employee's integration within the social and employment structure of a foreign Member State. This is particularly so regarding pension provision.

- **Employee benefits:** again, significant differences between Member States are likely to persist regarding the make-up of the 'standard executive package'. A good example is company car provision, which is much more common in the UK than in many European countries such as France, Spain and Italy.

Overall, it seems unlikely that these practical problems can be removed entirely, and that most managers – whatever their willingness to believe in pan-European mobility as a concept – will remain to a greater or lesser degree tied to their 'home' cultures. This presents a real problem for Personnel Managers, who will need to devise imaginative solutions to overcome the conflict between companies' corporate and managers' domestic requirements. They will need to consider both terms and conditions packages and career development schemes to support and encourage those who are prepared to 'buy in' to the changing mobility culture.

State of management development in UK

A further problem lies in the state of management development in the UK relative to other countries. A number of highly authoritative reports published in recent years have highlighted this, not the least of them being Professor Charles Handy's 1987 publication *The Making of Managers*. In this report Professor Handy examined management education, training and development in the USA, West Germany, France, Japan and the UK, and argued that management groups in the overseas countries are more likely both to have been educated to a higher level, and to have benefited from more formal and systematic policies for continuing education and development than in the UK. Whereas other countries have established traditions of management, education, training and development, Britain's system is still in a muddle. More recently, Osbaldeston and Barham's report entitled 'Developing Managers for a European Future' suggests that while there is a determination to improve management development in the UK, insufficient attention is being paid to the needs the Single Market will introduce.

The two important questions raised from this echo those expressed at the beginning of this chapter:

- The growing need for managers at all levels to be able to work effectively with people from other countries and cultures. How should organisations, management developers and business schools give this issue greater explicit attention?
- Managers may need attitudes loosely defined as 'openness and sensitivity' to deal with people from other cultures. What does this mean in practice and how can such attitudes be developed?

Michael Osbaldeston, Chief Executive of Ashridge Management College and joint author of the above-mentioned report, reinforced these messages at a lecture given to personnel professionals in late 1989, emphasising the vital importance for our management education system to target itself towards producing managers who are 'qualified internationalists' and not peculiarly British in their approach. Key characteristics needed in managers will be openness to foreign cultures, involving knowledge of the language, customer and social values and institutions of the countries in which the company operates. This can be developed through early exposure to foreign cultures and business practices, and participation in training events that bring together delegates from different European countries and where the tutors have international experience. Understanding how to manage cultural differences, to operate in an unstructured environment where line responsibilities are diffused, and to maintain a clear vision of the future will be essential qualities in the European business manager.

Executive pay and benefits

There is a widely held view that the salaries of UK executives are well below those of their equivalents throughout the rest of Europe, particularly at the most senior levels. This is certainly a conclusion reached by many of the commercially available surveys on executive earnings, which also on the whole tend towards the view that these differences are likely to increase rather than decrease throughout the 1990s. The corollary of this is that many of our brightest executive talents will be tempted away by European-based employers; a businessman 'brain drain' that will leave the UK with inferior talents to manage its major industries as they are faced with ever more formidable foreign competition.

How real is the evidence presented in such surveys, however? In coming to any view about the relative value of post-tax earnings, a large number of complex cultural and economic factors must be taken into account. It is far from easy to compare like with like, even more difficult to make reliable and valid predictions about the future. For my own analysis of the current situation, I have used the data in the Wyatt Company's 1989 survey entitled *Top Management Remuneration: Europe, USA* which, with an extremely large number of participating companies spread throughout the Community and close matching of job descriptions for executives in different functions and company type, I believe gives an accurate picture of the current situation. Even here, however, it is necessary to sound a word of warning. The company base for this survey is predominantly international rather than local, and it therefore gives relatively limited information on national salary practices and labour market norms. It is, therefore, of greater value to companies seeking to relocate a 'home' national abroad rather than one seeking to recruit a local national to a senior management position.

The survey concentrates on top management positions within different functions, categorising these further by company size and level of responsibility according to three definitions:

- *Level A* - an executive within a very large or diversified organisation, almost certainly with international responsibilities;
- *Level B* - an executive within a large organisation operating in one country only;
- *Level C* - an executive within a smaller scale organisation which may nevertheless have a significant part of its markets or operational bases abroad.

Remuneration levels

In looking at the total pay of executives across the Community I have picked three examples from the survey as giving a representative sample. These are as follows:

- Chief Executive: Level A: 'the most senior executive in the organisation, co-ordinating the full range of functions . . . reports direct to the Board or to Corporate Office. Responsibility for a number of countries or a large, divisionalised organisation in one country . . . normally at least 45–50'.
- Director of Marketing: Level C: 'reports direct to the Chief Executive . . . heads up marketing in a smaller sized operation, possibly for an international market'.
- Director of Personnel: All levels: 'reports direct to the Chief Executive . . . responsibility for overall direction and control of all personnel matters'.

Table 4.1: Chief Executive: Level A: Average Remuneration

Base Country	Annual Total Remuneration ($000)	Net Remuneration as % of ATR
Belgium	158.5	46
Denmark	164.8	42
France	165.3	64
Germany	214.5	53
Greece	71.9	65
Ireland	107.8	51
Italy	190.2	61
Luxembourg	159.9	57
Netherlands	147.8	45
Portugal	54.3	62
Spain	155.6	59
UK	174.1	58

This reveals that, as one might expect, the gross level of earnings of the German Chief Executive is some way ahead of the rest, although the differential is narrowed somewhat by relatively high deductions. Italy is perhaps surprisingly in second place, with earnings approaching those in Germany after deductions. The UK is at the top of the 'second rank' group which covers most of the other Community countries within a $145,000 to $175,000 range. At the lower end of the ranking come Ireland, Greece and Portugal.

Table 4.2: Director of Marketing: Level C: Average Remuneration

Base Country	Annual Total Remuneration ($000)	Net Remuneration as % of ATR
Belgium	63.2	52
Denmark	66.8	46
France	62.0	69
Germany	72.8	60
Greece	33.0	70
Ireland	56.9	55
Italy	55.3	64
Luxembourg	66.6	66
Netherlands	73.4	50
Portugal	25.6	64
Spain	53.8	66
UK	70.2	62

This table shows that, apart from in Greece and Portugal, the pre-tax earning levels for the average job holder across the Community fall within a range of $53,000 to $73,500. The UK is towards the top of this range at $70,200.

Table 4.3: Director of Personnel: All levels: Average Remuneration

Base Country	Annual Total Remuneration ($000)	Net Remuneration as% of ATR
Belgium	78.1	53
Denmark	72.7	74
France	75.5	71
Germany	94.3	61
Greece	31.1	75
Ireland	63.1	55
Italy	74.7	65
Luxembourg	78.0	68
Netherlands	74.9	51
Portugal	31.1	64
Spain	72.3	67
UK	67.2	63

In this table the earnings levels in Germany are again the highest; although appearing towards the lower end of the 'middle range' band, those in the UK are, as before, comparable with those in other major European competitors such as France, Spain, Belgium and the Netherlands.

The benefits package

The Wyatt survey includes bonuses and profit-sharing in its definition of annual total earnings, but analyses separately several other benefits included in the total remuneration package. Three components of the package are worthy of particular comment:

- *Stock Option/Purchase*: the proportions of companies by Member State that provide schemes varies relatively little. Overall, UK companies are identified as slightly above average.

- *Company Cars:* while the provision of a car to the Chief Executive is almost universal practice throughout Europe, at top management level the practice is far more common in the UK and Ireland than elsewhere. The proportions of companies providing cars is particularly low in France and Spain.

- *Company Pension Schemes*: these are far more common in the UK than in other Member States, the lowest providers being Spain and Italy. To a large extent this is a reflection of the different practices in state pensions provision.

Relative cost of living

The survey considers this separately in a table headed 'Comparison of National Living Costs'. It points out the complexity of calculating reliable indices, bearing in mind particularly different patterns of consumer spending; the table is based on actual prices excluding housing costs, applied to 'a standard manager spending pattern'. Against a UK base of 100 the following figures are given:

Table 4.4: Comparison of National Living Costs
UK = 100

B	D	F	GDR	GR	IRE	IT	L	NL	P	S
91.2	116.0	95.5	108.0	82.4	85.7	104.4	82.8	115.4	64.3	91.0

Clearly, this puts a rather different perspective on the figures I have abstracted from the survey in previous tables; however the index reveals that the cost of living differences between the UK and the major Community States (France, Germany, Italy, Spain) are not significant, none varying from the UK 'base' by more than ten per cent.

Conclusions

Overall, the figures presented in the Wyatt survey – and I have selected a genuinely representative sample – challenge the general conclusion that executive pay and benefits in the UK lag behind those in other Member States. On the contrary, the total remuneration packages that are available to senior managers within this country appear to be as competitive as in most others. Broadly speaking, three distinct remuneration levels emerge from the survey:

- At the top West Germany, where in two of the three examples of annual total remuneration shown the rates are significantly ahead of the majority. In some instances (e.g. Italy in the case of the Chief Executive example) these rates are matched due to lower deductions from gross earnings.

- In the middle the majority of Member States including all the other main industrial ones – France, Italy, Spain and the UK. While variations exist in remuneration levels and cost of living these are relatively minor and it would be hard to pick out any individual country as significantly above the rest. The UK is, if anything, slightly above average due to the more attractive benefits packages that tend to prevail (including, in almost all cases, the company car).

- At the lower end, the relatively underdeveloped Member States of Greece and Portugal where the picture is one of considerably lower pay and benefits for executives. The conditions that apply in the Irish Republic tend to place this country some way between Greece and Portugal and the countries within the 'middle' group.

In the face of this evidence, it is difficult not to form the view that, when people talk of UK salaries being below those of most of the rest of the European Community, what they really mean is that they are below those in West Germany. Certainly, looking at the overall picture one cannot see a drain of management talent from the UK to Europe taking place purely on the basis of higher levels of remuneration. I would emphasise again however that the Wyatt Survey information is of greatest value to those companies contemplating transferring executives abroad. For other purposes, international salary survey information should always be supplemented by local market information relating directly to the specific locality under consideration, the strength of its particular labour market and levels of pay for equivalent jobs in competitor organisations.

What of the future? Again, although many are prepared to predict that the UK will lose ground in providing an attractive package to senior management, the evidence is at best uncertain if not contradictory. On one hand, the 1987 and 1988 top marginal tax cuts have done much to maintain competitiveness, and post-tax increases at senior level were, at the end of the 1980s, running at about 26 %. On the other, commentators predict that other Member States may also reduce their employee tax and social security debts at the same time as their companies improve their benefits packages, while our inflation rate remains stubbornly higher than the rest of Europe. Taking a balanced view, OECD projections for inflation and total average salary increases show a fairly consistent pattern of increases running at about two to three and a half per cent above inflation across the major Community Member States.

In summary, the large-scale loss of professional and managerial staff from the UK into Europe may not be quite as big a problem as is generally supposed, purely from a remuneration point of view. This does not mean, of course, that employers do not need to exercise imagination in drawing up the most appropriate pay and benefits packages for the mobile executive, taking into account location, anticipated duration of posting, personal considerations in terms of individual tax, pension and domestic circumstances. I leave the last word on this issue to Richard Underwood, writing in the February 1989 edition of *Personnel Management* regarding expatriate pay:

'Employers will have to aim at maintaining systems which are flexible enough to cater for different national salary levels . . . These systems will also need to be able to cope with more frequent moves and job changes . . . A sensible constructed and flexible policy will be essential.'

Recruitment of professional/managerial staff in the wider market – a threat and an opportunity

Mobility of people in work

Early in 1989 the findings of a survey conducted by the *Guardian,* newspaper entitled 'Why work?' were published in *Personnel Management* magazine. With the primary objective of determining the attitudes to work of people already in work, a questionnaire published in the newspaper on which the survey was based provoked an enormous response of over 26,800 replies. The survey covered many aspects of employment conditions and employee expectations: one of the most surprising responses was to the question: 'Which of these (EEC and non-EEC, as listed) countries would you consider moving to for a job?' The overall response in relation to each of the EC countries listed was as follows:

Table 4.5: Response to Mobility Survey

Country	% of Respondents Who Would Consider Moving
France	48
West Germany	31
Netherlands	28
Italy	26
Denmark	22
Eire	21
Spain	21
Belgium	20
Luxembourg,Greece,Portugal	16

The commentary on this in the accompanying article in *Personnel Management* read:

'Even more surprising was the high degree of interest in working abroad. Over one in five stated that they would actually *prefer* to work in other EEC countries and nearly half would consider working in France or in Australasia. Interest in working abroad is even stronger among the young, among Londoners and among those at director level in their companies. Different countries also appealed more to different industry sectors. Interest in working in France was highest among the financial and business services sector, and West Germany appealed particularly to those in manufacturing.'

Of course, there is a world of difference between indicating one's mobility preferences in a questionnaire and actually being prepared to move when presented with the opportunity to do so. However, there is no doubt that the overall response to the questionnaire indicates an awareness of the wider employment market that could, potentially, be exploited by European as well as UK recruiters seeking to fill vacancies in other European countries. It should be borne in mind also that the survey respondents are exclusively *people already in employment* – no doubt predominantly professional and managerial but not including students yet to move into the employment market, who are rightly regarded as the group within the employable population most likely to consider themselves as fully mobile.

Employers and staff mobility

Increased staff mobility represents both a threat and an opportunity to UK companies. In a shrinking employment market, the likelihood of increasing numbers of staff being tempted abroad by European companies is unwelcome news. On the other hand, to UK companies that are themselves seeking to recruit staff for their European operations the news is good. A further positive factor is that, as far as it has been judged, it seems that increasing numbers of workers in other Member States also are keen to benefit from the wider opportunities to be gained in working abroad; the UK being, to many, a particularly attractive option.

Altogether, what this means is that employers who continue to take an isolationist approach, failing on one hand to recognise the threat from abroad and on the other to move into the wider employment market themselves will encounter ever increasing difficulties. Faced by a dwindling domestic employment pool being fished by new as well as established recruiters, failure to consider the options to recruit from other EC countries could, in some cases, spell disaster. Of course, recruiting from abroad will not always be easy; it is necessary to gain a sufficiently detailed knowledge of other countries' sources of supply, vocational qualifications, advertising mediums and recruitment practices. It is necessary also to think seriously about the kind of packages that are appropriate to foreign nationals living and working in the UK. This adds up to a growing market niche for recruitment and selection consultancies to investigate the issues and offer a comprehensive service to UK-based employers.

Are employers waking up to the challenge of the Single European Market for staffing? As far as filling domestic posts is concerned, there is little evidence as yet that many recruiters are turning their attentions to Europe to redress the imbalance between supply and demand. It seems likely that the labour intensive professions such as teachers and nurses, where domestic supply is already acutely short, will be the first where employers are forced to consider the wider options. There have already been several well-publicised cases of German, Dutch and Danish teachers coming to this country to fill vacant posts in state schools in the South East, and of doctors 'surplus to requirements' in Germany, The Netherlands and Italy being recruited by hospitals in the West Midlands. At managerial level, a number of executive selection consultants and headhunters are establishing themselves on a pan-European basis to be able better to respond to changing client needs.

There is altogether more evidence of international companies advertising within the UK for vacancies across Europe, although the number of adverts placed forms but a tiny proportion of the total numbers that appear in the quality national papers. Some newspapers 'swap' job advertisements with European equivalents and present these in a separate section each week – which is an indication of the publishers' awareness if nothing else. Some common features of these advertisements are:

- they are almost exclusively at professional and managerial level;
- a second language is often regarded as desirable rather than essential;
- the companies advertising range from relatively small and newly-established operations (including a high proportion of US companies) to well known and established multinationals with long experience of managing expatriates;
- British professional qualifications, which on the whole are highly regarded in most European countries, are a frequent requirement for many vacancies;

- the most commonly advertised functions are sales and marketing, finance and accounting, electrical/mechanical engineering (vacancies in West Germany predominating) and data processing.

A further development in recruitment advertising that reflects companies' growing interest in the European market is the increase in the number of UK-based vacancies advertised for executives to operate on a European sphere. Usually at senior level, such advertisements tend to offer higher-than-average remuneration packages and highlight international responsibility as a challenging and rewarding aspect of the job. Two good examples are:

- *European Marketing Manager* (Berkshire based, a US company 'one of the best known names in personal computer operating systems'): 'The position provides the opportunity for both European and US travel and offers excellent career opportunities'.
- *European Financial Controller/Marketing Manager/Human Resources Manager* (Hertfordshire based: again a US company, in the field of computer-aided systems engineering): 'Strategic roles contributing to success on the European stage': 'Outstanding individuals will thrive on the challenge of formulating European strategy against a background of rapid growth and varying cultures'.

The internationalist 'flavour' is apparent in both of these examples even through the standard hyperbole of executive recruitment advertising!

Finally, one should not forget the European Commission itself, which advertises regularly for administrators, translators, scientists and technologists among others throughout the Community. Applications from British subjects to meet the unofficial 'quota' – approximately 17 per cent of posts should be filled by UK nationals – are insufficient, a fact the Commission puts down to the poor press it receives in this country. The application procedure itself, however, does little to improve the Commission's bureaucratic image; the process of advertising, recruitment competition and interviews can take up to a year, and unsolicited applications – however suitable – are not considered.

Vocational, cultural and language training

There is no doubt at all that the broad area of training is one in which the UK lags well behind the rest of Europe; indeed behind the rest of the developed world. Survey after survey, drawing comparison with the educational, vocational and professional training systems in other Member States, has consistently revealed this. Government ministers themselves believe that between two million and five million new jobs will be created in Europe as a result of the Single Market expansion, but recognise that these will go to countries with highly skilled and trained workforces. Britain is recognised with considerable alarm as being below other European standards.

In part, the problem is historical. In the past our cultural focus has been too insular, our education system too little attuned to the needs of commerce and industry. Although awareness of the problem is growing and change is beginning to take place, much needs to be done if British enterprises are to maintain a competitive market pitch within the Community; and equally important, are to contribute to the full to the improvement of Community-wide trade with the rest of the world. The European Commission is well aware that education and training lie at the heart of the Community's ability to compete in world markets, emphasising the importance of developing links between schools and industry and closer co-ordination with the objectives of the Single Market Programme as priorities for the period 1989–92.

School level education

Looking first at school level education, research published in 1988 by the International Association for the Evaluation of Educational Achievement into standards in maths and science in 17 countries has revealed some alarming trends. In particular, the mathematical abilities of 13 to 16 year olds in this country are identified as between one and two years behind their West German equivalents, while the academic abilities of Japanese pupils are about three years ahead of those in the UK. In Germany, there is a well-developed system of providing vocational training to pupils not aiming at higher education in the last three years at school, including full-time attendance at vocational training schools in many cases. Responsibility for the transition from school to workplace is largely managed by a system of vocational training committees which (of greatest importance) take detailed account of the views of employers as well as educationalists. The introduction of young workers into the employment structure in Germany is indeed impressive; financial assistance is met largely by the employers themselves, and through a voluntary system of 'shared benefit' small firms with insufficient resources of their own are able to make use of the facilities and programmes of larger ones. The upshot is that almost all 16 and 17 year olds have benefitted from some form of vocational training from their future employers *before* leaving the education system.

University level education

Another significant difference is in the numbers of students going on to university level education. In the UK the figure is 15 per cent of the 18-24 year old population; in France it is 19 per cent, Germany 20 per cent, and the Netherlands 22 per cent. These figures are somewhat reversed by the numbers completing higher education courses, as the university drop-out rates are higher in most other Member States. However, in the UK there are critical shortages in engineering and technology placements, with applications for courses in these areas having fallen alarmingly during the last decade. Higher education research and development funding is also below that provided in France and West Germany.

Effects and remedies

Not surprisingly, the outcome of this is that when we turn to an analysis of the skills level of those in work we see some alarming shortages compared with the rest of Europe. A detailed CBI survey comparing the productivity of manufacturing industry in West Germany and the UK, published in 1988, found considerable evidence to support the conclusion that the much better performance of German firms is directly attributable to higher standards of education and training. Citing the cases of individual companies, the survey pointed out key differences between levels of qualification respectively at worker, supervisor and manager level, highlighting in particular the lower UK levels of post-secondary school qualifications amongst workers and supervisors, and the lower proportion of UK managers holding degrees. The survey concluded:

'The UK firms we have looked at do not appear to suffer any glaring deficiencies in comparison with their West German counterparts, apart from the levels of education attained by their labour force and management. . . Given the UK firms' poorer productivity record, we infer that this must be due in large measure to the lower quality of the workforce.'

The contrasts are as sharp with other countries. In France, where a concentrated effort has been made to develop technical skills, three times as many mechanical and electrical craftsmen are produced than in the UK. France has, in recent years, experienced a considerable increase to engineering industry output. Even at degree level, where the differences are less marked than at craftsman level, France produces slightly more engineering graduates than the UK while West Germany produces half as many again.

Of course, much is now being done to improve the vocational skills of our workforce. Employers, schools, colleges, universities and the Government itself through the Training Agency have launched many schemes to redress the balance as the skills gap becomes acutely wider and the establishment of Training and Enterprise Councils promises to take this activity considerably further. There are already indications of some success; the number of placements on the Employment Training Scheme, for example, now exceed the 200,000 mark. However it is a sobering thought that even the most sustained remedial action will take many years to be reflected in improved results; possibly as long as a decade, according to predictions by the CBI. Government surveys in 1989 showed that seven out of ten of Britain's 26 million workers left school at minimum leaving age, seven out of ten had only short initial training and seven out of ten had had no training since.

Regarding training towards 'a common culture', I have already described the ways in which the UK educational system has embraced such European Commission initiatives as the ERASMUS and COMETT programmes. The Commission has placed great emphasis on the need to create a new generation of Europeans more receptive to each other's cultural norms than past generations; although British attitudes have often been seen as narrow and unresponsive, the emphasis in our education system on the cultural and artistic rather than the technical has perhaps been of some benefit in this respect. Nevertheless, a report in the *Times* on the response of our universities and colleges to the coming of the Single European Market still concludes with the colourful remark: 'There are times when the prospect of 1992 looms like the date of some dread global exam'!

It will certainly be necessary for our higher education system, and indeed employers in drawing up their management training and development programmes, to adapt to the growing desire among graduates and young professionals for the skills to equip them for careers in the pan-European market. To quote again from the *Times* article mentioned above:

'Terry Garrison, MBA programme director at the very Europhile Buckinghamshire College, believes that there is "a yearning across the board" for more students to become properly versed in the commercial and cultural lives of our European neighbours. "The product for which we aim is someone with an international form of business passport" he says. "This is absolutely vital if we are to take the Single European Act at its face value."'

There are encouraging signs that some professions are taking significant initiatives in the direction of cultural exchange. For example, the European Law Students Association (Elsa) was established eight years ago and has grown quickly, now claiming to represent 150,000 young lawyers from countries throughout Europe including the Eastern bloc. The Association's last annual conference was held in London and some 130 delegates attended. The English legal profession, with its sharper focus on business development and marketing rather than academic debate, is clearly of considerable interest to European law students. It is also clear that the Single Market Programme has aroused awareness of the possibilities for wider European integration. Sinisa Rodin, the Yugoslav editor of the Association's journal *Elsa Law Review*, has been been quoted in the *Times* as saying:

'There are more and more legal issues becoming international . . . A generation of law students – currently studying in their law faculties throughout Europe – is going to help create an entirely new legal framework to provide a better future for coming generations of Europeans. Hopefully, here is one important item that lawyers have in common: the belief in the idea of law and equity.'

Cross-cultural skills

The ability to speak a foreign language is the most outward manifestation of cross-cultural skill, and in this area too we have been badly served in the past by our education system. Throughout most of Western Europe, particularly in France, Germany and the Low Countries, English is taught as a second language from nursery school level and this is reflected in the very high proportions of students coming out of the education system at 16 and older who speak English to a good standard. By contrast, the numbers of children in English schools taking GCSE and 'A' levels in French and German fell significantly during the last decade, there has been no development in the teaching of other Community languages such as Spanish and Italian and at university level – where the emphasis in any case is on literature rather than language – courses fail to attract their quota of students. The number of teachers qualified to teach a modern language is, amazingly, less than a quarter of what it was ten years ago.

And yet it is an obvious truth that improved language skills are going to be absolutely vital if the opportunities to develop trade created by the Single European Market are to be grasped. There are many graphic examples of this, such as that of the sales manager able to improve his department's exports to Germany by 70 per cent following the taking of a German language course. Some reports suggest that up to 50 per cent of companies consider that lack of foreign language skills has hampered their exports. Fortunately, there is considerable evidence to suggest that companies are waking up to the shortcomings of their executives and staff and are taking remedial action to correct them – or are at least thinking about doing so. Language training has been identified as the most commonly recognised personnel issue arising from the Single Market Programme which the majority of employers are seeking to address in one way or another.

There has certainly been an explosion in the number of commercial providers of language training services in the last two or three years. The 'London Language Show' Exhibition held at the Barbican Centre in June each year is able to present the full range of organisations each with their own methods of providing language training to a particular market niche. These methods vary considerably, from home and audio-based intensive learning programmes, to courses aimed at achieving competence at different levels based on standard tutorial techniques. Many colleges and universities, as well as the cultural institutions of foreign countries such as the Alliance Française de Londres, now offer services on a commercial basis. Some of the intensive methods offered by smaller, foreign based organisations appear the most interesting. One recently established company offers five or seven day courses in a French *auberge*, in which expert tuition is given in the context of total immersion in the French way of life. Delegates of the same nationality, and even married couples, are kept strictly apart to remove the possibility of any conversation in their native tongue. An exhausting means of learning to speak French, but one possibly having its compensations!

5 Demographic trends: a European problem?

The subject of the demographic downturn has probably occupied more column inches than any other in the pages of recent specialist personnel periodicals. As a major problem facing all employers throughout the 1990s, it has been identified and analysed in detail, and a wide variety of responses have been suggested to enable companies to recruit, retain and develop the staff needed to keep their businesses in operation.

Naturally, most commentators on the subject have tended to take a purely domestic perspective, concentrating on measures for employers to make best use of the local labour supply. This is appropriate as, whatever impacts the Single Market will have on labour mobility, the vast majority of non-professional staff will remain restricted to their immediate locality for domestic and cultural reasons and from personal preference. However, many of the issues to be faced apply almost uniformly across the European Community; in responding to others it is possible that currents of change will be created that are of impact on the Europe-wide labour market.

In this chapter I shall attempt, to a certain extent, to cover both these perspectives. Moving from an overview of the general issues I shall examine the measures being adopted by UK organisations to meet them, taking particular account of how these relate to employment patterns and conditions across the Community. I shall also examine two specific areas of concern:

- First, **graduates in the Single European Market**. This is an area where there is much conjecture as to how the wider opportunities available to graduates will affect British companies.
- Second, the **impact of demographic trends** on the widely differing forms of pension provision that exist between Member States.

Demographic trends – general issues

It is possible to identify two broad factors contributing to the 'demographic downturn' which will so affect the UK employment market during the 1990s. The first is the changing characteristics of the workforce itself. As the school leaver population falls, the number of new workers coming into the labour force will be insufficient to meet the increasing demand for labour; therefore labour demand must be fed by new sources of supply, particularly the unemployed and women of working age who have hitherto not been prepared or unable to enter the employment market. The second is the growing skills shortage; projections show that the main growth areas of employment throughout the decade will be the professional, managerial and skilled craft sectors, while the unskilled/operative sector will actually decline. This places an enormous burden on the Training Agency, employers and education establishments alike to provide increased training for the workplace to bridge the skills gap that will arise. The overall picture is a pessimistic one, in which employers will face considerable increases to staff costs if they are to meet their staffing needs. However, the Institute of Manpower Studies (IMS), which has carried out extensive research in this area, predicts that the problems are not insurmountable and that far sighted employers can meet the challenge, as long as they respond early enough and in appropriate fashion.

Changing characteristics of the workforce: Europe and the UK

Compared with the major 'competitor' economies of Japan and the USA, the European Community's deplorable unemployment statistics could prove to be a godsend in the context of providing an available labour pool – as long as the European economy can generate the jobs. The contrast is indeed stark. Unemployment in the EC in 1988 was just over ten per cent of the working population compared with five per cent in the USA and three per cent in Japan; the working population expressed as a percentage of the total population was 43 per cent in the EC against nearly 50 per cent in both Japan and the USA. Unfortunately, there are few current signs that the gap is being filled. Though European unemployment is falling slowly, the US rate has reduced more sharply by nearly five per cent of the working population in six years. The working population/total population ratio in Europe has also fallen since 1986, although it has remained virtually static in Japan and the USA. The clear conclusion to be drawn from this is that while a large labour pool exists in Europe to fill vacancies that may be created, the economy has not yet been able to create those vacancies in the right areas. This conclusion is supported by trade and industry trends: though growing, European industrial production remains well behind that of Japan and the USA, and the gap continues to increase.

The statistics hide considerable national and regional differences within the Community concerning unemployment and the changing composition of the labour pool. It is pertinent to consider where the UK stands compared with the rest of the Community in some of these key demographic areas:

• Looking first at unemployment, the UK rate expressed as a percentage of working population is some way below that of most major competitors as can be seen from the table below.

Table 5.1: Unemployment as a Percentage of the Working Population, December 1988 (Source: Eurostat)

Country	%
UK	7.4
France	11.2
Germany	7.9
Ireland	18.7
Italy	16.4
Spain	(20.5 – April 1988 figure)
Netherlands	11.8

Only West Germany has a rate comparable with that of the UK, while those in other Member States are at least 50 per cent worse than ours. A further significant factor is that UK unemployment was one of the few in the Community to show a fall during 1988; in Italy the rate rose by almost five per cent from April to December. These differences are also apparent when looking at the working population expressed as a percentage of the total population. Here, only West Germany (55 per cent) has a higher figure than the UK (48 per cent), while France (42 per cent), Italy (41 per cent) and Spain (36 per cent) all lag some way behind. At face value this would confirm the conclusion that, insofar as the unemployed are to be regarded as a source of labour, there is less of a pool to be exploited in the UK than in the rest of Europe. However, the strong regional disparities that exist reveal how closely unemployment is linked to economic strength; at risk of stating the obvious, the rates are highest in those regions where the economy remains incapable of generating jobs. Thus, the whole of Spain and

Ireland, Southern Italy and Scotland stand out as the regions where unemployment is highest. In Eastern France, most of England, Germany and Denmark, and Northern Italy and Portugal the rates are much lower.

- Regarding the employment of women as a proportion of the total population the UK is above average, coming second only to West Germany in this respect. Conversely, unemployment among women is significantly below the rates in most other Member States; Spain, Italy, Ireland and Belgium having the highest. Again, one might conclude that a greater source of supply continues to exist elsewhere in the Community than in the UK.

- It is the dwindling supply of young workers coming into the European employment market that gives rise to one of the greatest causes of concern, as the table below reveals:

Table 5.2: Percentage Decline in Supply of 15 to 19-Year-Olds, 1985 to 2000 (Source, OECD: 1984 = 100 %)

Country	1985	1990	1995	2000
UK	97	84	72	75
France	99	97	88	90
Germany	94	67	54	58
Ireland	101	109	109	111
Italy	98	92	77	63
Netherlands	97	89	72	70

Apart from in Ireland, the decline shown in this table is dramatic, although for most Member States it tails off after 1995. The UK is by no means in the worst position, with Italy and West Germany facing much more severe difficulties. However the overall conclusion is clear; across almost the whole of Europe there will be a significant drop in the numbers of young workers coming into employment for the first time from the education system.

In summary: British employers, in common with counterparts throughout the European Community, can no longer rely on a sufficient supply of labour being provided each year from schools and colleges. Our position in the UK in this respect is bad, but by no means as bad as in many other Member States. Employers must therefore turn to other sources of labour, of which the unemployed and 'women non-employed' are the two most significant. Here, our available pool is somewhat smaller than the

Community average; however with a relatively healthy economy capable of creating the jobs, a still considerable supply including nearly two million unemployed and an increasing willingness amongst women to return to work if the right terms and conditions are offered, it may be that overall the UK is not seriously disadvantaged compared with the rest of Europe.

The growing skills shortage

In the previous chapter I described how the UK is seriously deficient in the provision of technical and professional training, the contrast with West Germany and France being particularly sharp. Skills shortages is certainly an area where the UK economy is at a considerable disadvantage compared with our major European competitors. The problem is not that the shortages themselves are continuing to grow; rather that, despite the strenuous efforts now being made to train school leavers, the unemployed and those changing their career orientation, it is insufficient to keep pace with occupational change. Our economy needs more mechanical and Information Technology (IT) technicians, social and medical workers, professional, administrative and managerial staff. The demand for low-skilled industrial, clerical, service and agricultural workers is, however, declining.

This is not to say that problems do not exist elsewhere in Europe; the basic issues being faced, particularly the shift in employment sector growth from unskilled areas in agriculture and industry towards the service sector, are the same. The big European employers, such as Philips in the Netherlands, are also having to address the problems of declining graduate numbers and an insufficient supply of those with technological skills. But overall, skills shortages throughout the rest of Europe are less acute than ours. Many commentators lay the blame firmly at the door of our education system, pointing out how historically the links between schools and employers have been pitifully weak. This may not be entirely fair; there is an onus on employers as well as schools to declare their needs, and meet educationalists half way in ensuring that those coming through the system are adequately prepared for working life:

'Skills shortages are now affecting 85 per cent of West Midlands companies': "six out of ten employers report shortages of skilled personnel, with nearly one in ten rating the effect as severe".'

Headlines such as these demonstrate that awareness of the problem is growing and that companies are indeed devoting more time, money and effort to professional and technical training. It is interesting also that education ministers are looking seriously at West German models, particularly the co-operative ventures between schools and employers in craft training, as being a realistic way of making progress. A Department of Education and Science Minister has recently said:

'With 1992 approaching it is timely that we compare the best practice across Europe . . . There is an awful lot of curriculum development going on in the UK and I hope to get an insight into the way German curriculum is developed and delivered.'

The National Health Service – a case study

In order to illustrate these labour and skills shortage issues, I have analysed the demographic trends from the point of view of a major organisation in the domestic market. I have chosen the National Health Service for this purpose, as throughout the 1990s it will continue to have a requirement for large numbers of entrants suitable for professional level employment; and in the past has relied heavily on the school leaver output for its labour supply. Thus, the problems it faces mirror those faced by many other employers in the UK and in Europe as a whole. I shall put the issues raised, and the proposed responses to them, into a European context as far as possible.

Manpower planning experts within the NHS have concluded that staffing shortages will undoubtedly replace finance as the single biggest constraint on the provision of services in the 1990s. The key issues identified are as follows:

- In the 15 years from 1985 to 2001 the over-75 population will increase by 21.8 per cent while the total population will increase by only 4.6 per cent. This will massively increase the demand for health care provided by the NHS.

- The reduction in the number of school leavers throughout the decade means that the traditional source of labour supply for the NHS will be cut drastically. NHS entrants are predominantly female school leavers with between five 'GCSEs' and two 'A' levels: in addition to the problems caused by a falling birthrate, predictions are that an increasing number from this category of school leaver will go into further education rather than direct employment.

- The entry requirements for many professions are rising – for example, the minimum education standards for mental nursing and radiography were increased in the late 1980s.
- There is increased competition, particularly from the service sector, for nursing and other NHS professional calibre entrants and staff. At lower level where the NHS employs many part-time workers it is predicted that the growth in part-time working during the 1990s will also lead to increased competition.
- The unemployment pool as a labour market is unlikely to provide an alternative pool for the NHS. It is predicted that in future unemployment will mainly be confined to male unskilled and semi-skilled workers, largely unsuitable for the type of jobs that will need to be filled in hospitals.

Faced with this diversity of problems, what solutions are proposed by NHS planners? Taking a brief look at these there are three broad areas:

- improving recruitment and retention rates from the existing source of labour supply: measures suggested to achieve this aim include increased levels of pay, provision of childcare facilities, and a better working environment;
- looking towards new sources of labour supply: by reducing entry qualifications, operating with lower ratios of qualified/unqualified staff, recruiting more male workers and mature entrants;
- 'radical' measures such as reducing the demand for staff by, for example, increasing day care and patient throughput rates, and maximising the availability of staff.

Implications

What messages are there in this for, respectively, European social policy as driven by the European Commission, and the personnel strategies of organisations in the wider European Market? First of all, it can be seen that the responses prepared by the NHS do, in some areas, lend considerable support to the Commission's social initiatives. In particular:

- The NHS proposes measures that will improve the working terms and conditions of women. Directly, the provision of childcare facilities and measures to facilitate the return to work of older women are examples of this. Indirectly, improving rates of pay for professions that remain largely female dominated (e.g. the female intake of nurses is 90 per cent, radiographers 83 per cent, and physiotherapists 91 per cent in England and Wales) add great weight to the Commission's drive to create equality with male employees.

- In recognising that part-time workers are becoming an increasingly important element of the total workforce and will be sought more competitively by service sector employers, the NHS is committed to providing equality of opportunity in terms of training and promotion as well as pay. An NHS report declares: 'The NHS has a particular advantage in the part-time market. A higher proportion of its part-time jobs are in skilled, relatively well paid areas. Can we exploit this to our advantage?' This startling declaration is indicative of a dedication towards the improvement of part-time terms and conditions to achieve benefit for the organisation, reflecting very closely the European Commission's own ambitions to achieve improvements in this area.

Implications on a European level

There are European-wide implications, too, in other areas less directly linked to the NHS strategy for coping with demographic issues. Equivalence of qualifications will increasingly enable professional staff of all levels working within the health service to take up career opportunities arising throughout Europe. In the past we have seen a well publicised 'drain' of qualified nursing staff leaving this country, mainly for America. Although the remuneration levels for nursing jobs in Europe are unlikely to match those obtainable in the United States, nevertheless differences will exist and may well increase in those countries such as West Germany which face a growing need for health care provision as their population too ages rapidly. Equally important, the opportunity for European travel and experience is likely to remain most attractive to the young, single, professional element of the labour market which continues to make up the bulk of the NHS career entrants.

On the other hand, it is possible that the NHS may be able to go out towards Europe in order to increase its entrants to key professions. It is widely recognised that the NHS needs to reorient its recruitment publicity material and advertising campaigns, and there may well be some scope in doing so to target sources of labour supply elsewhere in the Community. The most obvious of these targets is the Irish Republic, which contrary to almost all other Member States actually shows an increase in the supply of school leavers during the 1990s. This, allied to close geographical proximity and lack of language barriers, means that the UK is uniquely well placed to make the most of this potential source of supply.

Professional training

Professional training is an area to which the NHS recognises it must devote more attention during the 1990s in order to reduce the balance of skills shortages. Though most nurse and other professional training of staff within the health service is widely recognised as setting high standards, it is interesting that a focus area is the setting up of TECS and other links with educational establishments. Once again, the models that exist in Europe, particularly in West Germany, France and Denmark, may provide valuable sources of information and study towards the development of worthwhile educational links.

Relocation of operation

One further response to demographic trends that cannot be considered by the NHS for obvious demographic reasons is the extent to which organisations can relocate their operations, or significant parts of them, into other regions within the Community where a bigger local supply of labour exists. This is an extremely complex issue, and companies will inevitably take into account a multitude of factors affecting their production and distribution costs and their customer bases before 'taking the plunge'. Availability of suitable labour may be a factor but in the final analysis is unlikely to be a major consideration except in industries where employment costs form a major part of total costs, and all other methods of meeting labour and skills shortages at the existing location have been exhausted. Even here, employers will have to assess the impact their relocation will have on the employment market in the proposed new location – their demand for employment may turn a weak local labour market into a strong one! The actual costs of relocation itself are also likely to be a strong influencing factor.

Graduates and the Single European Market

'A single European market may drain talent from Britain.' Thus the dire warning in the recently published book *Recruitment in the 90s* written by Professor Peter Herriot of Birkbeck College. It is one of many similar forecasts that predict huge problems for UK companies, as the decline in school leaver numbers and awareness of Single Market opportunities combine to make graduates increasingly sought after in the employment market place. In assessing the validity of these predictions we must consider two basic questions:

- First, is our domestic output of graduates likely to be sufficient, and graduating with skills in the right areas, to meet employers' needs as they compete for business in the wider marker?
- Second, will graduates become inclined to emigrate from the UK in significant numbers to take up employment with companies in Europe?

The adequacy of UK graduate supply: a comparison with the rest of the Community

Despite the declining UK birthrate, the Government is committed to the aim of doubling student numbers over the next 25 years. This is clearly a necessity as domestic demand for graduates continues to increase – statistics published by the Institute of Manpower Studies, the most authoritative source of information on labour market trends, shows growth of over 30 per cent over the last ten years, with banking/ insurance and the law recruiting almost double the numbers of 1979. Only the teacher training and engineering sectors have in this period shown a decline, the latter almost certainly due to lack of supply. Not surprisingly, fierce competition among employers is forcing starting salaries up well in excess of the rate of inflation. The most recent trends also show an encouraging increase to the number of graduates pursuing a career in industry rather than commerce.

The IMS predicts that, despite the Government's programme to increase student numbers, graduate shortages will become worse during the 1990s due to the two key factors of increased demand and the falling birthrate. However, in this potentially serious circumstance the UK is unlikely to be significantly worse off than its major competitor nations in Europe. As I have already indicated, the demographic downturn will take place almost universally throughout Europe with Member States such as West Germany and Italy being hit harder than the UK. The convergence of the Community's economy means that employers everywhere will be seeking the same thing – highly skilled, adaptable and intelligent recruits, capable of making an immediate impact on the commercial success of their companies. Throughout the whole of Europe, there will be a scramble at higher education level to turn out as many as possible of such recruits and among companies to secure their services.

In one respect at least the UK has a competitive advantage over most of the rest of the Community; our students graduate younger. Most European degree courses last between four and six years, with finals resits being common; the average graduating age in the UK is 21, whereas in France it is 23, West Germany 24 and Italy 25. A further factor in this equation is some Member States' requirements of young people to do National Service. In France, for example, almost all males are required to spend a year in the army before the age of 29. Employers may therefore face the cost and difficulty of losing key employees for a full year at a time when they are integrating into the values and objectives of the organisation.

Numerical comparisons

In purely numerical terms, what differences exist between Member States regarding graduate supply? IMS statistics on European student populations show the following pattern:

Table 5.3: Student Population (Total Enrolments on Degree Course as Percentage of 18 to 24 Population: 1983/84)

Country	%
UK	9.8
France	15.8
Germany	17.2
Italy	17.6
Netherlands	9.0

This shows the UK undergraduate population to be well below those of France, Germany and Italy. However, turning to graduate output the pattern is very different.

Table 5.4: Graduate Output

Country	(Thousands)	(As Percentage of Total Population x 1,000)
UK	132	23.2
France	164	29.5
Germany	127	20.7
Italy	73	12.7
Netherlands	16	10.1

Here, the UK output does not vary significantly from that of Germany and France, but is well ahead of that of Italy; the narrowing of the gap may in part be due to much lower 'drop-out' rates from degree courses at British colleges and universities. Overall, it seems again from these statistics that the UK is not seriously disadvantaged compared with the rest of Europe regarding its supply of graduates coming into the employment market.

Course comparisons

Differences in the characteristics of degree courses between the Member States are sometimes identified as a more significant factor. The Association of Graduate Recruiters puts forward the following views:

'A high proportion of British students study non-vocational degree courses. In Europe the philosophers, historians, social scientists and all the others whom British recruiters employ would not, initially at least, be acceptable. In Europe, arts graduates teach; pure scientists undertake research; lawyers go to the legal profession. Until European employers change their approach or until British students start to read relevant degrees, there may be problems.'

Although it is hard to be specific about the extent of these differences, the approach towards graduate skills and training does certainly vary. In France, for example, although university entry requirements are lower than ours and degree courses are on the whole more broadly based, there is more of a vocational slant which propels students, by the nature of the course modules they take, into specific career paths.

On the other hand, it would be misleading to convey the view that throughout the rest of Europe a better balance exists between the supply of graduates in key skills areas and the demand for those skills. The IMS in its report 'The Graduate Labour Market in the 1990s' contains the following summary:

'In terms of the balance between supply and demand we see a segmented market in many countries with high levels of graduate unemployment in the Netherlands, Spain, Germany, Italy and Ireland, for example, co-existing with shortages of engineers, IT specialists, and management graduates.'

Overall it would seem that, in the area of skills shortages also, the problem faced in the UK is only part of a larger, Community-wide problem.

Conclusions

What conclusions can be drawn from this? First, there is now clear evidence that graduate supply in terms of both numbers and key skill areas is not significantly worse than throughout the rest of the Community. The problem, therefore, is not so much one of UK companies being disadvantaged compared with European ones, as the European economy as a whole being disadvantaged compared with Japan and the USA. Here, the comparative statistics are again stark and unequivocal. In 1984 the total output of engineering graduates in Japan was over 40 per cent higher than the total of France, Britain and Germany combined, while the US output of science graduates in the same year was almost exactly double that of those three Member States. There is clearly much to be done across the Community if we are to compete effectively in world markets. But here there is a twist in the tail. 'One in ten of all university lecturers who changed jobs went abroad', according to a recent report. There is increasing concern that unless something can be done to arrest this trend our ability to produce more graduates in management sciences, economics, engineering and the natural sciences will be severely jeopardised. A warning to the Government in its academic funding and pay policy!

Graduates abroad: a growing trend?

All students in higher level education must by now be aware that graduates have been identified as a key resource in the European labour market. The cultural exchange programmes of the European Commission, and the many individual initiatives being taken by universities, polytechnics and business colleges have combined to create an enormous interest and awareness at this level in the purposes behind the Single Market. Naturally, this is being translated into expectation as new graduates – the least constrained of our workforce in terms of mobility – look towards Europe for career opportunity. A recent survey of 4,000 students revealed that half of them intended to work abroad after graduation, the most popular overseas destination being the European mainland.

The Association of Graduate Recruiters offers a number of reasons why British graduates are a particularly attractive target for European recruiters. These include:

- the obvious fact that they speak English, which is an important skill in international business;
- they are easily accessible because of the highly structured network of careers services here which has no counterpart in Europe;
- although the proportion of school leavers going into higher education is low, the quality is high;
- unlike their European equivalents, British students usually leave home to study. They are therefore more likely to be prepared to consider working abroad.

Constraints

A number of European recruiters, such as Siemens, Philips and Logica, are already active on the UK university milk-round, and undoubtedly their pan-European training and career development programmes make them extremely attractive to ambitious graduates. The Association of Graduate Recruiters does, however, identify two constraints on UK graduates which, to some extent counteract their marketability:

- first, the non-vocational nature of most degree courses (although as indicated earlier in this chapter this may not be so great an issue as is generally supposed);
- second, low standards of proficiency in foreign languages: 'Despite all the talk about English being the language of business it is difficult to imagine Britons with no command of German selling in Germany to German buyers, or working with German colleagues'.

On the whole, these disadvantages will be slight to any student determined to embark upon a European business career. The increasing numbers of enrolments on 'Eurocentric' degree courses, the interest in exchange and co-operation schemes between colleges and in Commission-led initiatives such as ERASMUS and COMETT are a clear indication that undergraduates are keen to develop the skills for the wider market by the time they finish their degree courses. At present, demand outstrips our colleges' ability to supply; for example, there are 2,000 applicants for the 50 places on Trent Polytechnic's business degree course run jointly with universities in France and Germany, while the largest enrolment of students to INSEAD, the prestige European business school at Fontainebleau just outside Paris, is British. The most telling statistic, however, comes again from the IMS. They show that managerial/professional emigration from the UK to Europe rose threefold from 5,700 to 17,700 in the ten years to 1986, while equivalent immigration from Europe during the same period increased from 4,100 to 5,200 – just 25 per cent. This is clear evidence of the increasing tendency of graduates – the managers and professionals of the future – to be willing to develop their careers beyond our national boundaries.

The IMS is equally pessimistic about the ability of British recruiters to penetrate the European graduate labour market, to redress the imbalances created by increased demand by companies at home. The European demographic downturn means that graduates will be in equally short supply in other Member States as they are here; furthermore, recruitment practices in some countries are difficult to adapt to unless local knowledge is obtained. Against this, many of our bigger international companies have been recruiting graduates across Europe for many years, and government and educational institutions do exist to facilitate placements in the colleges and business organisations of other Member States. The coming of the Single Market has created awareness and expectation amongst students throughout the Community, which may present a window of opportunity for employers far-sighted enough to research, plan and exploit the graduate labour market in countries other than our own. For example, a survey conducted last year found that nearly one in four French graduates had a specific interest in working in the UK. A high percentage spoke good English and regarded it as a key business language.

Pensions provision: a growing problem for Europe

The demographic downturn in Europe creates a major problem in the area of pensions provision, which will worsen throughout the 1990s and continue well into the twenty-first century. A number of individual factors contribute to this:

- Falling birth rates will reduce the number of workers coming into both state and private pension schemes at the 'bottom end', thus severely cutting the level of contributions.

- As a greater proportion of young people goes into higher education rather than directly into employment the average age of entrants to the labour market will rise. Again, this reduces the overall level of contribution into pension funds.

- At the same time, the proportion of over-65s in the population will increase throughout Europe during the next 40 years, as the table below shows:

Table 5.5: Share of elderly population projections
(Source: OECD)

Country	1980	2000	2010	2020	2030
Belgium	14.37	14.70	15.90	17.74	20.78
Denmark	14.41	14.87	16.67	20.11	22.56
France	13.96	15.28	16.26	19.45	21.76
Greece	13.14	14.97	16.76	17.80	19.49
Ireland	10.72	11.12	11.08	12.57	14.74
Italy	13.45	15.31	17.28	19.37	21.92
Luxembourg	13.32	16.74	18.12	20.15	22.38
Netherlands	11.51	13.46	15.13	18.89	22.96
Portugal	10.17	13.54	14.13	15.63	18.24
UK	14.87	14.48	14.61	16.27	19.24
West Germany	15.51	17.12	20.35	21.74	25.82
Spain	10.85	14.36	15.53	17.00	19.64

Thus, the amount of non-contributors receiving benefits from schemes will increase as the number of contributors in employment goes down.

- The average life expectancy of citizens of the Community is also expected to rise as better health care techniques and 'healthier living' increases. Pension schemes will therefore have to pay out benefits for longer periods of time.

- The range of entitlements provided by pension schemes has tended to become more generous during the past decade, again adding to total costs.

The upshot of this is that all Member States within the European Community are being forced to look hard at their methods of pensions provision, and to consider radical measures either to shift the burden by privatisation, increased contributions or reduced benefits. An article in the January 1989 edition of *Occupational Pensions* puts this starkly:

'One common thread emerging from any examination of social security in Europe is that it is in retreat . . . Many of the state systems are under severe financial pressure and steps are gradually being taken to reduce this burden and to shift the balance of making up income in retirement on to new, private arrangements.'

As with the issue of demographic trends itself, the problems of pension provision vary considerably between Member States. In countries such as West Germany and Italy the above-average birthrate decline has the additional knock on effect of increasing their share of the elderly population more rapidly than most; again in Italy, the continuing unemployment problem reduces the number of potential contributors into schemes. Unlike the UK, in many countries a higher proportion of the workforce is covered by 'pay-as-you-go' schemes funded jointly by the state, employers and employees rather than separately funded and insured private schemes. The burden of funding is therefore more directly related to the ratio between contributors (workers) and pensioners.

Different countries are addressing the funding problem in different ways. In the UK we have had the introduction of personal pensions and money-purchase contracting out; the CBI has also proposed a 'flexible' retirement age between 60 and 70. In France, Belgium and Portugal, measures to encourage 'third pillar' arrangements have been put in motion, while in Spain measures to contain the cost of social security have meant a ten per cent reduction in state pension. At bottom, philosophical as well as demographic considerations are of fundamental importance to the means of provision. This is most clearly illustrated by drawing comparison between the widely differing systems that apply in two neighbouring European states: France and Great Britain.

France and the UK: fraternité versus *laissez-faire*

The chief characteristic of French retirement provisions has been described as solidarity. All employers from manual level up to *cadres superieures* (i.e. senior managers) contribute compulsorily to schemes which top up the basic social security provision to a common level – up to 50 per cent of average career earnings in the 'highest adjusted pay years' for a maximum contribution of 37.5 years.

Employer contributions are around eight per cent, employees' around six and a half per cent. The system overall is completely unfunded, involving direct transfer of contributions from current employees to current pensioners. It is therefore heavily dependent on a steady stream of new workers coming into the employment market, to maintain contribution levels.

By contrast, the UK system is divided into the 'haves' and 'have nots' – those covered by an occupational scheme, and those who are not. To a French worker this would seem completely unfair – though the investment-related and insured occupational schemes provide pensionable earnings levels well above those attainable under the French system, the levels for those relying on SERPS are pitiful, leading in many cases to poverty and hardship in old age. At present, 10.5m. employees, almost half the working population, are not covered by an occupational scheme.

The pros and cons of the two contrasting systems vary greatly. In terms of what is provided, the French system offers no choice, but a reasonable level of retirement income for all workers. The UK system allows considerable choice, but no guaranteed security for the many employees not covered by occupational schemes who, for one reason or another, do not opt for a personal pension. In terms of funding, the French system is much less robust than that in the UK; totally dependent on the balance between workers and pensioners at any given time, as the number of new workers falls it is inevitable that contribution levels must rise or the system as a whole must change drastically. On the other hand, and to quote one commentator:

'The UK's financial provisions for occupational pensions by forward funding in segregated funds is the envy of France and other nations and provides employees who are members of such schemes with much greater security and certainty than they would get in almost any other European country.'

Implications for UK companies operating abroad

There are several implications in all this for UK companies operating in the European Market. First of all, the differences between Member States' systems of pension provision are so great that harmonisation of them is unthinkable except in the very long term. As the number of people working abroad for at least part of their working lives increases, companies employing staff across the European Market will need to consider how to handle the pensions issue – whether to keep such staff in the 'home' scheme, place them in the framework of the local scheme, or perhaps consider some other type of individual arrangement. From the point of view of the employees themselves, some form of 'multinational fund', co-ordinating the pensions liabilities of a company across the national boundaries within which it operates, might be the most attractive option. However, there are considerable difficulties attached to the setting up of such arrangements; not only the headache of assessing different tax regimes, exchange controls and social security arrangements, but also in rendering the scheme fair without harmonising upwards to the highest common denominator in each detail of the scheme.

At present Inland Revenue rules allow expatriates to be retained within the home country occupational pension scheme as long as they return to the UK within three years. This may become increasingly anomalous if, as is likely with the advent of the Single Market, executives spend longer periods of service away from their 'home' country or even move on to appointments in third or fourth countries in the furtherance of their careers. Unless the Inland Revenue changes its rules on this, most companies are therefore faced with little choice but to retain such staff in the home scheme and pay increased contributions to equalise the loss of tax relief.

There are similar issues for UK companies going into Europe and employing foreign nationals for the first time. To quote again from *Occupational Pensions*:

'The UK company's move into Europe may be the result of acquisition in which case the employees will already have pension arrangements. The UK company will have to decide whether to adopt an international pensions policy which is subsequently applied to all-country employees, or, as is more likely, how to adapt such a policy to local circumstances.'

Again, whatever the case, the complex issue of reconciling different state pension and tax arrangements and local employers' pension practices with the company scheme will be extremely difficult.

Finally, it is worth noting that the complex differences between pensions provision across the European Community creates a huge window of opportunity for UK insurance, investment and actuarial firms. Our system of forward-funded and insured occupational schemes is by far the most highly developed in the Community: the demographic downturn and increased need to harmonise across Europe will accelerate the trend towards money purchase type schemes that is already underway. The considerable experience of UK professional firms in this field presents them with a unique business opportunity provided they research the issues involved and market themselves appropriately to different client bases in Europe.

Part three
Responding to the challenge

6 The strategic personnel manager

I have sought to emphasise throughout this book that the main contribution a Personnel Manager can make to a business will be at strategic rather than operational level. In this chapter my intention is to give substance to this basic principle, putting the role of the Personnel Manager into the context of the senior management response to the challenges set by the Single European Market. The chapter looks back, therefore, towards the general issues raised in Part One, and suggests a management approach to these. It also looks forward to the specific operational issues that will need to be addressed as a result of the drawing up of the strategic plan.

Of course, no two companies will have the same approach. By looking at the issues in a broad context, however, it is possible to identify some common strands that need to be followed and to illustrate the ways in which personnel managers can contribute to the strategic planning process. The three sections within this chapter attempt to draw these strands together and put them in a logical sequence:

- In the first section, the key questions that will determine where a company needs to position itself within the European Market are raised. Although these are questions of business decision planning on the broadest scale, the responses to them must in most cases include a strong human resources element if all the issues are to be resolved thoroughly.
- In the second, the major strategic task of creating a European management structure appropriate to the needs of the organisation is given detailed consideration. Personnel professionals must play a major role in accomplishing this task.
- The third section looks in detail at mergers and acquisitions strategy for the Single Market. This particular approach to the challenge of increased competition is one that many organisations will consider and

again there is an important contribution to be made by the personnel professional.

Overall, it must be stressed that the resolution of these strategic issues is vital before operational issues arising from them can be addressed. The discussion here therefore sets the scene for subsequent chapters in this part of the book which consider specifically employment related responses in such fields as training and development, recruitment and staff mobility.

Position in the market

The first and most important step for any business is to decide exactly where it is to place itself within the Single Market. If you are already there in Europe, you may have developed a full business strategy underpinned by, among other things, a personnel strategy which aims to forestall all the potential problems and make the most of the opportunities. If you are going in for the first time, you need to decide how, where and on what scale; if you are staying out, just as important, you need to be able to place yourself best to respond to the new challenges you will face from foreign competitors penetrating your domestic market. Even in the latter circumstance, your response need not be purely defensive.

The Policy and Planning group at Deloitte, Haskins and Sells Management Consultancy (now part of Coopers and Lybrand Deloitte Management Consultancy Services) have produced a handbook on the impacts of the Single Market entitled *Deloitte's 1992 Guide*, which sets out very clearly the strategic approach a company needs to adopt in analysing its own market position. The main theme of this is that companies need to consider the range of their activities very carefully to ascertain which of them will face significant change as a result of the Single Market Programme, and which will remain largely unaffected. The conclusion is reached:

'Because the programme is very specific, companies will need, in many instances, to look at the individual parts of their business in some detail. Three basic ingredients will be required:

- a knowledge of the timing and content of community legislation;
- market research on areas of current activity and areas of new opportunities;
- an analysis of likely moves by competitors.'

As an appendix to the handbook, a checklist is presented which sets out in some detail the practical questions that need to be considered before reaching any overall decision. Although these relate to general business management and are not therefore personnel specific, many of them must be addressed by the personnel strategist in making his or her contribution to the direction taken by the business relative to the Single Market. I use the checklist, therefore, as a focus for my analysis of the personnel professional's strategic input to this process.

Timing and content of legislation

The impact on the home market

The first set of questions to be asked under this heading concerns the potential impact of EC legislation on a company's existing home market. In particular, is foreign competition restricted because of home market protection through either UK standards or restricted access by foreign firms? If so, is this protection likely to be removed by proposals in the Single Market Programme in the near future or over a lapsed period of time? If the answers to these questions are 'yes', the management of the business will need to draw up plans to minimise the threat of increased competition. For the Personnel Manager, the response is likely to be inward-looking, taking as its starting point the structure of the organisation and the attitudes of its management and workforce. Change here will be almost inevitable if the company culture has developed in a protected environment; specific measures necessary may include training and development programmes to create commercial awareness skills, the development of reward systems that link individual performance with corporate targets, or slimming down to create a leaner organisation with its attendant needs for redeploying, retraining, counselling and redundancy programmes.

The impact on major competitors

The second set of questions concerns the potential impact of EC legislation on major competitors, and on access to European markets. They can be categorised as follows:

- What will the overall effect on competitors be (one must think here of

US, Japanese and other non-EC companies as well as those within the Community); which proposals are likely to be of impact and when will these come into effect?

- Will the Single Market Programme make access easier to other EC or non-EC markets? Again, which proposals will have a major effect, how likely are they to go through and if so in what timescale?

- Will proposals in the Single Market Programme make it easier to obtain supplies from EC suppliers, i.e. by removing existing restrictions or barriers?

- Will the Programme allow reduction in the number of product variants produced for different geographical markets, allowing rationalisation or regrouping of existing production facilities, or easier/more competitive transportation systems?

In responding to these questions, the Personnel Manager needs to adopt a more outward-looking approach than with the first set of questions. If Single Market legislation is indeed likely to help the company to a more competitive position or open up new markets in Europe or elsewhere, an assessment needs to be made of the suitability of both the existing staffing arrangements and operational structure to meet this challenge. Again, much will come down to the question of skills, attitudes and abilities, and attention may need to be given to the following issues:

- First, management abilities. Technically, how does the company's management compare with that of major competitors in terms both of overall business management and in specific functional areas such as research and development, sales and marketing, quality control? Culturally, how will management cope with the demands of operating in new foreign markets? Do they have knowledge of the requirements and norms of these markets, and will they be able to deal with new customers (e.g., do they have the necessary language skills)? A detailed assessment will need to be made of these issues followed by the drawing up of an action programme to correct any imbalances between company needs and management abilities. This may include extensive training in technical, management or cultural skills, or the 'buying-in' of these skills by the recruitment of new professional or managerial staff; possibly from Europe rather than the UK.

- Second, the skills and abilities of the workforce. Again, assessment will need to be made of the appropriateness of the existing skills base in relation to new market opportunities, and plans drawn up to rectify any important shortfalls. It is likely that the focus here will be on technical training, although it is important to bear in mind the needs not just of production staff but of those working in other areas such as distribution, purchasing/supplies or general administration. Here, the new requirements may be more subtle by nature but just as crucial to the company's ability to penetrate its new market effectively.

- Third, the highly sensitive issue of whether to redeploy or relocate part of the company's operation in order to be closer to the new market, reduce employment costs or tap new sources of labour – for example, where the gap between existing workforce skills and company need is so great as to make retraining a non-option. In many cases this will be linked to the issue of mergers and acquisitions, which I consider later in this chapter; setting this aside, however, the Personnel Manager may need to become deeply involved in an extensive feasibility study encompassing such things as the cost of relocation; the cost to the company of the loss of key staff; the advantages and disadvantages in human resources terms of proposed sites, focusing on the availability of labour, local workforce skills, employment standards and norms and the impact of the company on the local infrastructure. Once a decision has been made, input into the strategic plan will include ways to mount recruitment campaigns and extensive training of new staff, plus the handling of 'slimming down' operations at existing sites possibly encompassing redundancy and retraining programmes.

The impact on employment and human resource issues

The third set of questions concerns, quite simply, those Single Market Programme proposals that directly relate to employment and human resources issues. These are set out comprehensively in Chapter 4 and do not need repeating here in any detail. The personnel strategist must, however, consider them carefully in the context of change to the business environment; those most likely to be of significance here are:

- Mutual recognition of qualifications: to what extent will this facilitate the employment of non-UK nationals?
- What are the language and cultural training requirements of your staff, and how can EC initiatives or funding be used to develop the necessary skills?

The message to be conveyed is that EC employment initiatives are not simply to be regarded as a threat to existing norms within the company; many of them are there to be made use of, and can be so in the interests of a company's business development programme in the wider market.

Areas of current activity and new opportunity

Under this heading, the first set of questions concerns, very broadly, the nature of the company's current products or services, the means by which these are stored, distributed and marketed to the customer and their suitability for or possibility of adaption to new overseas markets. Specific items to be considered include:

- an analysis of both current and planned product/service areas;
- an analysis of current and planned geographical markets;
- the degree to which products/services are highly standardised or customer designed;
- the quality and price-sensitivity of the products/services offered;
- the warehousing, distribution and selling arrangement for the products/services: again regarding both current and projected markets.

The analysis of these items will in most cases be extremely complex, but of crucial importance to the devising of an effective strategic plan for the business in the Single European Market. The contribution to be made by the Personnel Manager will again need to be a positive one, taking account of the company's ability in terms of organisation structure, location and staff skills base to make the most of new opportunities arising, and drawing up plans to achieve change where necessary. Specific areas of attention may include several of those already raised elsewhere, including technical and managerial training, the acquisition of skills appropriate to doing business across diverse cultures, recruitment in the European Market and reorganisation/redeployment.

The second area of questioning concerns both the feasibility and advisability of collaboration with European competitors in areas such as research and development, distribution and marketing. Cross-border joint ventures have not been common in the past, but for many small and medium-sized companies in the Single Market faced with increased competition from bigger rivals they may become the only way to survive. However, they are fraught with problems and complexities, many of which are personnel related and will call upon the skills of experienced and capable human resources professionals to surmount. These include:

- language difficulties;
- company culture/attitudinal differences;
- different approaches or legislative controls applied by different national governments;
- poor information exchange systems;
- rivalry between the partners, the passing over of blame, and in the instance of short-term ventures the possibility of 'poaching' of key staff.

Any decision to follow the joint venture route must surely involve the Personnel Manager in making an assessment of the attitudes and competences of any prospective European partner. This in itself can be a complex and sensitive task and may involve establishing a good level of trust and understanding with equivalents in competitor operations in order to obtain reliable information. Analysis of this information may be crucial to the final decision taken, and may include such factors as:

- The overall competence of the partner company's management and staff.
- The specific ability of its management and staff to adapt to new demands and circumstances.
- The willingness of the partner company to collaborate even-handedly.
- An assessment of the partner company's current and likely future market position as affected by factors such as staff turnover, employment costs.
- The effectiveness of the partner company's personnel systems and the impact they have, in a positive or negative sense, on the company's market position. Any audit of these systems must take a broad approach, but is likely to include, specifically, reward systems, health and safety policy (mindful here that legislation to improve standards may increase costs considerably for some European companies), human resource development practices and standards.

Analysis of likely competitor moves

There are two fundamental questions here. First, how to assess the degree of penetration from EC competitors into the company's existing market? Second, what responses are likely from foreign companies to any moves to penetrate their own domestic markets?

The responses to these questions are likely to be similar, involving a detailed analysis of competitor strengths and weaknesses *vis à vis* those of one's own company. To the Personnel Manager, this will mean a comprehensive audit procedure with the aim of pin-pointing all human resources differences that could be of impact. This will undoubtedly cover many of the issues already raised under other headings, including organisation structure, management and staff attitudes, significant skills shortages, demographic and labour market trends. From this should come a strategy for defence where significant weaknesses have been identified which could lead to successful market penetration by competitors, and for positive action where there are strengths that could contribute to the company's plans to move into new markets in Europe.

In analysing the strategic input of the Personnel Manager to business planning for the Single Market, I have taken competitiveness as my starting point; that is, I have looked at the ways in which personnel can contribute to the maintenance and improvement of a company's market position in the changing environment. Other approaches have concentrated on personnel's role in the development of management systems, although being equally practically based these have tended to throw up broadly similar conclusions.

Incomes Data Services, the research organisation which provides a wide range of reports and studies into personnel, employment and industrial relations issues, specified three broad conclusions for the personnel strategist facing the challenge of the Single Market as long ago as June 1988 (IDS Focus No 47). These were:

- First, the necessity to achieve 'compatibility rather than uniformity or diversity' in personnel systems for businesses operating in more than one country. This touches on the delicate balancing act between a centralised or decentralised approach to running the business, the need to maintain a corporate culture while remaining sensitive to different national practices and norms.

- Second, the need to maintain a central co-ordinating personnel policy authority in order to maintain control of line management authorities and in particular effective lines of communication between managers operating in different functions or similar functions but in different countries.

- Third, the need to assess the company's rationalisation and restructuring requirements. In an increasingly competitive environment this can, if not handled effectively, become an extremely bitter and divisive issue. Again it is important to maintain a balance; in this case between the sensitivities of staff and their representatives on one hand, the company's market needs on the other.

The Institute of Personnel Management has collaborated with Incomes Data Services in an important research project on the Single Market Programme, publishing its results in a handbook entitled *1992: Personnel Management and the Single European Market.* Naturally, the views presented dovetail with those presented in other IDS publications; broadly, the emphasis is on the creation of multinational management teams, the decentralised versus the centralised approach, and again rationalisation/restructuring. The conclusion is reached:

'European Personnel Managers have to be strategists not administrators. . . Such an approach means:

- getting the national and international systems right in order to develop a distinctive European management grouping;

- taking a Europe-wide view of management development and education and, increasingly, of graduate recruitment and training;

- looking at executive pay levels on a European rather than a national basis;

- treating transfers between countries as normal career moves and not as expatriation.

But for most firms there will need to be a balance between the development of European management and the definite national characteristics of individual markets or subsidiaries. The problem will be securing the right balance.'

The handbook differentiates clearly between the personnel strategy for a UK company going into Europe for the first time, and a company already established there. For the former the emphasis will be on developing the business from scratch: a major issue will therefore be the acquisition of reliable local knowledge into personnel practices such as recruitment and employment law, and obtaining the services of local professionals in carrying out preliminary audits is regarded as crucial. Others include the development of an appropriate management style, 'getting managers to think European', and the mergers and acquisitions question. For the latter, the emphasis is much more on consolidating and building on existing systems, and analysing the need for change in line with changing market conditions. A broad issue common to both types of company is, again, achieving the right balance between a centralised or decentralised structure. Going back to first principles, it is the IPM's view that this comes down to the question of 'compatibility', i.e. giving foreign subsidiaries or divisions sufficient autonomy to allow free business development in the local market, but not too much to allow them to break away from the corporate culture with its values, norms and systems.

To revisit Coopers and Lybrand Deloitte – how have human resources issues featured in the Management Consultancy's own European planning? A document laying out the European strategic business plan from 1989 to 1992 sets objectives in terms of growth, service/industry sector development and European networking. Among the individual strategies seen as key to successful achievement of the plan are:

- Measures to improve the skills base in specific functions/ geographical regions, either by the recruitment of new consultants or the acquisition of specialist firms.

- Measures to improve language skills; it is recognised that the main business language will continue to be English and therefore efforts must be targeted predominantly towards European consultants and support staff. However, UK consultants will also need to acquire skills in European languages.

- Most important, the maintenance of the right balance between the corporate culture and the culture of individual national firms. It is recognised that national firms must be enabled to retain their own entrepreneurial characters in order to achieve organisational growth; the strategy developed is to appoint leaders in each of these firms as 'European champions', responsible to a small, dedicated Deloitte Europe Management team for service area and industry co-ordination.

- Alliances with outside firms is seen as an appropriate strategy in some areas. This will involve detailed assessment by human resources specialists among others of strengths and weaknesses, skills and attitude bases and communication issues.

It can be seen from this that Coopers and Lybrand Deloitte has responded positively to the European challenge, and is heeding its own advice in the way it aims to develop its business in the wider market.

Creating a European management structure

'Creating a multinational management team is probably the most consistent thread running right through the process of internationalising a business. Creating that team is the responsibility of the whole board and top management, but the personnel department can make a unique contribution.' Thus the view expressed by Tony Vineall, Deputy Personnel Director of Unilever, in an article in the magazine *Personnel Management* in October 1988. It serves as a good introduction to the two key questions: first, what is European management? and second, how can it be developed and promoted?

The European business manager . . .

The key competences of a European business manager can be clearly and easily stated. Broadly, the four major attributes are:

- First, the ability to work within a complex operational framework, where there will frequently be potential for conflict and misunderstanding. An adaptable and cosmopolitan approach will be required to minimise these threats.
- Second, a sound understanding of change processes. It will frequently be necessary to work in an environment in which decisions cannot be based on facts and precedents and success in the old will not guarantee success in the new.
- Third, the ability to operate across cultural boundaries. This must include good communication skills as it may be necessary to lead or manage cross-cultural groups in areas of corporate strategy or product development.
- Fourth, quite simply, the willingness to accept a demanding lifecycle, involving frequent travel, relocation and other disruptions to family life.

These attributes are, of course, additional to the technical and managerial competences that would be expected of professional staff operating in a non-international environment. This being the case, they add up to a pretty challenging set of demands; it is interesting to compare them with those thrown up by the Saxton Bampfylde International survey which I quoted in Chapter 4. Though less exotic, the emphasis on cross-cultural openness and advanced problem-solving ability as the most important requirements is the same.

. . . and the Personnel Department

It is encouraging that, faced with such a complex set of variables in the challenge of creating a management team for the Single Market, many personnel professionals in leading international companies have responded positively. One of the key areas for attention is personal development; moulding a company's existing pool of management talent into a cadre of culture-sensitive business leaders who, in the words of one human resource development manager, are 'open, flexible, will listen, have vision and purpose, and are willing to take risks'.

Examples of constructive action being taken are numerous. At Shell UK, international as well as cross-functional career assignments are used to develop a breadth of experience. Olivetti has an extensive training programme for its international intake of systems support staff, involving contact with colleagues from different countries employed to do similar work, and foreign secondments as a stepping-stone to management appointment. The worldwide manufacturing group 3M has developed a workshop-based training programme for senior managers in all European subsidiaries, which will in time be extended down to more junior management levels. This includes analysis of leadership and influencing skills in a change environment, individual responses to new circumstances and the discussion of goals and action plans.

Altogether, it is clear that a significant number of companies have adopted a home-grown approach to developing international management talent, concentrating on improving their existing resources as far as possible. A major factor in this is undoubtedly that the output of graduates with European MBAs or equivalent qualifications is far too small to meet demand. A number of business schools, including Cranfield which is among the leaders in European management education, have also recognised this and have responded by developing a range of courses specifically for existing managers as well as direct links with major international organisations in the training and development field. It is likely however that the main thrust will continue to be companies developing their own internal training programmes, with foreign transfer or secondment featuring prominently among the techniques used.

Structure of the European management team

A second area of key importance in developing a European management approach is the structure of the management team itself. As I have already indicated, the major issue here is achieving the right balance between corporate and national management styles. All commentators are agreed this will necessitate a degree of complexity; to quote again from Tony Vineall's IPM article:

'Operations which cross national boundaries will almost inevitably run with matrix structures, whether or not they are called that . . ., more than one boss; activity-based working groups whose members have a primary reporting relationship in many different parts of the organisation; more time spent consulting and agreeing and building consensus than in issuing or receiving command-type instructions – all these will characterise the management style.'

For the personnel professional, getting the mix right will be no easy matter. It requires being sensitively attuned to the cultures and norms prevalent in different parts of the operation and in different countries, in order to draw on the most valuable attributes and mould them in to the corporate whole. It requires leaving national operations to think and act for themselves in areas where they are best able to develop aspects of the total business, while not leaving them feeling exposed or too distant from the policy-makers at centre. Experimentation with different approaches may be the only way for many companies to make progress. Above all, the basic premise must be that a headquarters-driven structure will certainly not be appropriate and that strategy and implementation are interlinked throughout the business process.

How are companies approaching this issue? I have already described the Deloitte 'European champion' system as one way of achieving the right balance. One client company I have worked with, a producer of complex sample analysis equipment with manufacturing or sales centres in most major European countries, has similarly appointed functional directors to take responsibility on a pan-European basis, choosing for these posts whichever national director is deemed to have the best attributes. These European directors meet regularly and are thus able to discuss at the same time specific national and broad corporate issues. The organisation development strategists at 3M have experimented with a number of approaches, including appointing a 'lead' subsidiary to develop a project on a pan-European basis, and giving a group of people in one country the responsibility for developing a brand or programme in another part of Europe. A particularly innovative scheme at 3M is the European Management Action Team (EMAT) programme. This involves bringing together teams of managers from different European subsidiaries to study the effects of the Single Market Programme on the business, identifying threats and opportunities, mounting business plans in response, above all devising ways to make best use of resources across individual subsidiaries and within the pan-European environment.

The development of appropriate personnel systems

The third area in which the personnel department has a key role to play in creating a pan-European approach is in the development of appropriate personnel systems and networks. Initially this may involve frequent visits to subsidiary operations in Europe, to gain information on existing practices, carry out audits and establish a presence. Arising from this should follow a strategic plan for the personnel function focusing on areas where a co-ordinated approach will be required to achieve compatibility across the organisation.

The specific systems needing co-ordination will of course, depend very much on the organisation's overall management style and areas of business. However, they may well include several of the following:

- achieving pay compatibility; this may involve the development of common grading systems, while remaining mindful of the different pay levels and costs of living in different countries;
- a standardised approach to non-cash benefits;
- a common job evaluation/indexing structure, possibly developed with the assistance of one of the major international consultancies specialising in this field;
- co-ordination of expatriate and overseas service policies;
- developing a common merit review/appraisal system for the whole organisation.

Creating a structure within the personnel department to address these and other issues will also be a factor of the organisation's management style. The IDS/IPM handbook *1992: Personnel Management and the Single European Market* gives many examples, including the following description of the approach taken by Philips, the Dutch-owned electronics and domestic appliances group:

'The pay of senior managers, for instance about 100 people in the UK, is determined after consultation between the corporate product division and the national corporation headquarters. Broadly speaking local specialists advise on a suitable range of increases in line with national circumstances and the HQ product divisions decide the amount. There is a centralised international personnel influence; for example the Corporate Staff Bureau recently decided there should be a common "potential appraisal" procedure for all graduate trainees. . . . This office also controls all expatriate conditions of employment . . . the aim is to ensure an equivalent home country standard of living. At a different level the European personnel manager in the Philips Telecommunication and Data Systems division recently set up a group to pool information and develop policies on performance measurement and management incentives.'

An approach increasingly being adopted by organisations with diverse European subsidiaries is the appointment of strategists without line responsibility but rather the brief of analysing individual practices across divisions and drawing up recommendations for change where appropriate to the main board. One major UK company with Europe-wide interests in the drinks and leisure industries, for example, has recently recruited a European Human Resources Manager at senior level to carry out audits of existing practices in all subsidiaries and work with individual personnel departments in developing compatible systems and practices. Such appointments represent a challenging role for personnel professionals with an interest in the European environment and the ability to take a strategic approach.

Mergers and acquisitions strategy for the Single Market

According to the European Commission, the number of major mergers involving EC-based companies nearly tripled between 1983 and 1987, and this growth rate is expected to accelerate. Undoubtedly, this is because many companies see this route as the easiest and most obvious way into the European market. The pitfalls are many, however, and the methods of going about the acquisitions process itself and of handling the post-merger relationship many and varied.

Not the least of the problems to be overcome has been the failure of the Member States to agree a policy on EC monitoring of cross-border mergers and takeovers. Broadly speaking the larger states of Britain, West Germany and France, which have their own monopolies commissions, have steadfastly resisted all proposals to lower the financial threshold at which mergers would automatically be referred to the Commission for scrutiny; and little progress similarly has been made on the issue of reciprocity in looking at mergers with third country companies – principally the US and Japan. Fortunately, a compromise proposal was agreed at the end of 1989, in which Brussels has the right to block or authorise mergers between companies with a combined worldwide turnover of more than five billion ECUs, although individual Member States' monopolies and mergers commissions will retain a right to block such mergers themselves if they can prove it would distort their national market. The proposals are regarded by some commentators as unenforceable, and in any case they are subject to review after four years' application; nevertheless for the time being they represent a way forward in an area that is clearly of vital importance to the development of trade.

Analysts from outside the EC have not been slow to point out the need for European companies to engage in cross-border mergers in order to strengthen their positions in the worldwide market. One of the biggest joint ventures to date has been that between the British electronics company GEC and its giant West German counterpart, Siemens. This has been hailed by a leading American consultancy, the Standford Research Institute (SRI), as a 'First class example of collaboration between two previously improbable partners'. Commenting on the results of a study it has made of the attitudes of 36 European, US and Japanese hi-tech companies towards alliances, SRI reached a number of specific conclusions:

- Partnering in continental Europe for many companies should be regarded as a 'must' rather than an option.
- European companies need to follow Japanese practice by adopting a more proactive role in the forging of alliances, and by setting clearer objectives at the outset.
- European companies need to negotiate with partners on the basis of 'reciprocity' – i.e. common advantages for both – rather than seeking opportunities just for their own products or services. Again, there is

divergence here from the Japanese approach, as many Japanese companies are themselves negotiating to establish a niche in the Single Market.

- There is a tendency to delegate merger project management responsibility to managers who are not senior enough, or have insufficient skills, to explore and exploit the full strategic potential. European companies in particular have therefore tended to lose sight of strategic objectives in the complexities of short-term legal wrangling, the problems of the negotiations themselves and of post-merger integration.

The problems inherent in taking the narrow perspective have been vividly expressed by one manager in what has become known as the 'ham and eggs' syndrome:

'The purpose of joint ventures is to produce ham and eggs. But while the chicken only has to lay an egg, a pig must be slaughtered to produce ham. Thus the pig does not want to make its contribution. The same is true in a joint venture – neither partner wants to be the pig.'

In the rest of this chapter I shall try to illustrate some of the ways by which these problems can be avoided in a European merger, and how the Personnel Manager can contribute to this. I look in turn at the two phases of, respectively, the acquisition process itself and post-merger integration.

The Acquisition process

The purpose behind the merger

To be successful this will necessitate detailed planning across a number of phases. The first, and probably the most important of these, is to clarify the purpose behind the merger. This will relate to issues of broad business strategy such as definition of future markets and the likely extent of foreign competition. Crucially, it will establish the type of relationship sought with any European partner. This may at one extreme be to leave it relatively free from central control, in the belief that a corporate culture will evolve naturally over time; or at the other to see the merger process itself as an opportunity to bring about cultural and attitudinal change, and 'go in hard' with centrally devised processes and systems. All the signs are that service sector companies are tending to favour the former approach, manufacturing companies the latter; a clear reflection of the differences in the nature of their markets. A prime objective for many manufacturing companies will be to offer a standardised product across the Community, and therefore a much more co-ordinated approach will be required. For financial, legal, marketing and business consulting firms on the other hand the aim must be to be able to offer a broad range of advice appropriate to the different national frameworks, and they will tend therefore to adopt much looser structures. A good example is provided by the legal firm of Lawrence Graham which, with a strong business advisory orientation, is aiming to create a 'federation' of European firms which only in the long term could end up sharing a common corporate image. Various leading firms across Europe have been sounded out on possible membership.

Merger negotiations

The second phase involves the actual merger negotiations. A considerable amount of research into employment-related issues will be necessary here if the process is to go ahead smoothly. Merger negotiations between two domestic partners can be tricky enough; bridging the cultural gap between companies from different Member States adds a further set of complexities and is likely to take even the most seasoned of negotiators into new territory.

Assessment of the merger partner will be a key task here. In most circumstances this will start from the initial establishment of rapport, moving on to an understanding of motives and intentions and from this into the more detailed work of auditing the partner's adequacy for the new venture. The personnel department is likely to be deeply involved in this. Auditing will certainly need to cover such areas as management strengths and weaknesses, the adequacy of pay and any collective bargaining arrangements, health and safety standards, training and development.

An equally important task will be assessment of the environment in which the proposed partner operates, taking account of both cultural and legislative circumstances. This will need to be extremely detailed and since most companies will not have the resources in-house to carry out in-depth research, it may frequently be necessary to obtain the services of local, independent experts to give advice. Again, much of this advice must cover employment-related areas. Examples include:

- national employment law and its impact on the company;
- demographic issues, including the strength of the local labour market and skills base;

- employment practices and norms including recruitment, pay and grade progression, pensions and social security, employee relations;
- the subtleties of attitudes to work and the employer, and the relationship between work, leisure and everyday life.

Some of these areas may at first sight appear esoteric, but it cannot be emphasised strongly enough that detailed insight into issues of this nature is essential. An article by Richard Sarson in the *Times* concerning Anglo-French mergers highlights some of the details that have created practical problems for companies during negotiations:

'Language appears to have been a particular problem where the same word has different meanings in the two languages. Profit in France means profit after tax, whereas in the UK it often means before tax . . . The French are more secretive about salaries and company plans than the British. And the French cannot see the point in company cars . . . Meetings tend to last a certain length of time in Britain, but in France they go on as long as it takes to reach a consensus. So does lunch.'

It is appreciation of finer points such as these that can, ultimately, mean the difference between success or failure in concluding merger negotiations.

Preparing management and staff for the merger

The third phase is the preparation of the organisation's management and staff for the merger. A number of key exercises involving the personnel professional can be identified here:

- First, communication. It will be necessary to give comprehensive briefing to the organisation on issues such as the nature of the merger partner's background, structure and objectives; the culture in which it fits and how this is reflected in the attitudes and values of staff; the objectives of the newly merged organisation and individual roles within it. It should not be forgotten that communication is a two-way process, and that to be effective it must present staff with the opportunity to air concerns. Communication links will need to be established at all levels between the merger partners at this stage, in order to gain understanding of local sensitivities, present the right image, and lay the foundation for working relationships.
- Second, a training programme to equip the staff with the skills to deal effectively with new colleagues will be required. This will undoubtedly

cover language training but may also extend into many other areas of management or vocational skill.

- Third, the need for adaptation of the organisation's personnel systems and procedures to fit with those of the merger partner. The extent of this will depend on the nature of the merger itself, in particular the degree of central control exercised; the cultural differences will again add a dimension not present when two purely domestic merger partners are involved.

In most cases, it is likely that the bulk of the staff will have been completely unaware of the merger plans before this phase of the pre-merger process is set in motion. To many it will come as a surprise; careful management of their concerns and expectations can be crucial. If handled properly, a feeling of new opportunity can be created which can contribute enormously to getting things off to a good start.

Post-merger integration

If all aspects of pre-merger planning have been successful, the initial stages of post-merger integration should be something of a honeymoon period. An expectation will have been created; the main issue therefore will be how to keep this moving in the right direction. Above all, this will require the Personnel Manager to be sensitively attuned to prevailing moods and circumstances, in order to foster those that are positive and influence to the good those that are negative. Training and integration programmes commenced during the pre-merger stage will need to be continued and, in some cases, stepped up. Some adjustment from original plans will be inevitable, perhaps requiring that new programmes in certain areas be devised and implemented rapidly.

A longer term perspective will evolve over time, and this too will inevitably require some adjustments. The focus here is more likely to be on achievement of corporate objectives than the management of individual sensitivities, although career counselling programmes must surely feature prominently on any Personnel Manager's agenda. Organisational issues will however be of greatest importance, involving the identification of real lines of communication and of key players, achieving balance in giving the right degree of autonomy to local or line management, above all implementing the appropriate systems and reporting structures. Getting the right management style can be a long drawn-out process, inextricably linked with longer-term corporate performance. The Personnel Manager can have a major role to play in the achievement of corporate success, and may in many cases have to adopt an innovative approach and develop entirely new systems that reflect the objectives of the new organisation. For example, the implementation of an entirely new performance-related pay system, in which the pool of money is determined by group profits and distributed through an innovative merit review scheme, has made a major contribution to the cementation of a merger between two larger European organisations in the financial service sector.

7 Recruitment and resourcing

Two significant factors will combine during the 1990s to make the recruitment and retention of staff throughout Europe more difficult for employers. First, the Commission's measures to increase labour mobility on a Community-wide basis, and the growing awareness among graduates and professional/managerial staff of career opportunities in the wider market, means that increasing numbers of potential recruits will be tempted abroad. Second, the downturn in school leaver and qualified graduate numbers will drastically reduce a source of supply into the labour market that has traditionally been the main target for recruiters. Quite simply, there will be too few school leavers chasing too many jobs.

Most organisations will initially adopt a domestic approach in addressing these issues. This is only right and proper; building on experience of UK employment norms and practices as they have developed over time, the forward looking personnel professional will be able to devise imaginative and fully appropriate solutions to new problems of labour supply and turnover. However, even for those organisations whose markets for goods and services will continue to be purely within the UK, it would be unwise to take too narrow a view. This would be to ignore the key dynamics of the European labour market situation – the shrinking pool of candidates within the UK on one hand, but on the other the wider range of options created by the Single Market Programme itself, including the possibility of recruiting from elsewhere in the Community as potential employees from other Member States seek the experience of working for a UK company.

Overall, it is impossible to divorce the domestic from the Europe-wide perspective in the area of recruitment and resourcing. In almost all circumstances the Personnel Manager will need to consider a range of options to ensure that manpower needs continue to be met. In this chapter I shall consider three broad areas:

• First, possible ways of redefining an approach to the domestic labour market. This will include concentrating on sources of labour supply previously given little attention, such as married women returning to work; creating a better match between employers' and employees' needs; and reviewing pay and benefits policies. There may be implications for European Community Social Policy in some of these, and more importantly there may be lessons to be learned from the employment practices that prevail in other Member States.

- Second, the ways in which British companies operating in Europe, including those going into the European market for the first time, can make use of their position itself as an attraction to potential recruits. There is growing evidence that the evolving mobility culture will make pan-European employers more sought after than purely domestic ones, particularly to graduates and staff of professional calibre. This is a situation that many companies are already capitalising on.

- Third, the opportunity to attract staff from other Member States. The evidence to date, though limited, suggests that this opportunity will grow. Again, it is a route that many employers may wish to consider, building on the experiences of multinational and other organisations that have already followed it to some degree.

Many of these issues – particularly those relating to domestic labour shortages – have been given extensive coverage in recent books, articles in personnel management and other magazines, and seminars and conferences. I do not propose therefore to consider them in any great depth, but rather to present a broad overview of the options available. The particular circumstances in which an organisation is placed will determine which of them are genuine possibilities for implementation.

The UK labour market – a mirror image of Europe?

In his influential book *Recruitment in the 90s*, Professor Peter Herriot of Birkbeck College warns that British employers will lose many of their professional staff to Europe unless they radically rethink their policies on recruitment and retention. The message is clear – better practice in relation to domestic labour supply is essential if a strong market position is to be maintained:

'Employers must stop using the word selection and start using the word negotiations and contracting, implying a two-way relationship which begins before the employee joins.'

Not only must companies become more flexible in their attitudes towards staff, they must also take steps to sell themselves better, both to potential recruits and existing employees. 'Selling' the company as an employer does not however mean making extravagant promises that cannot be kept. Rather, it involves the drawing up of coherent personnel policies and company values that staff can buy into, and the effective communication of these. Companies with a clear vision that marks them out will have a head start – particularly those with values and philosophies that prospective candidates wish to be associated with.

Personnel Managers faced with the task of meeting companies' manpower needs during the next decade should not lose heart. Despite all the dreary predictions concerning the demographic downturn, the problems are not insurmountable. It should also be remembered that many of them are common throughout Europe, and that employers in countries such as Italy and West Germany are even more severely disadvantaged in certain respects. There may be lessons to be learned, therefore, from comparing the responses to labour supply problems being proposed in the UK with those being proposed elsewhere in the Community. Looking first at the UK, a summary of the main areas to which attention is being given is set out below.

The UK situation

A major area must be improved liaison between employers and schools, colleges and universities. The well-publicised compact schemes in which employers guarantee jobs to students in deprived areas in return for attainment of specified goals such as attendance, punctuality and work experience periods represent one of the most formalised steps in this direction. For many employers, however, the schemes will be too elaborate, and will provide too little in the way of return on investment, to be a worthwhile proposition; many are likely to fall back on tried and tested schemes such as YTS, improving their management of placements and integrating trainees better into the company structure. Other, more informal means of communication with local schools and colleges will also need to be explored, perhaps without any guarantee that vacancies occurring will be taken up but nevertheless raising the profile of the company as a 'caring' employer with sound values and attitudes and a real interest in job creation and skills improvement in the local environment.

Graduate recruitment

At graduate level, a number of innovative schemes have been developed recently which may become a blueprint for future industry/education partnerships. These include the building of degree courses specific to industry sectors, by consortia of employers and universities or polytechnics, often linked with sponsorship of students by individual companies within the consortia. This is seen as developing skills in areas where they are needed by employers – civil engineering, for instance – and of course, a job is guaranteed at the end of the period of study. Many prospective employers who engage in sponsorships do not however insist, or even expect, that all those sponsored will take up their guaranteed job offers; this is particularly true amongst the big accountancy firms, major recruiters of graduates who anticipate that only about one in eight sponsored students will join them on graduation. The predominant aim is rather to convey the message of being an enlightened, forward-looking employer, in order to attract the interest of other undergraduates and those sponsored when they think of changing jobs at a later stage in their careers.

Improved graduate recruitment packages themselves are a second area. It is at graduate level that the biggest gap is likely to exist between supply and demand, and it is already apparent that the salaries and benefits on offer to new recruits are starting to spiral. Many employers now offer benefits to newly qualified graduate recruits that would only previously have been available to experienced staff, such as company cars and preferential loans. More imaginative employers have concentrated on attractive career development and training schemes rather than direct benefits in the attempt to attract better quality graduates. High quality development programmes for staff at all levels is indeed an area to which attention is being given, both to overcome specific skills shortages and sell jobs to potential recruits.

Women returners

Perhaps the most vaunted area is the increasing focus on attracting women back into the employment market, particularly older women with families who may be interested in part-time or more flexible methods of work. As far as recruitment is concerned, action has included 'the roadshow' approach in which individual companies or groups of employers set up recruitment fairs in town centres or other locations; indications are that this means of selling the company can be most effective in attracting new recruits. Many companies have also specifically approached ex-employees who have left in the recent past to start families with a view to bringing them back into employment. As far as employment conditions themselves are concerned, these are inextricably linked with equal opportunities for women. At one level this means offering equivalent levels of pay and benefits, improved services including childcare, career break and transport facilities, and flexible contracts such as part-time work or job sharing, flexible hours, homeworking and short-term contracts. At a second level it means improved training and development opportunities and equal consideration with male employees for promotion to senior positions. Treatment of women in work is changing partly because of demographic needs and partly because the values and standards within our society are themselves changing; there are major implications therefore for social policy, both within the UK and on a European scale.

Removal of restrictive selection practices

A fourth area which has attracted attention is, quite simply, removing restrictive selection practices which prohibit many otherwise suitable candidates for jobs from consideration. Restrictive phrases in advertisements such as 'must have a degree', irrespective of the essential requirements of the job, will disappear as companies realise that such phrases bar 80% of the employable population. The practice known as 'ageism', setting age limits for applicants typically of between late twenties to mid-thirties for many professional jobs, is also likely to be greatly reduced; many leading employers including British Telecom and the Civil Service have dropped age limits in advertisements altogether. Indeed, many employers have recognised that older members of the population represent an untapped source of labour in their own right and have dedicated recruitment campaigns towards them. Well-publicised examples include the recruitment and training of middle-aged professionals from commerce and industry into the teaching profession, and of older people – even pensioners – by retail chains to take up part-time clerical positions in shops and supermarkets. Experience is showing that such people are often prepared to be very flexible in their approach to work, enabling employers to maximise their use of labour most effectively to meet customer needs.

The situation in the rest of Europe

What messages are coming through from employers elsewhere in Europe concerning domestic labour supply? Broadly speaking, the pressures are the same, creating similar effects such as increases to pay levels that are well ahead of inflation and the need to redefine and develop standard employment packages. A fairly random look at practices in some other European countries confirms this, while also throwing up some interesting responses of which British employers might take note.

West Germany

In West Germany, the high subsidiary personnel costs brought about by a collective bargaining system that in many cases covers statutory contributions and fringe benefits adds further pressure to an extremely unfavourable demographic situation. Strenuous efforts have been made through this bargaining machinery, however, to make working time more flexible, particularly by developing part-time employment and increased Saturday working. Attempts are also being made to increase the employment of women in technical trades. These latter two areas are both ones to which more attention might be given by UK employers.

I have highlighted in earlier chapters the system of dual vocational training involving close liaison between school and employers. West Germany does indeed lead the world in this area, and the German model is one which should be considered carefully by UK employers. To be fully effective, efforts to improve school/employer liaison will need co-ordination on a wide scale, involving support by the government; however nothing precludes individual employers taking initiatives at local level that, on a smaller scale, mirror the German model.

France

In France, the growing diversity of graduate recruitment methods in response to greater competition for graduates is worthy of consideration. Many organisations have traditionally used APEC (Association Pour l'Emploi des Cadres), the state-sponsored professional recruitment agencies, to meet their needs; other methods that have shown an increase recently include:

- the use of the well-developed Minitel computer information network, into which job advertisements or CVs can be placed to be viewed by candidates or potential employers respectively;
- a growth in the number of recruitment fairs, many of which are organised by specialist or national publishing companies;
- fresh styles in job advertisements, for example including recommendations by existing staff to 'sell' the company;
- the use of personal contacts including recommendations by existing employers; some companies pay a 'bounty' to staff who are able to identify a suitable potential recruit who is subsequently appointed;
- a very high incidence of use of employment agencies for recruitment at graduate level;
- direct contact with higher education institutions, and the provision of training courses to newly qualified graduates as 'trials' to identify suitable candidates for appointment.

Many of these selection methods are very little used, if used at all, by UK employers. However some of them could certainly be introduced at little effort or cost to add an edge to a company's graduate recruitment campaign in a market which, just as in France, is becoming highly competitive.

The Netherlands and Belgium

In the Netherlands and Belgium, strong economic growth and the dominance of Brussels as a magnet to employment has created particular problems in executive recruitment. These have been further compounded by the growing reluctance of professional staff in both countries to relocate, a major symptom of the increase in dual careers. Belgium has a particularly well-developed network of recruitment agencies, many of which are highly specialised around particular industry sectors or job functions. A further employment trend has been dramatic growth in the number of part-time employees. In Holland this has been given impetus by the government which has developed a range of initiatives to help companies analyse the scope for introducing more flexible working practices, both to increase their attractiveness as employers and to improve productivity. The signs now are that companies have themselves seized the initiative – particularly in the service sector – and that part-time working is widely seen as the way forward in maintaining economic success.

Spain

In Spain, where the economy is also booming on the basis of the increasing diversification of its industry, skills rather than labour shortages is the main problem. One result of this is that young people coming into the employment market have begun to regard training and career development as essential and have therefore become highly selective in choosing their employers.

Forward-looking companies are responding to this by developing means of gaining access to the most promising and highly qualified potential recruits, including forging close links with university careers services and offering fixed 'trial' contracts, typically of a year's duration, to graduates. Recruitment at executive level is highly competitive and one result of this is that pay levels have rocketed in recent years. Fifty per cent of executive jobs are filled through 'networks', although selection agencies have gained a strong market niche and are continuing to expand rapidly.

A number of clear messages emerge from this comparison of recruitment and resourcing practices between UK and other European states:

- First, many of the broad areas being addressed are the same. Increased working flexibility, innovative recruitment practices designed to sell the job to the employee and better links between companies and educational institutions are all being considered, in one way or another, by employers in most countries.

- Second, there are lessons to be learned from the specific practices being developed in other Member States in response to the issues they face. I have presented here only a limited sample of these, but it should be clear even from this – in the system of schools/employer liaison in West Germany, for example, or the diversity of graduate recruitment practices in France – that there are many methods and techniques worth considering. Professional recruiters would be wise to conduct their own more detailed studies into specific areas before drawing up an action plan to meet business needs.

- Third, there are a number of Community-wide implications as recruitment and resourcing practices become more competitive. The Commission's programmes in the field of equal opportunities for women and part-timers are being given a considerable boost as employees concentrate more on flexible working and the provision of benefits and services to attract women back into work. The transition between education and work is clearly an area where more careful management by both governments and employers will be of great benefit as European companies compete with Japanese and US rivals in the worldwide market-place.

The British company in Europe – a key advantage

As an executive mobility culture develops during the 1990s, British companies that operate in the pan-European environment – whether already well-established, or entering the Single Market for the first time – are uniquely placed to capitalise on the graduate, managerial and professional recruitment markets. On the one hand, they can offer ambitious recruits all the advantages of being truly international, with the expanded career development opportunities this presents. On the other, they will retain an approach to many employment norms and practices which is essentially British, and with which potential job candidates will be familiar. This familiarity can be a source of comfort to the most seasoned of Euro-executives, particularly in complex areas such as tax, pensions and social security!

Many companies have already recognised this, as any scan of the appointments pages of the quality press will reveal. Advertisements for positions with job titles such as 'European Marketing Manager' and 'European Financial Controller' abound; offering exactly the sort of inducement likely to be attractive to those keen to operate in an international sphere, such as the challenge of formulating European strategy, the opportunity for international travel and to promote products and services on an European basis. Most such advertisements are nevertheless based in the UK, which in some cases does call into question the veracity of the career opportunity they claim to offer. Most of them, also, are pitched at senior executive level, offering little hope for those who would wish to embark upon an international career, but who do not have any of the more apparently obvious requirements such as overseas experience or command of foreign languages.

Two major considerations

I raise these points specifically to illustrate two of the major considerations for employers seeking to recruit for a European sphere of operations. In the first place, the term 'European' attached to a job title must be meaningful and real; there is evidence that some employers use it merely to attract candidates, and that the jobs themselves contain little to distinguish them from those with a purely domestic slant. Candidates bent on developing a truly pan-European career are unlikely to be caught out by this. More particularly, employers must think seriously about the nature of the jobs they have to offer, and how they fit into the overall structure, before plunging into the market. This does not mean that positions must be located abroad, or even involve extensive European travel; however they must entail responsibilities that allow the job holder the scope to influence policy across the European market, and to co-ordinate the activities of different parts of the business.

The second consideration is, quite simply, the level at which to pitch recruitment activities. The market for candidates with European experience at senior level is already highly competitive, and will become more so during the 1990s. The upshot is that for many companies the search for a ready-made executive with relevant international knowledge and expertise will be a fruitless one. Forward-looking organisations will take a lateral view and aim to recruit people either at a lower level or with relevant functional expertise in a domestic environment, who additionally show the qualities necessary to adapt successfully to the demand of the international environment. They will aim simultaneously to draw up training and development programmes to make such recruits conversant with the values of the company and the different cultural and operational backgrounds of the parts of the business located in different European Member States.

This approach is one that many of our major international companies have adopted, particularly regarding recruitment at graduate level; new appointees are recruited specifically on the basis of their ability to undertake a frequently rapid and challenging development programme which will include working with people from different cultures and backgrounds and learning new skills.

Pan-European career prerequisites

What, therefore, should recruiters be looking for in trawling the domestic employment market for candidates suitable for a pan-European career? Clearly, knowledge of foreign languages must be a help. However, the pool of candidates with language skills specific to the market of a particular company may be limited, or if the company does business across Europe the ability to communicate with people of several different nationalities may be required. On the other hand the acquisition of skills in this area sufficient to do business with foreign-based colleagues or customers is not so difficult a matter. Many companies would be better advised to seek candidates with the willingness and adaptability to develop skills in the specific languages likely to be of greatest benefit to the company, rather than amongst the much smaller number who already have such skills.

Many commentators see previous international experience as a drawback rather than an asset in prospective candidates. This may be taking too blinkered a view, in assuming that the expatriate culture creates a mentality in which people become set in their ways and unwilling to accept change. While this is undoubtedly not true in many cases, recruiters may find again that there are relatively few prospective candidates in the market whose experience matches their exact requirements.

They will certainly have a better choice if they widen their net to take in candidates who can demonstrate the ability to cope with the demands of working with people from different cultural backgrounds, without necessarily having previous experience of this. While this may be difficult to assess in prospective recruits, it is surely not beyond the bounds of possibility to devise a personality test to measure, for example, attributes such as willingness to accept rapid change and disruption to family life and analytical and decision-making ability in an unfamiliar working environment.

Recruiting in the wider market

Entering the European recruitment market will be a challenging new step for many UK employers, yet a necessary one if they are to meet effectively the threat of increased competition. Fortunately, several of our major multinationals have established long experience of recruiting in Europe, and the practices to be followed and pitfalls to be avoided are well-documented. A first step for any company, however, must be to analyse its specific needs of foreign nationality staff before embanking on the search.

Needs analysis

Many companies will identify a need for foreign nationals at senior executive or director level in order to build a multinational top management team. This has been recognised by a number of major European organisations, such as Daimler-Benz and Shell, as key to successful expansion activities and the development of a broader perspective. A survey conducted in 1987 by the Ambrosetti Consulting group revealed a much lower incidence of foreign directors in UK firms than in their counterparts throughout the EC. At a lower level, companies diversifying their product base or expanding into the European market may need to recruit foreign managers or professional staff to be based in their home country and add their local expertise to the developing operation. Here, the company's requirements may be highly specific concerning such factors as geographical location, technical skills and managerial ability.

A further reason for extending the search for labour into Europe is to recruit staff to meet domestic labour shortages. A number of organisations have followed this course and there must be some scope for building on their experiences – both to fill established vacancies and add a European perspective to a company's outlook at professional and managerial level.

Problems with foreign recruitment

Whatever the circumstances, companies attempting for the first time to recruit foreign nationals from abroad face a number of problems, stemming from their lack of detailed knowledge of the environment. The most significant of these can be summarised as follows:

- How and where to advertise: the basic methods of recruitment may be very different from those in the UK.

- How to determine a level of pay and conditions that will be attractive to candidates as well as appropriate, again given the differences that may exist between the UK and the 'home' country.

- How to assess the technical skills and abilities of candidates; not only will academic and professional qualifications be different from their nearest UK equivalents, but candidates' careers may have developed in entirely different ways. It will be necessary for recruiters not only to understand all this in general terms, but to arrive at means of assessment of the specific skills of candidates within this framework. It is in this area where the 'cultural divide' – i.e. the lack of understanding on the part of the recruiter of a candidate's real worth to the organisation – may be widest.

- How to assess the willingness and ability of the candidate to adapt to the cultural norms of the recruiting organisation. At basic level, evaluation of language skills or willingness to relocate may not be too difficult. More of a problem, however, will be evaluation of how the candidate will 'fit in' to a culture of which he/she may have little knowledge or familiarity. Experience has proved that the majority of foreign nationals employed by UK firms who fail to make the transition do so through cultural and communication problems.

These considerations will vary considerably in significance depending on the nature of the position to be filled. Take first the example of a company needing to recruit a line manager to run a subsidiary operation in the home country. Here, given that he/she will be dealing mostly with compatriots rather than the UK head office, the need for fluency in English or detailed understanding of the UK business culture will be less important than pure professional and management ability and relevant 'home country' experience. Relocation to the UK will not be an issue. These factors will in turn influence the precise means of recruitment. Advertising will need to be on a local basis, almost certainly in the mother tongue rather than English. It will be necessary to reach a fairly detailed understanding of pay levels and methods and employment conditions for local nationals in the exact geographical location; equally, it will be necessary to find out a great deal about the nature of professional and managerial training likely candidates will have been through, and the value of their professional qualifications.

On the other hand the considerations for a company seeking to recruit a foreign executive to sit on its Board or join the top management team will have an entirely different focus. The most important attributes of candidates are likely to be:

- fluency in English, as well as one or more other Community languages;
- international experience, possibly cross-functional rather than in one specialist area;
- the willingness to relocate throughout Europe, both immediately and in the future, to meet company requirements;
- the adaptability to be able to deal with business colleagues and clients from different cultures and backgrounds.

Of lesser importance are likely to be the specific qualifications of candidates, or their precise nationality. These very different requirements from those given in the first example will place a different emphasis on the methods of recruitment. Advertising may be carried out in more than one European country, in order to attract a range of candidates. The advertisement itself may be written in English, or may require candidates to reply in English. Selection procedures are likely to take place in the UK rather than at local level. Above all the selection process will place much less emphasis on functional experience and expertise gained in a local environment, and much more on general qualities such as adaptability, approachability, open-mindedness and long-term planning ability.

Who will do the recruiting?

A key issue arising from all these considerations that most companies will face is whether to carry out foreign recruitment activity themselves, or whether to contract it out to a specialist consultancy. As far as local recruitment of foreign nationals is concerned, those who adopt a 'do-it-yourself' approach will, of course, be much better placed if they already have an established personnel function within the foreign country. Otherwise, if selection procedures are to be conducted by the UK Head Office personnel department, there is a major learning curve to be gone through. This is graphically illustrated by Keith Allen in an article in *Personnel Management* magazine, in the context of a UK company recruiting a manager for a Dutch production unit:

'The personnel director then began to list the questions that seemed to him to be relevant. Where should he advertise? Or were jobs like this in Holland filled in other ways? What language should be used for the advertisement? Should he use the company's standard application form? What were the customs relating to invitation to interview – during the day or in the evening? Which language would be best for the interviews (the personnel director spoke no Dutch)? What were the customs relating to continuity of fringe benefits? What kind of contract was usual?'

Local recruitment agencies

This illustrates that for many companies the only realistic option will be to contract out its foreign-based recruitment assignments. Selection of consultants can be an assignment in itself; for 'home country' appointments it is probable that local rather than international firms will be most appropriate. It will also be important to establish early on the basis of the relationship. Will the consultants be handling the assignment from start to finish, or supplying the company with a list of candidates? Does the company wish to know about local selection procedures, and levels of pay and benefits in a general sense? Of paramount importance, as indeed with similar domestic assignments, is the issue of the building up of trust between client and consultant.

UK recruitment professional

The recruitment of executives for a multinational management team, requiring as it does much less detailed knowledge of local employment practices and conditions, would seem at face value an easier task for the UK recruitment professional to undertake. In reality it is probably more difficult as the issues to be faced, though less obvious, are much more complex. In the round a much broader approach will be required of the recruiter, if he/she is to avoid such pitfalls as assuming that the values and beliefs of candidates are similar to his own, or misunderstanding the complexities of international relocation. The price of failure can be high and here again the best course of action for many companies will be to appoint a recruitment consultant. It is likely that in this context an international firm with offices and contacts throughout Europe will be more appropriate than a local consultancy, the former having the expertise to carry out multi-country search and assessment of candidates' cross-cultural adaptability.

Headhunting firms

The good news in this is that many headhunting firms have recognised that recruitment at top management level is becoming increasingly international in focus, and are responding accordingly. For example, the firm of Berndtson International has carried out a detailed analysis of its clients' needs relative to the Single Market, in order to be in a better position to respond to these. A partner in the firm, Geoffrey Forester, has been quoted in the *Times* as saying:

'We needed to start collecting data about the way our clients are feeling about 1992 . . . We have to react to the marketplace. Our responsibility is to consult, not just to action a recruitment requirement . . . European headquarters of US corporations based here are wanting more of a cultural mix amongst their senior management . . . you have to have a viable, linked office network to do it properly.'

Berndtson International has 14 offices spread across Europe and is therefore in a strong position to be able to offer international recruitment advice. The evidence suggests that an increasing number of headhunters are developing a co-ordinated European approach to their profession. The ways and means they are going about this include:

- Increasing specialisation in functional areas across Europe. Some firms are developing a 'practice system' in which individual consultants specialise in key business areas such as financial services and IT, and liaise with colleagues with similar specialisms in other European countries.

- Developing stronger all-round consulting skills and thereby a deepening basis of trust with key European clients.

- Greater co-ordination between offices in different countries, particularly in the area of co-ordinated computer networks to enable the rapid and efficient transmission of information.

When to recruit foreign professional staff

The recruitment of foreign professional staff to fill vacancies in the UK is probably only worthwhile on a large scale if two circumstances apply:

- first, skills shortages within the UK make domestic recruitment, or the training of staff up to the required level, particularly difficult;

- second, there is a readily available pool of such skilled labour elsewhere in Europe, and few suitable vacancies in the home country for which they can apply.

A prime consideration for any personnel professional thinking of embarking on this course of action is, therefore, to carry out research into each of these areas. The examples to be followed are those of some of our education and health authorities, which have identified surpluses of, respectively, teachers and doctors in countries such as West Germany, the Netherlands and Italy and have mounted recruitment campaigns to attract them to the UK.

Employers in the health service in particular have adopted a proactive approach towards foreign recruitment. Steps taken have included:

- making use of European contacts within the medical profession, initially to scope out the possibilities but also to take an active part in the selection process;

- the placing of advertisements in foreign medical journals;
- the offering of short-term contracts, as a means of allowing both hospitals and appointees to test each other out before establishing more permanent commitments;
- offering trainee specialists the chance of valuable experience in their chosen areas in order to equip them for more senior appointment at home or abroad.

Some Area Health Authorities have been so successful in their campaigns that the level of unsolicited applications has removed the need to continue advertising abroad!

Graduate recruitment in Europe

This is an area to which increasing attention is being given, particularly by multinational companies. Until recently, the prevalent view was that the education systems of the different Member States were so incompatible as to make pan-European graduate recruitment an impossibility. That this view is changing has a little to do with EC Directives concerning mutual recognition of qualifications; however it has a lot more to do with the perception by many employers of the need to develop an international management style at well below senior executive level. Graduates entering employment for the first time and with the potential to reach middle and senior management positions relatively quickly are seen as the key to this.

There is also a growing perception, largely validated by reputable survey information, that European graduates are highly positive about international career mobility with UK companies being particularly sought after.

Suggestions by the Association of Graduate Recruiters

A number of specific suggestions have been made by the Association of Graduate Recruiters among others to employers mindful to recruit from abroad. Many of these are particularly relevant to companies that do not have the resources to mount full-scale, pan-European campaigns. They include:

- Making full use of the ERASMUS and COMETT programmes, in a positive way so that foreign students coming to the UK for work experience are encouraged to return as permanent recruits.

- Establishing programmes to handle applications from the growing number of European students who, independent of ERASMUS and COMETT, are seeking work placements in the UK. A striking example was given in the December 1989 edition of *Personnel Management* of a number of companies that have successfully taken foreign students on work placements via Anglia Higher Education College's European business diploma course. One company, Thermos Ltd of Brentwood which does a significant amount of business in France, has made effective use of placements for some time and has engaged French students to undertake an extensive and extremely valuable market research project on French consumer preferences.

- Making contacts with international student bodies that arrange overseas placements. The 'Eurostage' placement service, in particular, has been established recently to act as an intermediary between students and companies for placements of up to six months.

- Establishing which countries in Europe produce the most graduates with the skills required for specific jobs being filled. In some Member States skills shortages in particular vocations are just as severe as in the UK, whereas others produce, for example, a glut of engineers or computing specialists. Having identified suitable countries as potential sources further research may be necessary to identify the best colleges and universities, and the general tendencies amongst the student population in terms of attitudes to mobility and language skills. Significant differences exist between Member States here; for example, French or Greek graduates are more likely to consider working abroad than their Italian or German equivalents.

The Irish Republic has been identified as one particular Member State which can provide the solution to employers' graduate recruitment problems, in the UK and elsewhere in Europe. Graduate output is high – some 2,000 Irish students attend universities and polytechnics in Britain, while around 4,000 graduate annually from the Republic itself – and there is a strong sense of Europeanness which reinforces the traditional tendency among young Irish people to emigrate to seek work. Ireland has a growing, young population, and due both to geographical proximity and common language, the UK is the most frequent destination for expatriates. The main educational growth areas are IT, engineering, electronics and construction; 40 per cent of IT and electronic engineering graduates, and 70 per cent of newly-graduating architects are now emigrating, mostly to mainland Britain.

- Identifying the key differences between UK and other European graduates regarding both characteristics and career expectations. Age differences are one of the most obvious of these; in Germany for example many students do not graduate until 26 or 27 years old. This in turn can influence expectation in terms of level of responsibility or salary on appointment.

- Making use of foreign careers services such as government employment services in Germany, or placement departments in French business schools and grandes écoles. Unfortunately, many other European countries have little in the way of co-ordinated graduate placement services, and in some cases the controls can be restrictive. Again, knowledge of specific practices will be a valuable prerequisite to any recruitment campaign.

- Direct recruiting, perhaps making use of informal contacts with academic departments or professional bodies. The Association of Graduate Recruiters warns however of the difficulties to be faced in this, including the requirement to gain knowledge of different European qualifications and education systems, the age of students on graduation and military service requirements. Timing can also be crucial, as each country has its peaks and troughs in graduate output.

To add to this list, a further development which may well lead more companies into European graduate recruitment is the growth of international recruitment fairs. An early and well-publicised example of these was the International Graduate Recruitment Fair for Engineers, held in Toulouse in December 1989. Many of the predominantly French graduates who attended are reported to have expressed a specific interest in working in the UK, citing the opportunity to develop their English language skills as a key benefit.

Your foreign recruitment campaign

Focusing on direct advertising and selection, how can the smaller company, perhaps going into Europe for the first time, establish a campaign that meets its needs for growing international integration? Research in this field suggests that a key issue is recognising the different recruitment practices that prevail in different Member States, and adapting to these while retaining a strong semblance of the company's individual culture. This can be done in a number of ways, including ensuring that advertisements, application forms and recruitment literature are appropriate to local norms rather than being just standard translation from English, and fostering relationships with academics to reach students in countries where careers services are less sophisticated than in the UK. Another key issue is the need to explore in depth candidates' suitability to adapt to an international business culture. This may require sophisticated testing procedures being carried out, to measure such attributes as the ability to communicate with foreign nationals, and to reason and persuade in a second language. Needless to say any such tests must be expertly monitored and free from any culture or language bias.

Olivetti's example

Among the practices of the larger multinational recruiters, Olivetti's 'No Frontiers' graduate recruitment programme for systems engineers provides one of the best examples to be followed. The focus of this is to sell the company to students on a worldwide basis, emphasising both the high quality technical training Olivetti can offer, and the benefits to be gained through working for a company with worldwide horizons and above all, consistent selection and career development standards throughout the world. A career with Olivetti, indeed, is described as 'a professional and cultural melting pot'.

Advertising is carefully designed to give a consistent company message across all countries, with minor adaptations in response to local conditions. The wording of advertisements aims to emphasise the fusion of the benefits to be gained by employee and employer alike:

'In strengthening our market positions around the world, Olivetti, technology, business diversity and people are crossing new boundaries '. . . And the cement which binds each part together is a simple philosophy of people management: we believe in total integration coupled with individual freedom.'

Initial screening of candidates takes place from a well-defined set of basic criteria, which specifies among other things that candidates must have no previous work experience, be single and mobile, and with some English language ability and an interest in information technology. While some of these criteria may seem unnecessarily restrictive, they have been developed from many years experience of matching graduate skills with the specific business needs of Olivetti. They should not, therefore, be regarded as universal but underline the need for each company to identify its own set of basic attributes in graduate recruits.

One of the most impressive aspects of the 'No Frontiers' programme is the final selection process, which involves a day's attendance at an assessment centre and the evaluation of candidates against behavioural criteria in a series of exercises. Both group and individual exercises are carried out, in order to assess such qualities as problem analysis, listening ability, teamwork, interactive communication, flexibility and practical learning. Many of these are particularly relevant to working in an international environment where the establishment of rapport with foreign national colleagues can be crucial.

A further key aspect of the programme is that it is carried on into employment once the selection of candidates has been made, thus fulfilling Olivetti's part of the 'bargain' in the employment contract. In addition to specific training and development programmes this aims to integrate new graduate recruits into the company's ways and values over a period of time, by treating them as professionals and emphasising the importance of critical attributes such as tolerance and adaptability.

Overall, the 'No Frontiers' programme stands out as a model which all international recruiters should take note of. Many of its individual components are ones that those intending to move into the European graduate recruitment market would do well to copy; on a broader scale, there are perhaps messages to be derived from it of relevance to those recruiting from abroad at all levels.

8 Training and development

According to Richard Underwood, in his article in *Personnel Management* magazine on the broad issue of personnel and the Single European Market, training and development 'is the area which poses perhaps the greatest challenge of all for UK employers'. It is difficult to argue with this conclusion. The article continues: 'Survey after survey has shown the enormous gulf between the UK's training effort and that of other European countries. For example, five times as many people in West Germany's building industry gain vocational qualifications than in Britain; France trains nearly ten times as many sales and office staff as we do'.

The message coming through from this is clear; employers need to spend much time and effort on training staff in managerial and technical competences if they are to compete effectively with European rivals in the wider market. For those companies actively extending their operations into Europe in order to be closer to their new markets, there is the additional complication of preparing staff for the demands of working in a cross-cultural environment.

In this chapter I shall examine both these issues. Looking first at managerial and technical training, a number of ways have been suggested by commentators to draw upon the techniques being developed in Europe and elsewhere in the world, and graft these onto our own domestic systems. These are worth considering in some detail. Preparing staff to work with European clients and colleagues is a more diverse area, but again a number of specific responses are being developed and implemented by forward-looking employers. Here, I shall consider the three specific areas of management development and training, the preparation of graduates for a European future, and language skills training.

Managerial and technical skills requirements for the Single Market

The most authoritative report on management education, training and development published in this country in recent years is 'The Making of Managers' by Professor Charles Handy ('The Handy Report') which, taking as its foundation a detailed examination of practices in the USA, West Germany, France, and Japan, suggests ways in which aspects of these can be blended with our own culture and traditions to bring about improvement. That improvement is necessary is spelt out in no uncertain terms in the report:

'Britain has neglected her managerial stock. . . quantity does not guarantee quality, but in crude statistical terms we should probably need to be doing nearly ten times as much as we now are as a nation, if all would-be managers and executives were to be relevantly educated before they start and were each to spend 40 hours a year in off-the-job training in addition to all the other less quantifiable aspects of development.'

The report distinguishes clearly between *business education*, the gaining of basic knowledge and analytical skills, and *management development*, which is the acquisition of planning, resource management and implementation techniques. Different emphasis is given to these by the different countries surveyed, the report states: 'the UK has need to give greater emphasis to both'.

To review briefly the findings of the report in each of the countries surveyed.

France

In France, the output of graduates from *grandes écoles* (approximately 18,000 per year) has traditionally formed the backbone for senior management positions in commerce and industry. The training given at these institutions has centred on intellectual problem-solving ability and logic rather than technical ability. Education at other universities and business schools combines generalist as well as specific areas; this is so even in engineering and technical colleges.

French law requires that all organisations with more than ten employees spend a minimum of 1.6 per cent of the wage bill on induction and continued training. In practice many organisations spend much more than this, devoting a high proportion to management training.

A major shift of emphasis has taken place in France in attitudes to management education in recent years. There has been a move away from reliance on purely technical skills, and towards the development of business methodology and leadership/decision-making ability. Overall, French society has developed an increased respect for professionalism, defined as 'not the mere possession of skills, but to include the competence to use these as a means to a professional end and to collective success'. Continuing education into employment is therefore regarded as highly important, and many courses run or sponsored by private companies have been developed to provide managers with well rounded abilities.

West Germany

In West Germany, on the other hand, the emphasis is much more on a long, preparatory education followed by a functional career at management level, rather than continued development and training. This reflects both the traditional German respect for technical, 'master craftsman' skills, and the unwillingness to move from a system which, though rigid, has served the country well in the building of its post-war economy.

German managers are almost exclusively graduates. They are extremely unlikely to have reached employment before the age of 27, having been through a long degree course, a business 'apprenticeship', military service and a further course in business management, probably including economics. They would be expected to be fluent in at least one other language. Their careers would be likely to develop in only one, or at best two or three, different functions.

Continued management education appears to be regarded by many German organisations as an expensive luxury. Little induction training is given, and ongoing development is largely confined to junior management levels within the larger companies only. Overall, the long period of preparatory training managers undergo is regarded by most employers as quite enough, particularly as they come into employment so late at a time when school leaver numbers are falling so sharply.

The USA and Japan

In the USA and Japan, huge amounts of time and money are invested in continuing management education. A quarter of all US graduates major in business studies, and there are numerous in-company educational centres and university courses used by major companies to develop their managers. The Handy Report states:

'Behind this emphasis on early and continuing education is a market-driven system both inside and outside the firm, one typified by the slogan "individual initiative and corporate support" where the corporation makes opportunities available and the individual is responsible for his or her own learning and development.'

In Japan a highly structured system of on-the-job training takes place, built around the content of the job itself and involving supervisors and managers in monitoring roles. It takes many years for this process to be completed and recognised by promotion to a managerial position.

Quite clearly, the practices and attitudes towards management education in each of these four countries vary greatly, and each system contains its own problems. The problem with the UK system, according to the Handy Report, is a more general one in that it fails to fit neatly into any coherent pattern, thereby leaving the development of managerial skills largely to chance. On one hand, many of our biggest companies invest considerably in management education, and there has been sustained growth in the number of MBA graduates and of universities/colleges that offer postgraduate business diplomas. However, compared with countries such as France and Germany, few of our managers have degrees or professional qualifications, a considerable proportion have had little or no management training since starting work, and much training that does take place can only fill the gap created by inadequate school and university education, rather than building on established knowledge. The report concludes:

'Many British managers are uneducated in business and management terms. . .It must also be true that management training in Britain is too little, too late, for too few. It is finally probably true that most management development is left to chance in a Darwinian belief that the fittest will survive.'

The longer our management development is left to chance, the more difficult it will be for UK companies to compete effectively with French, German and other European competitors in the wider market – survival of the fittest in a broader context! The Handy Report suggests a ten-point plan of action in order to rectify this situation, building on the best practices in each of the four countries surveyed. These actions points are grouped under six broader headings, each of which is worthy of consideration in its own right. The headings are:

- the educational base;
- business education;
- management development;
- delivery mechanisms;
- the information base;
- required cultural change.

The educational base

The report proposes that more students should stay in the education system to age 18 and beyond, and should receive a broader range of learning. The French system provides a model to be followed here: 'Three A levels and a degree in the humanities is a poor match for a "baccalaureat" followed by a *grand école* in business or engineering with a "stage" of work assignment'. Formal work experience as part of school level or degree education is also proposed. Overall, the Handy Report sees it as essential that means should be found to link relevant work experience with both general and specialist learning at degree level; this would inevitably require degree courses becoming longer.

Business education

Under this heading are proposed measures to give managers of the future a grounding in core management competences, possibly linked with attainment of 'articles of management' with diploma status. Specifically, this could be achieved by a two-part management diploma, the first part containing standard business topics such as accounting, marketing and organisation behaviour, the second concentrating on the application of skills in a practical context. The 'MBA Part I' could be developed to become a requirement for those seeking management careers in large organisations, and could become an integral part of other professional qualifications in such fields as accountancy. The Part II would be directly linked to the work of an individual within a company, and would therefore require considerable support from that company in order to be worthwhile.

Management development

Here, the report proposes a public standard of five days off-the-job training per year per manager, and the aim of promoting the bigger, more forward-looking of our major companies as 'leaders' providing advice, consultation and training to others. These companies could form a 'Charter Group' with a specified code of practice, to set standards to be attained by others. This code would include such items as a personal development plan for every manager, and guaranteed time off work and reimbursement of fees for managers engaging in self-development programmes.

Delivery mechanisms

The report emphasises the importance of co-operation between companies and with business schools. In terms of funding, the French and West German models are cited here: 'the British need the equivalent of the West German Chambers of Commerce, statutorily funded by subscription, controlled by industry, concerned with training and education, and now, increasingly, management development'.

The information base

The report comments on the need for a centrally co-ordinated database in order to monitor patterns of activity. A statutory requirement for companies to provide details of training and development activity to this database is suggested.

Required cultural change

This item is probably of most immediate significance in the context of the position of UK companies with regard to European competitors. The report emphasises the need for a change in thinking to take place; the need for companies to regard individual management development as an investment rather than a luxury, and to give staff both early responsibility and support in their self-development programmes. The proposed Charter Group is seen as of key importance in this, leading from the front and encouraging organisations in commerce and industry to change in their thinking.

The management development and training debate generated by the Handy Report has moved on since the report itself was published in 1987, but the recommendations it makes – particularly the ten-point action plan – remain as a blueprint for the comprehensive improvement of attitudes and practices in the UK. I make no apologies for making such detailed reference to it, as it is highly relevant in the European context. Not only does it derive many of its recommendations from the study of practices in two of our major rival European countries, but, more important, it is made abundantly clear that our current level of practice is well below that prevalent in those countries. The measures proposed in the report are, therefore, absolutely vital if we are to compete with European companies in the wider market.

The Handy Report suggests a national framework for management training, education and development, requiring a high degree of co-ordination between government bodies, higher educational establishments and major private sector companies in order to produce benefits. What do individual companies see as being the main priorities for the future? The most authoritative piece of research in this area is Ashridge Management College's 'Management for the Future' project, which has obtained the views of leading European and UK organisations on their future management needs and how they are developing their managers to handle such challenges. A summary of the project findings was published by two of the authors, Mike Osbaldeston and Kevin Barham, in the *Journal of European Industrial Training* during 1989.

The companies surveyed in the project included ACCOR, BMW, Electrolux, Norsk Data and Shell UK. The views of managers were obtained concerning three broad areas; future challenges, the needs of managers to meet these challenges, and action being taken by the companies to meet these needs. The findings are summarised as follows.

Future challenges

Increased competition largely stemming from the wider European market is seen as the main challenge. This will require companies to be more flexible and market-responsive, in turn requiring increased decentralisation. Maintaining the company infrastructure and providing corporate direction will be a key task for senior management. A particularly strong requirement will be 'the need to become more internationally oriented in response to the growing internationalisation and globalisation of business'.

Management needs

In this changing environment, managers too will need a more flexible approach with less reliance on hierarchical or 'vertical' structures. They will need to have a sound understanding of the external environment and its influence on the company. In terms of person management skills, a major requirement will be to handle lateral rather than 'direct line' relationships and to lead and motivate staff on this basis.

Management development trends

The project identifies a major trend away from a 'fragmented' approach in which training given has no direct relevance to the manager's work within the organisation, towards a 'focused' approach in which continuous learning in the context of on-the-job development is a key factor. Thus, a manager is given challenges and responsibility at an early stage in his or her career, while the company provides a supportive environment in which risk taking is encouraged and mistakes tolerated as part of the learning process. This is a very American concept according to the Handy Report, but the examples given of European companies that have adopted it illustrate how far it has been taken up this side of the Atlantic:

'Norsk Data provides young managers with important challenges and responsibilities, allows them to find the best way to achieve their objectives, and provides very open lines of communication to top management. While Norsk Data invests in training, it is up to the managers themselves to determine their own training and development needs. . . ACCOR recognises the manager's role in training and development by putting managers through a course entitled "Training the Trainer" and expects every manager to set up a training programme for his/her people. Its top management also openly espouses a central value of the learning organisation: "droit d'erreur" – the right to learn from mistakes.'

The message from this is clear: learning and development linked to overall business strategy, and nurtured by the organisation as such, has become recognised by major European employers as essential if competitiveness in the wider market is to be maintained. Leadership, people management and international management skills, based on flexibility and quality of service, will be at a premium as companies become decentralised and pan-European in their approach.

Vocational training

Turning to the issue of vocational training for young workers and those leaving school, a number of proposals have been made by various commentators to bring about skills improvement in the UK. The European Commission has for many years called for measures to be implemented within Member States to provide more work experience for those about to enter the employment market; in this country the Technical and Vocational Education Initiative (TVEI) has been one significant move in this direction. This provides the opportunity for employers to become directly involved in course design by the linking of work placement modules with course modules that put emphasis on technological competence and problem-solving skills. Work shadowing is another initiative that some companies have adopted in this context.

It is perhaps fortunate that Mr Michael Howard, the Secretary of State for Employment, has driven forward so vigorously his predecessor Sir Norman Fowler's establishment of Training and Enterprise Councils to develop the higher skills among our workforce that the Single Market will demand; it is planned that 82 TECs will have approved funding and be operational by the end of 1990, two years ahead of schedule. These will give employers across all sectors a predominant voice in framing training efforts to suit local needs across the country, and it is vital that Personnel Professionals become involved in the process of establishing and developing the Councils. The National Training Task Force, the co-ordinating body responsible for driving the work of the TECs, is moving towards the implementation of a plan which, based on National Vocational Qualifications, will give all employees specifically-targeted skills and qualifications. This will involve:

- placing the emphasis in youth training on acquisition of skills rather than provision of jobs;
- a programme aiming to offer school leavers qualifications at level two of the National Vocational Qualifications geared towards specific work areas, e.g. factory, shop or office employment;
- the aim of bringing every young employee up to a minimum of five GCSEs equivalent, with as many as possible up to NVQ level three of two to three 'A' levels equivalent.

It is in this area where the West German model of vocational training, with its shared conviction between schools and employers that such training is both economically worthwhile for firms and a means of reducing unemployment, deserves closest scrutiny. Although it would not be possible to transfer this lock, stock and barrel to the very different governmental and industrial framework of Britain, the keystone to its success is the high level of commitment given to it by employers. It is not the model itself, so much as this conviction in the value of training among companies of all sizes that is worthy of imitation in the UK if better skills levels among young workers are to be promoted.

One of the most graphic examples of such commitment to date has been provided, interestingly enough, by the UK subsidary of a German chemicals firm – Hoechst UK. Hoechst has begun a programme in which a number of scholarships are offered to British sixth-formers to take part in the dual apprenticeship scheme run jointly by the parent company and the West German government. 'Apprenticeship' is perhaps not the right title for the scheme, as it encompasses not just craft skills but also specific business skills such as law and bookkeeping, direct exposure to the company's business and production functions, language training and a period spent at the company's computing training school. A high prestige industry qualification, recognised throughout West Germany, is the end result of the two years' study.

The company selects for its placements candidates who can demonstrate maturity and confidence as well as a minimum of three 'A' levels including German. The programme reflects Hoechst UK's commitment to training and growing their own managers of the future, in particular to meet the demands of the Single Market. Those qualifying from the scheme could expect to take up positions either within the UK or elsewhere in Europe, possibly as part of a pan-European development or marketing team. Though the programme is expensive (and at present only five trainees a year are selected to join), Hoechst UK regard it as an investment for the future, and no more expensive than the cost of post-recruitment training. The company is able to say this, even though there is no obligation on trainees to join Hoechst at the end of the programme; the publicity generated on Hoechst as a forward looking and staff development oriented employer is regarded as justifying the cost in itself.

Of course, this initiative requires resources that are way beyond those of many smaller companies, or are simply not available to those with a purely domestic slant. Here again, however, it is the level of commitment to training rather than the programme content itself, that is most worthy of attention. Even within the UK, the means exist for employers to meet educationalists half-way, and to provide work-related training that is of value to colleges, students and employers alike. Companies should not be afraid to invest money and resources in this. It will tell prospective recruits a good deal about them, and most importantly will mean that such recruits come into the company better trained and attuned to the values and realities of its culture and working life.

Management development and training in the pan-European company

Preparing managers for the demands of working in a pan-European environment can be a complex matter. However, a common strand running through the programmes of all major international companies is that as part of the development process, managers must work with – if not be trained with – colleagues from different countries and backgrounds. Thus, for many companies, international secondments are seen as a must in order to promote the right attitudes and abilities. Within Shell UK, for example, overseas postings are carefully targeted towards those who are seen as likeliest to develop into a long-term international career with the company. Other companies see the need for the careful nurturing of corporate values at centre, in addition to international experience. An example of this approach is IBM, quoted in an article in *Director* magazine as follows:

'Although the company appreciates the value of an overseas posting in terms of the breadth of experience it can give and the entrepreneurial thinking it can inspire, the feeling is that really *international* attitudes are best developed at a major corporate headquarters. The opportunity, for example, of working closely with the chief executive helps to give "universal" perspective.'

Many organisations supplement on-the-job 'internationalist' experience with more systematic training programmes. Here again, the focus is always to draw together staff from different countries, and working in parts of the organisation with different functional and cultural backgrounds, and present them with case study material that reflects the European, inter-cultural perspective. Team building is inevitably a major objective of such training programmes, in which emphasis is placed on interpersonal skills and the need to accommodate different cultures and personalities.

I have already mentioned, albeit briefly, the training initiatives being implemented by 3M in order to develop managers for a European future. Looking at these in more detail, two particular programmes worthy of note are described by Paul Davies, Human Resource Development Manager of 3M, in an article in the magazine *Training Officer*:

- First, the 'Leadership for Growth' programme, launched in 1989 with the objective of providing senior managers from across the organisation with training in appropriate skills; a key element of the programme is a three-day workshop, led by a team of international consultants. The first day is dedicated to an analysis of change processes focusing on the company itself and identifying leadership issues and the use of power and influence in this context. The second day considers human aspects of change, including leadership styles and individuals' reactions to new circumstances. The third day considers the learning process and requires the setting of action plans appropriate to group objectives.

- Second, the training of European Management Action Teams (EMATS), teams of managers drawn from 3M's European subsidiaries to study the effects of the Single Market on business objectives: 'EMAT training workshops focus on group behaviour and the effectiveness of group interaction by assigning skilled facilitators to live working sessions based on real business issues. Brief periods of more structured training are interspersed with these sessions, and constructive feedback provided to individual team members'.

It can be seen that both these programmes fit into the model for international management training described earlier, in that they bring together multinational groups and focus on team building and interpersonal skills in the learning process. The approach is one that other companies with an interest in international career development would do well to follow.

Staff transfers to foreign locations

Returning to the issue of the transfer of staff to foreign locations in the interests of career development, an innovative way of providing such experience is through exchange programmes with other companies. Such exchanges have been given some publicity recently, being highly regarded by companies that have 'taken the plunge' as developing very wide-ranging knowledge and experience in different functions, cultures and operational environments. The Volvo Car Corporation in Sweden has been particularly active in this area, placing key managers in organisations outside Sweden for two-month periods. The managers, on return, have been reported to be 'highly motivated, more cosmopolitan in their outlook, and full of new ideas'.

This is an area to which many companies within the EC could give greater attention, following on from the Volvo example. Although having placements arranged by an independent company on a commercial basis (as

Volvo has done in some cases) could prove expensive, companies that are able to reach reciprocal exchange agreements with organisations in other economic sectors in other countries are bound to reap many benefits. Not only will their own managers return to their jobs with new and interesting perspectives, but the company will have the services of the 'exchange' manager from a foreign country for a period of time on a consultancy basis. With careful handling, such placements can in themselves become a means of generating fresh ideas and possibly valuable business contacts in other areas with the reciprocating organisation.

A programme devised by Interchange International, a commercial company operating in this field, provides a useful model. This consists of three phases:

- First, a preparation seminar with the purpose of initiating the participant in the ways of the company being visited. This is seen as a confidence-building as much as an information-giving exercise.
- Second, the placement itself, in which the participant may be involved in functional activities different from those in the 'home' job. Additionally, he/she may undertake site visits, give presentations on the 'home' company environment, and become involved in workshops or strategic development projects giving detailed insight into corporate objectives and decision-making processes.
- Third, a follow-up seminar in which the manager relates the experience gained to the 'home' company on return. This is a vital step if the valuable lessons learned are to be passed on first-hand.

Overall, a programme of this type could be a cost-effective way for many organisations expanding into the European market to gain a valuable insight into the business practices and objectives in other Member States.

Sponsorship for European management programmes

Another possibility for companies to develop pan-European abilities in their managers might be to offer sponsorship on part-time or full-time European management programmes. Again, this is a route that few have followed as yet, but as the number of business schools offering programmes grows and as the courses themselves become more sophisticated and tailored towards companies' needs, there is little doubt that it will become more popular.

Many programmes now being developed recognise the pressures on senior managers, and therefore offer concentrated training over a relatively short period of time with as much exposure to foreign business cultures as possible.

A good example of one of the more forward-looking course programmes is Ashridge Management College's European Management programme, developed in conjunction with the Centre de Perfectionnement aux Affaires in Paris and the Universitätsseminar der Wirtschaft of Cologne. Building on the benefits of the links with these equivalent business schools in Europe, the programme focuses on strategic and operational issues facing organisations in different countries, and encourages participants to improve cross-cultural management skills. Details of the programme are as follows:

- It is a 16-day, fully residential programme, split equally between the two venues at Paris and Cologne. The principal course language is English.

- The participants are 'high potential, high calibre senior corporate officers, . . .who have the responsibility for formulating and implementing European-wide strategies'. Ashridge applies strict selection criteria and limits the number of participants to 33 per programme.

- The programme 'focuses on strategic and operational issues facing organisations in different countries and different sectors in the new European context'. Cross-fertilisation of ideas and experiences from different cultures is regarded as particularly important. The European continent is identified as one part of a network of world centres of influence.

- Participants and speakers come from the different European countries, in order to foster a truly broad approach: 'the EMP is principally a learning experience for executives by executives'.

- The programme itself is highly intensive, requiring an average of ten to 12 hours per day attendance at modules throughout the 16 days. These modules encompass lectures, syndicate work, and company case studies. The subjects covered are very wide ranging, from specific areas such as distribution and marketing policies, to issues of broad concern such as pan-European corporate identity, key factors of competitivity, and priority planning.

Although expensive, programmes such as this can be used to create detailed awareness among senior executives of cultural and business issues of significance as the Single Market Programme takes hold. In the words of the EMP brochure:

'In future, managers will have to think strategically in European terms. . . To survive and succeed, business strategies will also have to take account of the skills managers will need in order to analyse and assess new opportunities in the EC. Flexibility, the ability to think in inter-cultural terms, and a desire to learn new ways of working will be essential qualities for the successful European manager.'

International management consultancies

A number of organisations have forged links with international management consultancies in order to develop the right approach. British Steel, for example, has drawn up a management succession policy in conjunction with the PA Consulting Group, based on key competences which reflect the company's requirement of managers to be internationalist in their approach. Another good example is provided by Grand Metropolitan, which has commissioned Price Waterhouse to undertake a project examining the development issues surrounding international market awareness, language skills and European regulations and training standards. Areas under consideration include cultural awareness programmes, and ways of helping managers to cope with the demands of international assignments.

Finally, another cost-effective way for smaller companies in particular to gain understanding of the business practices prevalent in other Member States might be to participate in the activities of European professional associations, or even to form such associations themselves in conjunction with like-minded foreign organisations. The European Law Students Association (ELSA), which I described in Chapter 5, is a good example of one of these. ELSA continues to look for sponsorship and support from legal firms across Europe, and would probably welcome the prospect of one or two major international firms taking the lead in some of its activities. In return, it is able to offer a number of services to member firms. These include:

- quick access to a network of overseas contacts;
- schools and seminars held at international venues to discuss particular aspects of European law;

- a short-term exchange programme (STEP) in which young lawyers have the opportunity to spend the summer working in a foreign law office;
- a regular journal to which members can contribute and containing articles on a wide range of subjects;
- an annual conference giving the opportunity to meet lawyers from European firms and debate issues of particular interest.

For those companies too small to establish European contacts on their own, active participation in an association such as ELSA could provide an unrivalled opportunity to gain pan-European awareness.

Graduate training in the pan-European company

'The adaptability of young graduates is a powerful factor in persuading companies to start up European recruitment and training programmes.' This statement, taken from the IDS/IPM handbook, 'Personnel Management and the Single European Market', is certainly true as far as many of the large multinational organisations are concerned. There is less evidence, however, that British employers have begun to follow suit. This is strongly underlined by Dr Lynda Gratton of London Business School in an article in the *Times* entitled '1992: Are we missing the boat?':

'Yet in all this (graduate resourcing) activity, too much time is spent in recruitment and not enough on development. The companies who are most likely to succeed in the race to find and develop an international cadre of executives are those which understand that job experience, not personality tests, is the main determinant of future potential.'

The powerful message coming through from this is that companies intent on turning their graduate recruits into European business managers must put in place detailed training programmes to ensure that the right attitudes and abilities are developed. They must act quickly; this is essential if graduates' initial adaptability and readiness to absorb the social and business norms prevalent in other countries is not to be dulled. According to Dr Gratton, exposure to different cultures and environments should therefore be given to newly appointed recruits as soon as possible into their careers. One method suggested to achieve this end is to arrange exchange schemes with non-rival European companies, a course of action I have discussed earlier in this chapter with regard to the development of more senior and experienced managers.

Examples of European companies

Dr Gratton gives a number of examples of European companies that have established international development programmes for graduates. These include Fiat, which prepares its graduates to operate in the wider market by arranging regular visits to other countries, supplemented by language training and briefings on different countries. Ford has a database on its graduate recruits throughout Europe, which is used to determine individual training needs and the placement of these recruits across the continent at different stages in their careers. One of the most sophisticated examples given is that of Electrolux, which deploys its workforce widely throughout Europe:

'Like Ford, it has designed an integrated selection and development programme for its new graduates. An international assessment centre assesses high potential people to a similar set of criteria across Europe. These are supported by management audits and task forces which ensure key people work together.'

For companies like Electrolux and Ford, the precise nationality of the graduate recruit is, quite clearly, of relatively low importance to their career development programme. Of far greater importance is the initial willingness to adapt to different cultural values, and the specific technical ability of each recruit. These attributes can be built on by the provision of appropriate training, a major part of which will be deployment into different functions or subsidiary operations across Europe in the interests of both career progression and company need.

In the previous chapter I described Olivetti's 'No Frontiers' recruitment programme for graduate system engineers. In fact, the screening and selection of candidates is only one part of this programme, as it is followed up by a sustained and highly specific integration and training process. The programme as a whole, therefore, provides a classic example of how to handle an international graduate intake; rigorous selection processes, but just as importantly an extensive induction and training programme aimed both at easing recruits into the corporate culture, and developing them as true internationalists.

A key message given to new recruits is that, from the day they join the company, they remain as participants in the 'No Frontiers' programme. Thus, although coming from many different countries across Europe and indeed the world, they stay together for many aspects of training and are therefore able to gain understanding of each other's different backgrounds and cultures. This in itself is of great benefit to the development of an internationalist approach; the actual programme, which unfolds over several years, also encompasses four lengthy periods of international classroom training and three stages in the field for practical training. These practical training stages, each of approximately two to three months' duration, are invariably spent in different parts of the company's operation in different Member States.

Responsibility for the training given is held jointly by Olivetti's corporate centre which designs the programme content, monitors quality and measures training effectiveness; Olivetti subsidiaries, which carry out the field training; external education consultants who validate the results; and Olivetti schools which develop and deliver the classroom modules. The overall framework is the classic one in which individuals are encouraged to take responsibility for their actions, while the company provides sponsorship and support. Each participant in the programme is assigned a field tutor whose role is to assist in the integration process, give professional guidance and support, and ensure that the field training programme is followed.

The 'No Frontiers' programme provides us with one of the best models to date of how to go about the task of training and developing graduate recruits as internationalists capable of operating comfortably throughout the wider market. While much of the training itself concentrates on the specific technical details of the system engineer's work, three aspects of it are particularly worthy of note:

- First, new entrants to it stay together as a team. Working alongside each other for several years in the classroom and the workplace, they learn about the cultural similarities and differences between them, and become able to adapt to these.

- Second, on-the-job training is carried out in different countries. Again, through this the programme participants develop sensitivity to different cultural norms and environments, and are required to apply this culture sensitivity to their methods of work.

• Third, the programme itself is driven by the corporate centre. Thus, even when undergoing training in subsidiary operations, the overall direction and scope of learning given to scheme participants is focused towards corporate business objectives rather than local ones. Participants are encouraged to think of themselves as part of the worldwide Olivetti management team, rather than as individual systems engineers carrying out their jobs in different parts of the business.

It seems likely that the 'No Frontiers' programme will be extended by Olivetti into other functional areas of the business, building on the success of its launch in the systems engineering function. The programme is undoubtedly improving the company's ability to operate effectively in the wider market, giving it an edge in attracting career-motivated graduate recruits, and in developing them as corporate-thinking, culture-sensitive business managers. It is a model that many UK companies would do well to follow.

Language training

The English language has always been, and is likely to remain, the predominant language of international business. This is undoubtedly why, in the past, British businessmen have been castigated as being lazy and unwilling to learn how to converse with European clients or colleagues in their native tongue. Fortunately, this perception is now changing. Language training is clearly identifiable as one of the major areas to which attention is being given by UK companies as they prepare for the coming of the Single Market.

That there is a growing need for such training should by now be beyond any doubt. The former German Chancellor, Willi Brandt, once observed that if he wanted to sell to Britain he sold in English, and if Britain wanted to sell something to Germany it had better do so in German. Despite the continuing predominance of the English language, Europeans will increasingly consider it downright rude if no attempt is made to converse with them in their own languages. Furthermore, given the high levels of foreign language ability amongst European managers, British firms are at a considerable disadvantage if their own managers do not have comparable skills.

A survey published by IRS Employment Trends in March 1989 revealed the extent to which language training is being taken seriously by major

British companies. Of 21 companies surveyed, almost all had put in place some form of provision, ranging from limited support for senior executives arranging their own tuition, to permanently available placements on intensive courses with external language schools as well as in-house provision for all staff.

The main findings of the survey, as summarised below, make interesting reading:

- most companies rely on external courses provided by language schools or linguistics units in colleges/universities, though a significant number have developed tailored, in-house programmes;
- in may cases training is partly carried out during work time, and partly outside working hours;
- the priority languages are French and German, with Spanish and Italian receiving much lower attention;
- training is often limited to senior management staff, but in some cases is offered to lower levels on a selective basis (e.g. where staff have regular contact with foreign customers or subsidiaries during the course of their work), or indeed to all staff;
- the demand for and take-up of placements on courses is very high;
- most companies are thinking of expanding training provision in one way or another;
- language skills are being seen as a factor of increasing importance in the selection process.

These findings will be of some value to any company thinking of launching a language training programme, in compiling its initial checklist of needs and purposes. It should be emphasised, however, that each company will be approaching the issue from a different business standpoint, and that the specific details of the programme will need to be tailored to meet these business needs. The main considerations to be taken into account are set out below.

Prioritise training

First, it will rarely be appropriate to adopt a 'blanket' approach to training provision. Priority for training should be given to those staff who need it most; clearly, in many cases this will include the top management team where there may be a requirement to conduct business at corporate level with foreign colleagues, customers and even rivals. There is likely to be a need for language skills at lower level, however, amongst salesmen operating in the wider market, even amongst engineers, IT specialists and other functional managers who, for one reason or another, need to communicate with foreign counterparts.

At lower levels even than this, there may be a need to offer training to staff such as receptionists and telephonists who are at the front line in presenting the right company image to foreign customers. It hardly needs to be said that the specific languages targeted should be those in which the company is most likely to need to conduct business. Thus, a company like Hoechst UK concentrates exclusively on German, whereas companies that operate more widely across Europe may need to offer a range of languages for training to staff.

Determine skill level

It will be necessary to decide on the level of skill required of staff in foreign languages. Again, the approach here should be highly specific; a salesman or buyer who may need to negotiate with foreign dealers and to have detailed technical knowledge of a product or market is likely to need much higher order skills than either a managing director or a telephonist, who may need little more than social skills. These considerations will be instrumental in determining the most appropriate training methods as well as the degree of investment required in setting up the programme.

Decide on language training programme

The experiences of most companies to date suggest that, to be effective, language training programmes should be intensive with, if possible, periods of total immersion in the foreign culture. Local tuition, even involving the whole family where appropriate, is clearly a rapid means of making progress but may be expensive or inappropriate for many employees. On the other hand, leaving staff to get on with it on their own is most unlikely to bring results. A sound approach for many companies may be a middle course, in which a group training programme based on audio material and a participative approach forms the backbone of the training. There is clear evidence that, by bringing together people of similar abilities under the guidance of an experienced tutor, rapid progress can be made. Course participants are encouraged to learn from each other and to develop foreign language communication skills that can be transferred directly to the workplace.

Almost all companies will need to make use of external suppliers in putting together a language training programme. The search for a suitable supplier should, needless to say, extend well beyond looking purely at local evening classes, though in some cases these may provide cheap and effective basic training. Any commercial language training school being considered should be thoroughly vetted as to suitability before a final decision is reached. Basic questions will concern the training methods, the number of training hours within the programme and cost of provision, but more precise areas may include:

- Are the teachers native speakers, and what experience do they have?
- Are courses tailored to business needs?
- Can language laboratories be used outside tuition hours?
- Does the school teach English to foreign business people, thus allowing the opportunity of meeting people from abroad who speak the language being learned?

Where to get help in choosing the right programme

An independent, non-commercial organisation that exists to help employers identify their language training needs is the Centre for Information on Language Teaching (CILT) based at Regent's College, London. CILT is able to offer an advisory service tailored to individual company needs, starting with the giving of general advice and the scoping of the organisation, leading to a consultative role to develop the most appropriate policy, through to the identification of potential training providers. This is an extremely valuable service that many employers would do well to make use of. Among the general advice given by CILT is the message that quick, easy and neatly packageable language training will rarely work. A tailored language programme in the context of the organisation structure, though more expensive, will always be a worthwhile investment.

A further source of valuable advice just becoming available to many companies is the European Commission itself, via the Lingua Language Programme which was introduced at the beginning of 1990. The declared aims of this programme are, first, to improve the quality and quantity of foreign language training in the Community, and second to assist companies in providing the workforce with foreign language skills.

A number of specific measures proposed are of potential significance:

- the promotion of 'foreign language audits' to help small firms in particular to determine needs and methods of provision;
- a pilot exercise to promote and develop language training materials in different economic sectors, again particularly in small firms and the new technology sector;
- support for certification of language qualifications for specific professions and sectors;
- assistance to small and medium-sized companies wishing to engage in exchange schemes, and to language trainers actively working to develop skills in companies.

Audit of existing skills

One final consideration for any company thinking of embarking on a language training programme for its staff is, quite simply, to carry out an audit of existing skills levels before deciding on a specific course of action. Experience has shown that many companies have been surprised to discover the extent of language skills already held by their employees; furthermore, such an audit is essential if the company is to be able to assess accurately the training needs and from this draw up a suitable programme.

A good example of a language training programme implemented by a major company is that of Rowntree Mackintosh. The impetus for the programme arose from Nestles' takeover of Rowntree in 1989, following which a need was identified to provide senior and middle level managers in regular contact with the Swiss Headquarters with French language skills.

The company's initial approach to the target group produced a huge response, so much so that it was necessary to narrow down the initial selection to a group of 40. Following this a major audit of the company was carried out by independent experts, to establish business needs and existing levels of competence. Interviews with the 40 managers selected were conducted to ascertain how quickly they could be expected to learn new skills, and to identify individual needs and suitable training methods.

The learning given has therefore been highly specific to these individual needs and abilities. Features of it are:

- groups of four to six managers of similar levels of ability have been put together to form tuition units;

- all training has been provided by French native speakers;
- a conversational approach has been adopted, involving listening to tapes and participating in a classroom environment;
- the training requires some commitment from the managers concerned, the tuition taking up to two or three hours outside working time per week.

The Rowntree Mackintosh approach to language training represents an expensive option, but the company is reported to be highly satisfied with the results and likely to develop its programme further.

9 Remuneration and benefits and mobility policy

Despite the plethora of surveys, reports and articles concerning pay and benefits across the European Community, there is perhaps more confusion in this area than in any other on the human resources agenda. To a large extent, this is due to the amount of detail required in order to make valid comparisons between the earnings levels of nationals in different Member States. Quite simply, how does one compare the take-home pay of, for example, a mechanical engineer in Milan with that of an equivalent in Stuttgart, or of a software programmer in London with a counterpart in Toulouse? In addition to the basic packages, how far should one consider such factors as differences in the cost of living, lifestyle and spending patterns before reaching a conclusion?

For many companies, such questions as these will be purely academic. A CBI spokesperson has said:

'Our initial talks with companies suggest that they are not ready for harmonisation of conditions with West Germany where pay rates are a lot higher. This would put billions of pounds on the wage bill and companies cannot afford that.'

The basic issue of cost is clearly identified here; without doubt, rates of pay in West Germany are generally higher than in any other Member State. This may be less of a factor for British companies that are setting up operations in countries where the broad level of earnings are comparable with, or even less than, our own. Here, the issue of how far to harmonise pay, benefits and conditions may be more related to management style and the degree of autonomy given to European subsidiaries. It may also, quite simply, be related to the degree to which it is possible to change local working and payment methods that have built up over time due to a combination of custom and practice, government intervention, and labour market forces.

In this chapter I shall try to adopt a logical approach to all these complex issues. The chapter falls into four parts:

- First, a review of possible sources of information on pay and benefits in other European countries. These are many and various, but some are more appropriate than others to the specific needs of different companies.

- Second, the issues of harmonisation of pay itself. The circumstances in which this may or may not be appropriate will be examined, and methods of going about the process given consideration.

- Third, an examination of some of the key differences in benefits and working practices between the UK and other European countries. Some of these are highly complex, making harmonisation extremely difficult. Social security and pension arrangements, in particular, could prove to be a major headache for many employers.

- Fourth, a review of mobility policy and the makeup of benefits packages for expatriates. There is some evidence that practice is changing in this area due to the increasing effect Europeanisation is having on our major multinational companies. This is an interesting issue in itself, but one also that may signpost the way ahead for the harmonisation issue generally.

Salaries and benefits in Europe: where to obtain information

In Chapter 4 I used the Wyatt Company's survey 'Top Management Remuneration: Europe and USA' for my analysis of executive pay comparisons across Europe. This survey is, I believe, as reliable as any due to the breadth of the database from which information is obtained, and the accuracy of job matching. However, the findings vary considerably from the results of several surveys produced by other major remuneration and benefit consultancies. For example, P-E Inbucon have recently participated in a survey by a consortium of consultancies called the European Remuneration Network. This reports that in some cases the total remuneration packages of executives in the UK are substantially below those of counterparts in countries such as France, West Germany and Italy.

To some extent the differences between survey findings are simply a factor of the precise differences between the type of jobs being matched. A key consideration for any company wishing to use such survey information, therefore, is to ensure that its own circumstances match as closely as possible those of the survey participants. Many of these surveys are expensive to buy and preliminary research into the methods used, the level of positions compared, the extent of detail regarding specific functions and industry sectors is highly advisable prior to purchase. A further consideration is whether or not the information is derived predominantly from jobs filled by local nationals or expatriates, or by an equal mixture of both.

Surveys such as these are usually confined to senior executive levels, where it should be remembered pay levels can be highly volatile due to the effect of changing income tax levels, bonus and share option schemes and non-cash benefits. For companies seeking information on European pay, benefits and costs of living at lower levels, they are not really appropriate. The choice here appears to be threefold: subscription to published information updated on a regular basis, a bespoke survey related specifically to the company's circumstances in terms of location and market sector, and direct access to local sources of information.

Subscription to published information

The first of these options is only really of value in this context as a supplement to more precise data. Although the information supplied is in many cases highly detailed, the breadth of the subject-matter covered leads to a somewhat piecemeal approach to its presentation. Perhaps the greatest value in subscribing to published journals is in the overall picture that can be gained, over a period time, of the employment practices prevalent across Europe including the individual Member States' differing approaches to pay and benefits.

The most widely known of these journals is the *IDS European Report*, which has been published on a monthly basis for several years. Each edition contains an update of employment news in each European country, as well as latest information on employment-related developments at the EC.

In addition there are feature articles focusing on individual countries, or issues of significance across Europe such as employee participation practices or childcare provision in different Member States. There is also a regular update of statistics, including prices, unemployment and purchasing power comparisons. The style of writing in IDS journals is consistently readable, informative and logical in presenting what are at times highly complex issues.

Bespoke surveys

Bespoke consultancy services providing detailed and specific pay and benefits information on other European Countries are offered by a number of well known professional companies, such as Hay Management Consultants and Towers Perrin. Such services are often available in addition to off-the-shelf country reports, regular newsletters and telephone 'hotlines'. It is surely essential that any company employing staff in another Member State has access to one of these databases, if it is to understand the fine detail of local employment practices and market rates.

Employment Conditions Abroad Ltd (ECA) is one company that has established a sound reputation in this field. It derives its data from a worldwide 'membership network', made up of more than 500 different companies both large and small, and covering all industry sectors including banking, pharmaceuticals, software, manufacturing and engineering. It is effectively owned by its participating members, claiming therefore that it is non-profit-making and able to put all its resources to the development and improvement of its services.

Company details service

Broadly speaking, ECA offers two distinct services to its members. The first involves contribution of company details to its database on a confidential basis, in return for which detailed information on all other participants' policies and practices is given. Individual company identities are never disclosed. This information is specifically related to expatriate rather than local national terms and conditions, and is produced in various forms including country reports (giving details of remuneration comparisons, tax, social security and labour legislation and expatriate cost of living indices) and expatriate remuneration surveys (comparing the packages of individual job holders in different services, and computer-based salary/tax comparison programs. Users of this service include companies planning a foreign venture for the first time and medium sized operations without the resources to conduct their own research, as well as most of the big multinational employers.

Advisory service

The second area of service is an advisory capacity offered on a straight forward consultancy basis. ECA consultants operate in a number of areas to do with overseas remuneration policy, covering both expatriates and local nationals. These services are probably most useful for companies setting up in a foreign country for the first time. They include:

- Conceptual design, including the effective design of remuneration systems for expatriates and local nationals employed by foreign companies.
- The implementation of cost effective packages, taking account of fringe benefit and tax.
- Cultural awareness advice, covering such areas as managing and negotiating across cultures, and organisation design.

This kind of bespoke service can be invaluable to a company in determining the extent of the differences between the remuneration systems of two different countries, and deciding on an effective strategy to handle those differences within the company culture.

Obtaining local employment market information direct from local sources can be difficult for a company unless a concerted effort is made. In many cases, the resources simply will not be available to carry out sufficiently detailed research, in others issues of secrecy or confidentiality will preclude much investigation. However, the experience of some companies has shown that, where the effort has been made, the results have been worthwhile. Sources of information have included local or national employment services, professional associations and other employers. In some cases highly valuable information can be gained by pooling company information with like minded companies in foreign countries, particularly if in the same industry sector. The data obtained via these sources can sometimes be more detailed and specific than that provided by even the most sophisticated of third party sources.

The harmonisation of payment systems

The paradox for companies operating across Europe in this context is clear. How far should they maintain differentiation between operations in various countries where pay levels and employment practices may be widely different, while at the same time developing systems that are compatible, and reinforce the corporate approach?

The strategy

Individual companies' responses to this question will be ranged along a continuum which, at one extremity, will mean leaving local operations strictly alone to follow their own separate policies, and at the other to implement all-embracing grading and salary systems. In practice, almost all employers will fall somewhere between these two extremes. Factors determining exactly where they need to position themselves will include the following:

- The nature of the product or service they have to offer, in particular its specificity. Companies that are aiming to sell the same product across the whole European Market are likely to need greater compatibility within their employment systems than ones whose products are highly specialised to the different markets of individual countries.

- The size of the company: large multinational companies may have a more highly developed corporate culture than smaller and more fragmented ones. Companies that employ just a few local nationals in different countries are unlikely to have a major need for harmonised payment systems.

- The extent to which relocation of managers and staff takes place. Companies that have adopted an active policy of international career development will have a stronger need for compatibility.

- The company's management style itself; some are, quite simply, historically more centralised than others. The precise way in which the European operation has developed can be a major factor here, with organisations that have grown through a series of mergers and acquisitions likely to be less centralised than those that have developed organically. There is a great danger, particularly prevalent among American parents that are remote from their subsidiary operations in Europe, to adopt a blanket approach to Europe and thus fail to recognise the many cultural and employment differences that exist between individual countries. This can lead to inappropriate systems and procedures being imposed on highly diverse parts of the operation.

- The precise degree of differences between pay and conditions norms in different countries where sites are based. Quite simply, it is much easier to harmonise across some European Member States than others. To attempt to adopt a co-ordinated approach to pay and working practices between West Germany and Greece, to give an extreme example, would be almost impossible.

These factors will need to be considered carefully by any employer in determining a strategy for European payment systems. As with so many other items on the Single Market Agenda, the fundamental question is that of company style, structure and position in the market.

The implementation

Obtaining information

Having decided on an appropriate strategy a number of further questions come to the fore concerning implementation. The first of these is the basic question of obtaining information. I have already outlined some of the most readily available sources but what is also important is co-ordinating and classifying the details obtained, and above all ensuring that they are kept up to date. Focusing purely on basic salaries, it is clear that many factors contribute to the situation in which, for any particular job, levels can vary widely both between different countries and between different localities within the same country. These include:

- The strength of the national economy, which may have the effect of pushing up salary levels generally (it is quite clear, e.g., that salaries in West Germany tend to be higher than in all other Member States).
- Economic trends such as cost-of-living and average earnings increases.
- The demand for the job within, respectively, the national and local economy.
- The type of person doing the job in terms of age, experience and qualifications. For example, although graduate starting salaries tend to be higher in countries such as France and West Germany than in the UK, this is partly due to the differences in age on graduation (nearer 25/26 than the 21/22 in this country).

Arriving at genuinely valid comparisons is a complex matter, requiring a combination of professional support and reliability of local sources of information.

The need for conformity. . .

A temptation to be resisted is that of allowing local operations to tackle their short-term, individual differences on a piecemeal basis. Except in the very smallest operations, such a policy is likely to destroy any chances of achieving the right balance in the long term. There is considerable danger of creating conflicts and schisms between different parts of the operation in different countries, severe constraints could arise in recruiting and retaining staff in different parts of the business; such moves can wreak havoc with any coherent international mobility policy. Above all, there is the high risk that an upwards spiral in the levels of pay across the company will occur, as continual claims for parity lead to harmonisation upwards to the highest common denominator. This situation can create a perpetual air of tension and, of course, will add considerably to employment costs.

The corollary of this is that, even for companies whose multinational operations are diverse in terms of their products and markets, a central personnel authority must be vested with the responsibility for developing and ensuring implementation of a co-ordinated, long-term payments policy. Only a function of this type will have the necessary resources, and the breadth of vision, to take a view that is appropriate for the whole operation. This does not, however, mean an 'ivory tower' approach. A vital requirement is to maintain communication with all line and local personnel functions, in order to respond quickly to changes and ensure that new policies and practices are broadly in line with overall company policy. There is a strong case to be made for the European Remuneration Manager's job to be that of a roving consultant, visiting the different sites on a regular basis in order to monitor trends and develop appropriate, company-wide responses.

. . . and flexibility

Some companies are actively working towards the harmonisation of salaries and benefits across Europe on a long-term basis, seeing this as a likely requirement of the Single Market Programme itself. Others are more circumspect, believing that the differences in social security systems between Member States will, in itself, make major changes in this direction impossible. The one thing that seems clear from the various approaches of most multinational employers is that compatibility rather than uniformity is the watchword. In the words of Richard Underwood, writing in *Personnel Management*:

'Employers will have to aim at maintaining systems which are flexible enough to cater for different national salary levels while avoiding continual claims for parity. These systems will also need to be able to cope with more frequent moves and job changes, with variations in the size and scope of comparable jobs in different countries and with differing approaches to performance-related pay.'

In order to achieve this flexibility, many multinational employers have adopted the approach of building a common framework for their payment systems across Europe, while allowing local operations to fill in the detail. The grading structure applied is one area that has come in for particular attention. Many companies, both large and small, have applied a common job evaluation system for their management grades so that jobs in different locations across their European operations can be measured accurately against each other. These systems range from relatively simple in-house schemes to the application of the more sophisticated, matrix-based systems developed by specialists such as HAY.

Achieving corporate unity

There is some evidence to suggest that formal job evaluation systems are more common amongst major US multinationals such as Gillette and Heinz, which apply them across Europe in a manner that, to some extent, subverts local differences in the interests of corporate unity. For European-based companies, it may be more appropriate to develop their own systems that recognise these differences and build them into the organic structure of the organisation.

One key advantage to this more organic approach to job comparison is that the grading structure can be more closely linked to local market rates of pay. Whatever system is applied, it is essential that the actual rates of pay for each grade can be adjusted to reflect both national and local market conditions. I use the word 'local' in its true sense here; just as in the UK, the going rates for equivalent jobs in other European countries can vary by as much as 20 per cent in different regions. Some companies apply standardised but extremely wide salary bands, allowing local operations to set levels as appropriate within these; others have separate salary bands for the same grades at different locations. Whichever option is chosen, it is imperative that the central personnel function maintains a firm monitoring role, to ensure that local operations do not run away with themselves and start applying rates of pay that are at variance with local norms, or movements in the cost of living.

Appraisal systems

Common appraisal systems are another means of developing corporate unity while being responsive to local employment practices. Again, many companies have applied standard systems across their European operations and have seen benefits arising from this. This is particularly so where appraisal has been linked to performance-related pay. In some of the more sophisticated schemes a pool of money generated by profits is distributed partly on the basis of overall group performance and partly based on local performance. Thus, staff receive an equal percentage award according to the success of the company as a whole, and a differential award according to the success of their local operations. The link is made between corporate identity and individual success.

Profit-sharing or bonus schemes

Some companies have developed profit-sharing or bonus schemes to apply across Europe, indeed there has been an explosion of such schemes during the 1980s, and this is likely to continue throughout the 1990s. This is a more difficult area, as different attitudes towards profit sharing prevail in different Member States. However, when applied to senior management levels and based on company wide measures such as sales targets or corporate results, they have proved to be highly effective in developing positive attitudes towards the corporate culture. As with other elements of the payment structure, care needs to be taken in implementing any new system. Most companies that have harmonised have only done so over a considerable period of time, carrying out extensive research and ensuring that each initiative is fully appropriate to overall requirements before implementation.

The IDS/IPM handbook *Personnel Management and the Single European Market* gives many examples of the ways in which different organisations have tackled the issue of pay harmonisation. One of the best of these is the approach taken by Air Products:

'Air Products is an example of the undiversified company with a Europe-wide evaluation, appraisal and performance-related pay system, although the UK has gone much further in relating pay to performance than other countries. There is a strongly co-ordinated HAY-based evaluation process which enables the company to have a good scheme for senior management beginning at the same grade point in each European country based on corporate results. There is also a Europe-wide stock option scheme, but the benefits differ according to the local tax regime. Air Products has a highpay salary policy coupled with competitive benefits, but how this is achieved is up to local management on the basis of common guidelines discussed in regular co-ordinating meetings of personnel managers. The pay policy line is set once a year with local personnel on the basis of local survey information and salary clubs. The company aims to conduct an outside review of salary levels every five years or so with the aid of consultants.'

The benefits package: a suitable case for harmonisation?

If anything, in this area the differences in practice between Member States are wider and more irreconcilable than with pay. There must be a temptation for many companies to leave well alone but, just as with pay, there is a need for the definition of common standards and a consistent philosophy without necessarily attempting to achieve uniformity across all operations. Again, the company's style, size and market position will be significant factors in determining what position to adopt. There is also the additional factor of pressure coming from the European Commission, which would seek in some cases to introduce legislation to harmonise basic working rights and conditions, irrespective of the cost to individual employers.

Pensions

Nowhere are the difficulties to be faced more severe than in the broad area of pensions provision. As I indicated in Chapter 5, the differences between Member States are considerable, stemming from very different philosophies concerning social security in old age. It seems very unlikely that harmonisation at national level will take place except in the very long term, leaving multinational employers to decide whether or not to make their own arrangements to bridge the cultural gap. There will be a particular need to do so when the transfer of managers and staff takes place between countries on a regular basis.

Where small numbers of transfers are involved, it may be most practical to issue guarantees to the staff concerned, effectively retaining them in the 'home country' scheme. However, for larger numbers or where individuals are transferring on to second or even third foreign countries in their careers, restrictive Inland Revenue rules will make this more difficult. Here, a more effective possibility may be to co-ordinate all of a company's pension liabilities in different countries into a multinational fund. A number of companies are looking at this option, although few such schemes have been established at present. They may become more popular if the taxation and social security systems of different Member States come closer together as a result of EC legislation.

Multinational funds may also be the most effective option for companies employing local nationals in different Member States, although inevitably these will need some adaptation or approximation to suit local circumstances. The problems are likely to be most severe in cases where European growth has taken place through mergers and acquisitions, where existing pension arrangements, probably very different from those of the parent company, are already in place.

Stock ownership

European stock ownership plans have been a growth area during the 1980s, and this growth is likely to continue during the present decade. To some extent, their popularity has been a factor of the growth of pan-European grading systems, as it is necessary to have in place a method of comparing jobs between different countries in order to decide a common minimum level for participation in such plans. In many cases confined to management levels, they are being regarded increasingly by multinational companies as an effective means of creating corporate awareness among staff employed in local or subsidiary operations.

Naturally, the provisions for employee share ownership plans vary between different countries, particularly regarding tax treatment; broadly speaking, they are made more attractive to UK employees than elsewhere in Europe. However, the experience of several major companies has proved that the problems arising from this can be worth overcoming. It is essential to enlist the services of specialist consultants in the area of employee share ownership and tax harmonisation in drawing up the details of any plan, and equally essential to communicate the details effectively to qualifying staff throughout the organisation.

Company cars

The provision of company cars to staff is still more widespread in the UK than elsewhere in Europe, although there is some evidence that the gap is beginning to narrow. In Germany, for instance, whereas in the past cars would normally only have been available to very senior executives, some companies are now providing them for managers at the middle-to-senior level of authority. Despite this it remains unlikely that other European countries will extend provision all the way down to the relatively junior levels that prevail in this country, and therefore the scope for harmonisation of the benefit across Europe in the short term remains limited. In the longer term, the steady erosion of the UK tax advantages in this context as well as changes in European practice may lead companies to revise their policies, providing scope for compromises which effectively iron out the differences between practices in different Member States.

Terms and conditions of employment

Many of the more basic terms and conditions of employment are the subject of attention by the European Commission; pressures to harmonise are likely to come about indirectly rather than directly, particularly through trade unions which have become highly aware of the content of the Social Charter, and the lobbying of governments by ministers in Brussels. There are further external pressures which, through having nothing directly to do with the Single Market Programme itself, may lead to harmonisation in some areas occurring over a period of time. A brief review of some of the more significant of these will illustrate this point:

- **Childcare provision** is one area that has received considerable attention recently, highlighted by the demographic downturn and the need, therefore, to attract women with children back into employment. The UK is a long way behind much of the rest of Europe regarding both parental leave and the provision of workplace nurseries, and has come in for severe criticism from Vasso Papandreou, the European Commissioner for Social Affairs, as a result. Ultimately, more pressure on employers to improve facilities to levels that exist in other Member States is likely to come from the economic need to recruit and retain experienced staff. The easing of the UK tax restrictions on employees who make use of workplace nurseries, following the 1990 Budget, will surely facilitate an increase in the provision of such facilities.

- **Standard working hours** vary to some extent between Member States. The UK is the only country in the EC that does not apply statutory maximum weekly hours, but in all countries norms are set by industry sectors and the UK is not widely divergent from these. Throughout Europe there is a trend to reduce standard weekly hours, and it seems likely that over a period of time downwards movement to 37.5 or 35 hours per week may occur.

- **Notice periods** is a further area where differences exist between European countries, particularly at management level where, in some cases, the notice required of both employee and employer can be much longer than in the UK. Many employers are likely to seek standardisation of the contracts offered to managers working in different countries, leading to convergence in the levels of notice entitlements.

- **Holiday entitlements** is one area where standardisation can be very difficult, and many employers may be advised to leave well alone. Looking first at public holidays, these vary widely both in terms of the number of days per year (the UK comes near the bottom of the table with only eight days, compared with 14 in Greece and 11 in Portugal and Belgium) and the dates on which they occur (Bastille Day, 14 July, would be a welcome addition for some, coming mid-way between our May and August Bank Holidays!). The UK is also the only Member State with no statutory minimum annual holiday entitlement; although our standard practice at senior or long service levels (28 to 30 days) is as generous as most, at lower levels the 20 to 22 days per annum norm compares unfavourably with countries such as France and Denmark where the minimum is 25 days. Any harmonisation would, from the UK point of view, be in an upwards direction and in addition to the question of cost there is considerable pressure to maintain levels as low as possible by US companies operating in Europe. Holiday entitlements in the USA are rarely more than ten days per year.

The Single Market has led to an increased awareness among UK companies of the differences between standard benefits practice in European countries. In determining whether or not to standardise individual items a multiplicity of factors will need to be taken into account, not the least of which is cost. It will be important to monitor trends and plan carefully in order to achieve compatibility as appropriate to the business, but also in such a way as not to harmonise upwards to the maximum level of benefit.

Expatriate packages and management mobility

A recent survey by P-E Inbucon, the remuneration consultants, has concluded that many employers are paying expatriates far more than they need to, as general attitudes towards working abroad begin to change. The survey reveals that, for many foreign postings, UK executives are earning between 150 and 200 per cent of their average UK take-home pay, even after cost of living adjustments. This is becoming increasingly anomalous as foreign postings become more regarded as valuable in themselves for career development purposes, and local nationals compare their own packages with those of expatriate colleagues. The recommendation is made that paying expatriates at local rates is unlikely to diminish the desire amongst ambitious staff to work abroad, will reduce costs and remove a cause of friction between expatriates and local nationals working alongside each other.

Of course, some of the biggest expatriate packages are paid to executives seconded to countries where living and working conditions are particularly difficult such as Saudi Arabia, Nigeria and Japan. In the context of European transfers, there is some evidence that the approach taken by employers is beginning to change. More people are on the move, and are being moved in order to build up pan-European attitudes within the company rather than just to carry out a specific project or assignment. The accelerated promotion prospects for the individual arising from this are regarded as sufficient incentive in themselves. Willingness to relocate is seen as part of the natural desire for career development, rather than unusual or exceptionally demanding.

Expatriate packages within Europe

Within Europe, therefore, there is a major trend away from traditional 'home build-up' type policies and towards packages based on 'host country' levels of salaries and benefits. This is particularly so regarding longer-term assignments of more than two to three years' duration; for shorter assignments, the issues surrounding housing (house purchase in the foreign country is frequently not an option) and pensions and benefits differences can create major difficulties.

Even here, however, attitudes are changing. Whereas in the past many employers would have covered accommodation costs in full, several now expect a contribution from the staff member, in recognition of the fact that the staff member's own home will probably be let during the period of transfer at some personal profit. Regarding pensions, companies still tend to keep employees in the 'home country' scheme as long as possible, but then insist on some sort of transfer or deferral with no automatic guarantees built in.

The trend towards expatriate packages in Europe that are based on national pay structures has been confirmed by Employment Conditions Abroad, who give a lot of consultancy advice in this area. ECA sees the costs of expatriate packages coming down on average by as much as 15 per cent as a result. In part, this is becoming possible due to the changing mobility philosophy, in part also to a perception of increasing commonality in national pay structures in Europe especially between capital cities and in certain functions such as IT. However, for the time being differences remain and these in particular cause problems in developing harmonised mobility packages:

- It is easy enough to transfer a manager from a lower earnings to a higher earnings country – from the UK to West Germany for example. The manager receives a substantial salary increase in line with the pay of local national colleagues, and everyone is happy. Problems arise in transferring a manager from West Germany to the UK however: few people, whatever their nationality and whatever the circumstances, are willing to take a drop in salary! In theory several major companies do move salaries downwards to reflect local levels but in practice various 'cushions' are often built in to compensate.

- The taxation differences between European countries cause a major headache to employers in this context. Although the contrasts are greatest with the non-EC Scandinavian countries, they are still significant within the EC. Harmonisation of the different tax regimes does not appear to be high on the European Commission's agenda for the Single Market Programme.

- The costs of mobility packages are more easily absorbed by service sector companies than manufacturing companies, where small increases to product price can hugely affect sales and profits. Manufacturing companies may therefore find it difficult to transfer staff in significant numbers in the interests of developing individual careers and an overall European business culture.

- European secondments are also much easier for big multinational organisations that have more to benefit from the development of a European Business culture and, again, are better placed to absorb the costs.

European mobility policy

In determining a strategy for a European mobility policy, a basic principle must be to establish what benefits the company expects to gain from transferring staff to different locations. In many cases, there will be a 'mix' of functional reasons (he/she is the one we need to do the job), skills-base reasons (these engineers will learn a lot from how our subsidiary in Germany does things) and cultural reasons (we need our people in different countries to understand and communicate with each other better). From this a number of key questions will emerge, raising such issues as – who? where? how long for? to do what? – and from this an ideal plan, not, one would hope, a million miles from the company's overall manpower plan.

Having established requirements, the next step must be to determine the attitudes and values of the staff towards mobility. This would aim to answer such questions as:

- How many staff are prepared to relocate across Europe?
- What are their individual preferences in terms of location, timescale, etc.?
- Are they the right staff in terms of functional area, career to date and ability to fit in with other cultures?
- What rewards and benefits will they seek from international career moves?

Only when, through this analysis, the degree of overlap between the company's requirements and those of its key staff has been established should the terms of any international relocation package be drawn up. Key features of it might be:

- Changing the perception of reward, with emphasis on career as well as

salary progression coming from international moves.
- Adopting 'European best practice' – not necessarily most expensive practice – to pay structures and benefits.
- Providing competitive rewards in relation to local standards.
- Recognition of family constraints and aspirations, including providing rewards or job opportunities for older children and spouses.
- Active development programmes as part of the relocation experience, including the provision of language and cultural awareness training.

These, and other aspects of forward looking packages are perhaps best illustrated by looking at some of the many examples of relocation schemes provided by major multinational employers. I have chosen just two; the giant UK chemicals company ICI, and the European Division of IBM.

ICI: comprehensive support from start to finish

ICI sees itself as a European-based international company, and has a long history of transferring employees about the world. Most of these international transfers are of relatively short duration – two to three years being about the norm – and at the end of the transfer period the employee usually moves back to his or her home country. The details of ICI's international transfers policy reflects all this.

A key feature of the policy is the amount of preparation given to employees prior to the transfer taking place. Briefings given and written material supplied provide detailed information on cultural norms and practices in the country being visited, taxation, housing, politics and language. While the company's international personnel group takes responsibility for amassing and updating this information, dissemination of it is the responsibility of divisional personnel departments which liaise with relevant departments overseas and can relate to the transferee's personal situation. The focus is very firmly on smoothing out the domestic problems associated with international transfer. The circumstances of the whole family are therefore given detailed consideration, and care is taken that spouses are included in the briefing process. A family trip to the country being visited, prior to the transfer taking place, is always arranged. Education of children is seen as the biggest difficulty to be overcome and detailed counselling is given in this area in addition to financial support.

Regarding pay and benefits, the contractual arrangement made is that home country contract is suspended during the period of transfer. Gross salary is paid at the rate for the job in the local economy; in netting this down a complex calculation is made, which effectively relates part of pay to domestic commitment in the home country and part to living expenses in the host country. The driving principle is that no transferee should be worse off than if he/she had taken up the same post in home country, while ensuring that living standards are in line with those of local staff of equivalent status. Although an international location allowance of up to 40 per cent of home gross salary can be paid this applies predominantly to locations beyond Europe where climate, security, medical risks and leisure facilities are such as to make the transfer particularly stressful. Free housing, and allowances to cover relocation and home visits form part of the overall package.

ICI ensures that employees transferred abroad are kept in regular contact with their home country operating units, and above all are given detailed preparation for the return home. This relates both to the change in domestic circumstances that will occur, and to career development. Considerable thought is given by the international personnel group throughout the period of transfer to suitable job opportunities for the employee on return, which means that job offers can be made well in advance of the return itself. This facilitates the transition process, and also ensures that the experience gained abroad is put to best use from the company's point of view.

IBM: mobility–an aspect of corporate culture

The approach towards international career assignments within IBM is carefully planned and structured to fit in with the company's overall culture. This is founded on the belief that the individual is to be given the opportunity to develop his or her own career, and will be appraised and rewarded accordingly. Two-way communication, career management and redeployment are significant aspects of this.

International deployments take place for three reasons: to ensure the transfers of technological and other skills between operations, to provide expertise locally and to develop careers within the company. A feature of most assignments is that they are of relatively short duration, two to four years being the norm, and as with ICI are usually followed by transfer back to the home country rather than on to a third location.

Unlike ICI, remuneration and benefits are based on home-country levels, with the company providing assistance towards any measured excess costs. This system works well in an organisation in which international mobility policy is universally applied, and understood by all. Although the company does not compensate directly for the loss of any income from the spouse following transfer, housing is provided free to a consistent level to different nationalities.

In many ways, IBM expects its staff redeployed abroad to be more self-reliant than does ICI. However, the degree of support provided to reimburse transferees for actual costs and disruptions arising is impressive. There are a number of specific areas:

- All travel from home country to work location is paid for, including a preliminary visit and any emergency returns.
- Relocation costs including hotel expenses, meals, etc. for up to three weeks, shipment and storage of household goods as required.
- Supervision and maintenance of the home during period of absence.
- The cost of education up to secondary level, including tuition, transport and materials and two foreign trips per year where education is continued in the home country.

IBM also provides a comprehensive tax consultation service for its expatriates. It has an 'excess tax' plan in which any taxes and social security contributions incurred above home country levels are reimbursed.

IBM goes to considerable trouble to ensure that expatriate staff are integrated quickly and easily into the new work location. A preliminary trip to the new location for employee and spouse is arranged, and briefings both pre-departure and on arrival take place covering such areas as terms and conditions of employment, local working practices and sources of information and support. Language training for both employee and spouse is provided where appropriate. Ongoing support to the family continues throughout the duration of the assignment, including mechanisms to ensure that readjustment to the home country lifestyle is as smooth as possible.

Career monitoring throughout the assignment is an impressive feature of IBM's overall policy, facilitated by the common systems of appraisal and merit pay that apply throughout the company. Every expatriate is designated a home country manager for the duration of the assignment, who has primary responsibility for monitoring performance and the progress of the job itself, and awarding pay increases. Responsibility is also taken to ensure that, on return, the employee is placed in a suitable position to continue his/her career development within the IBM corporate structure.

It will be seen that there are many similarities between ICI and IBM in their approach to expatriate policy, although in the area of remuneration and benefits they differ quite markedly. It should always be remembered that, fundamentally, it is individual people who are being relocated, rather than the company's corporate philosophy; therefore, the support mechanisms that need to be put in place will relate just as much to individual needs as to the company view.

10 Other human resources issues

In this chapter my purpose is to review, briefly, a number of issues that may become of greater importance to the Personnel Manager as the Single Market begins to take effect. It is highly unlikely that any of them will be at the forefront of anyone's mind; though deserving only a brief mention in their own right some of them may nevertheless form a significant part of a comprehensive European human resources strategy for some companies.

They are respectively:

- health and safety;
- employee communication policy;
- employee involvement;
- responses to trade union initiatives;
- business relocation within the European Community.

Health and safety

The European Commission has pressed hard for legislation in this field, recognising that the Single Market should not be associated with a free market for unsafe products, or exploitation of lower standards in some Member States for reasons of competitive advantage. It has stepped up its activity since 1988, when the proposals for a new safety framework directive and five subsidiary directives covering minimum workplace standards, machinery safety, VDUs, heavy loads and personal protective equipment were published. As decisions concerning health and safety matters can be taken in the European Council on a majority basis it seems likely that progress towards the translation of these directives into European law will proceed relatively quickly, although the Commission has been careful to consult with employers and governments as well as unions through the organ of its International Labour Organisation.

Many of the Commission's specific proposals are already covered by UK legislation concerning health and safety. In two areas, however – VDUs and heavy loads – it is possible that new EC legislation may go beyond that already in place in the UK:

- regarding VDUs, proposals would necessitate evaluation of the ergonomic design of workstations, compulsory training of employees and eye examinations;
- regarding heavy loads, the directive would require employers to provide mechanical methods of lifting wherever possible, and to adhere to strict safety standards to prevent back injury wherever not.

Employers cannot, therefore, afford to be too complacent about current standards in these areas, and should review their existing practice against the proposals laid down. This may include an evaluation of the costs of improving standards in specific instances, and methods of effecting such improvement over a period of time should this be deemed necessary.

Employers operating across Europe

Employers who operate across Europe face a much more complex task in evaluating their own standards against proposed minimum European standard practice. A careful study of health and safety practices in subsidiary operations in different European countries may be advisable, followed by an action plan if significant differences between operations are found to exist.

Many employers will find aspects of the European Commission's programme unacceptable, and may wish to make these views known. Health and Safety legislation is an area in which the Commission has proved to be responsive to lobbying, wishing to take a balanced view between acceptable standards on one hand and the costs of improvement faced by industry on the other. The CBI and other trade organisations have consistently opposed the Directives concerning VDUs and heavy loads in particular, and adding weight to this opposition may, in the end, lead to proposals being modified in ways more acceptable to employers as a whole.

Employee communication policy

The experiences of some large multinational companies (e.g. ICL, whose pan-European initiatives I shall consider in more detail in the next chapter) have proved that comprehensive communications policies reaching all their employees across Europe can be highly effective in developing awareness of the wider market, and of the values and objectives of the organisation within that market. Such policies can be developed for a number of specific purposes:

- To advise staff of initiatives being taken by the company, either in a pure business sense or directly relating to the staff themselves.
- In particular, employees can be made aware of promotions being undertaken in areas such as training and development or cross-cultural exchange schemes.
- To raise awareness of general areas of interest and developments within the European community, for example initiatives being taken by the Commission or purely cultural information (e.g. country profiles on different Member States).
- To seek the views of staff on specific issues, or ascertain their general attitudes towards working within the Single Market. Questionnaires or checklists can be used to carry out preliminary audits into such areas as the extent of foreign language ability amongst the workforce, and the extent to which staff have travelled throughout Europe either on holiday or for business reasons.

Overall, communicating effectively with the staff can provide strong indications as to the level of interest in European affairs and in specific work-related issues. It can be an important precursor to more directly targeted human resources initiatives that aim to build on interest generated to develop cross-cultural sensitivity and career patterns.

Attractively presented written material is probably the most suitable medium, as it lends itself most readily to translation into different languages. Periodic magazines, statements and newsletters can all be used to build up the image of a company as a European rather than a domestic employer. Needless to say, the translations should be done professionally, if the right image is to be presented! It is also essential that information is distributed consistently throughout the organisation, and at the same time to staff working in different locations. If not handled efficiently, communications programmes can have a divisive rather than a unifying effect.

Employee involvement

Involving the company's employees in its business planning and its success can take two forms; worker participation and consultation, and financial involvement through share option schemes or profit-sharing. Both have been vigorously debated at government level, with the European Commission and some Member States strongly favouring Community legislation to impose the former, and in this country the latter being promoted as a more effective option by our Conservative Government and the CBI. In the pan-European context, neither option is as simple as it might seem.

Worker participation and consultation

The West German model is most often held up as the prime example in Europe of employers and employees co-operating in the interest of company success. In fact, many Community countries have formalised systems of employee representation. Works councils form part of the overall framework in Belgium, France, the Netherlands and Portugal; in Denmark, Spain and Luxembourg as well as in Germany, appointed employee representatives or directors are obligatory for most companies. One result of these varying national requirements is that multinational companies may be required to inform and consult with their staff to differing degrees in different subsidiaries – a situation which, it is argued, can have a destabilising effect and create tensions between one part of the organisation and another. Some commentators see this as becoming an increasing problem as trade unions across Europe communicate more closely with each other and become more aware of differences in approach.

In practice, a number of factors combine to make this less of a problem than it would first appear. First, consultation is related only to issues concerning the local environment, such as technical change, relocation or job losses as well as the application of terms and conditions of employment. Since almost all multinational companies leave such matters to be negotiated at local level anyway these issues are hardly ever relevant to workers in subsidiaries located in other Member States. Second, there is no direct link between workers councils or representatives and trade unions, as representatives are directly elected by the workforce. In some countries including Germany the degree of influence of trade unions is, indeed, considerably limited as the legal obligations of works councils effectively act as a filter between a company's management and trade union representation.

The different approaches to employee participation in different countries are, in any case, a factor of the social attitudes towards work and the workplace in each of those countries, and therefore – despite the declared intentions of the European Commission – are unlikely to be easily transformable into some common standard. To look more closely at the much vaunted West German model, for example, the key to its success rests in the nature of trade union relations in West Germany which, unlike in the UK, are political and non-sectarian. German trade unions are not wedded to the cause of a socialist government; they are industry rather than craft-based, so that a cleaner working in the engineering industry will be a member of the same union as an engineer. Workers in many public service jobs are forbidden to strike, and are not permitted to be communists. Above all, to quote one commentator writing in *Times*:

'Trade unions themselves are not the arbiters of worker representation in German management. They do not appoint (or even elect from their own ranks) delegates to serve on boards, nor do they orchestrate a collective position to be adopted by such representatives. Workplace employees, whether unionised or not, elect their spokesmen, who may or may not be union members. It is difficult to imagine British unions relinquishing this degree of power to "non-organised" workers' delegates, quite apart from the difficulties of organisation presented by most major industries' myriad array of craft unions.'

In conclusion, employee involvement is unlikely to be a major issue for either UK-based or multinational employers, as the Single European Market takes hold. There are two reasons for this:

- First, the differences between Member States are so fundamental and specific to their own social structures that any attempt to introduce harmonisation through Community legislation can only be of diluted form. It is likely that individual national practices will continue to prevail, even if some overall framework is put in place.

- Second, even multinational companies operating across the whole of Europe have had no difficulties in coping with the complex differences to date. They have tended to leave individual plant or subsidiary consultation to local level, thus ensuring that local issues or concerns are effectively dealt with by those most familiar with their background. This too is unlikely to change in the future.

Financial involvement

The British Institute of Management has promoted financial involvement as a more acceptable alternative to the European Commission's proposals for legislation on worker participation. The BIM's own proposals call for expanded share ownership and profit-related pay schemes, as well as the provision of more detailed and regular information concerning profit forecasts and results.

Two problems regarding financial participation on a Europe-wide scale have been identified. The first is that the different taxation treatment of employee share ownership or profit schemes in different countries leads to complexities and inequalities. The second is the potential for employees in one particular country to hold a disproportionate number of shares, and therefore to exert too significant a degree of influence over the company's affairs.

The experiences of the many multinational companies that have implemented financial participation schemes of one form or another tend to indicate that these potential drawbacks are not significant, if the schemes themselves are properly drawn up and controlled. Profit-share schemes are considerably more common than employee share options, no doubt largely because they are easier to administer, can be more readily understood by employees working in diverse areas and are subject to more consistent tax treatment. The value of share options as a motivator of staff is, in any case, increasingly coming under question and it seems likely that such schemes will diminish in popularity throughout this decade.

Responses to trade union initiatives

It is only relatively recently that trade unions across Europe have developed a concerted approach towards the Single Market. However, a head of steam has now been built up and, on a number of fronts, unions are pressing employers and governments for a bigger say in employment related developments, particularly those covered by the Social Charter. This growing activity has been evidenced in the UK by the publication of the TUC's guide 'Europe 1992: Progress Report on Trade Union Objectives', presented at the September 1989 Blackpool Conference. This recognises the need for Unions to develop expertise in making cross-border comparisons in levels of earnings and employment conditions, and forge links with counterparts in other Member States.

A number of general issues have emerged as the major concerns:

- The possibility of 'social dumping' taking place: that is, employers relocating their operations in Member States where employment costs are lower. This is an issue raised most forcefully by the European Trades Union Congress (ETUC).

- Harmonisation of minimum employment rights across the Community; again an issue raised by the ETUC but also vigorously taken up by our own TUC and, in some cases, individual unions. The TUC guide for example, supports a process of upwards adjustment of earnings levels across Europe towards those levels that prevail in the higher-wage countries, while recognising that progress will be slow and differences will persist due to differences in productivity, efficiency and investment. The guide also seeks legislation to introduce a maximum working week and minimum holiday entitlement to the higher levels of some other European countries.

- The improvement of terms and conditions of employment, particularly between workers employed in different Member States by the same organisation, and for women through the provision of better maternity leave rights, childcare provision and equal access to training and promotion opportunity.

- Increased employee representation, a cause espoused vigorously by the TUC which would in particular wish to see workers councils in place throughout industry in this country.

Despite this increased activity, there are two major reasons why, for the time being at least, the trade union voice is likely to remain ineffective in bringing about major change:

- First, most concerns raised are derived directly from the Social Charter. They are therefore secondary by nature, and depend very much on the success of the European Commission in gaining acceptance to the detailed measures proposed in Charter and from this ensuring that its aims and purposes are implemented throughout the Community. The second objective may prove to be much more difficult to achieve that the first! Therefore, even were the Charter universally approved, the ETUC and individual national trade unions may face a difficult task in bringing about any real change.

- Second, the degree of co-ordination between the ETUC and trade unions in different countries is still low, which is no more than a reflection of their different aims and priorities. Despite the TUC's published views there is little evidence to suggest that unions in this country are aware of the detail of employment structures and norms in other Member States, which tends to call into question the practicality of some of the measures they propose.

A good example is provided by the TUC's drive to persuade employers to set up European-style works councils for consultation and bargaining. Unilever in particular has come under fire from unions across Europe to set up works councils to discuss such issues as collective bargaining and exchange of financial information. However, as I have already explained earlier in this chapter, 'works councils' and 'trade unions' are far from the same thing. It is a moot point whether the unions concerned have considered how the establishment of works councils might erode their own bargaining position, and whether, therefore, they would be prepared to carry through their demands when the detailed consequences become clear.

Overall, it seems unlikely that trade unions will have a significant part to play in changing the thinking of employers in a pan-European sense, or even in importing European employment practices into the UK. This will probably remain so unless the unions adopt a far more sophisticated and concerted approach, or far-reaching Community legislation concerning employment reaches the statute book.

This does not mean, however, that unions can be safely ignored in the context of the Single Market. They are, as they have always been, a catalyst to change, responsive to general trends and developments and keen to create awareness of these where they can be harnessed to the benefit of the employee. Many of their claims, as also many constituent parts of the Social Charter itself, are worthy of more detailed consideration by personnel professionals in the interest of consolidating employee/employer relationships and creating the right working environment.

Business relocation within the European Community

'Executives at General Motors have given unions until next Monday to agree a deal on working practices which will allow all disputes to go to arbitration, or lose a new £200 million engine plant . . The proposed Cheshire plant is competing with a site in West Germany. GM's decision to invest in the UK hinges on union agreement to end restrictive practices, increase job flexibility and put all disputes to arbitration . . . A Vauxhall spokesman said last night that problems still under discussion included altered shift patterns and a "continuity-of-supply" agreement to end the threat of wildcat strikes.'

These words, taken from a report concerning Vauxhall's proposed new plant to make V6 engines for its European executive cars, show just how important labour relations and working practices have become in decisions concerning the location of manufacturing bases. In many cases indeed they can be seen to be the predominant factor, just as much so for non-EC companies setting up new plants within Europe as for those already established in the EC.

Involvement of the personnel professional in the location of a new production site

Little if any detailed research has been carried out into the factors that cause employers to choose their new production sites, although many of these must be fundamental to personnel and industrial relations managers. Costs must clearly be high on the agenda, although the Vauxhall example shows that many of these will not be obvious or direct; here the main concern is to ensure sustained production by minimising the threat of damaging industrial action. The message for the personnel professional is clear; he or she *must* be involved in this planning process, if the right decision is to be made and implementation to proceed smoothly.

To describe this involvement in detail is beyond the scope of this book: it would make a substantial research project in its own right! However there are likely to be three broad phases:

- first, evaluation: this will involve detailed investigation into the employment norms at possible sites in different countries, including direct and indirect labour costs, labour supply, local and national industrial relations practices and employment laws;

- second, negotiation: the actual drawing up of proposed working practices that are acceptable to the workforce and their representatives, but equally meet the company's initial and likely future needs;

- third, implementation: the lengthy process of recruiting, training, organising and managing a new workforce, ensuring both that production targets are met and that employees understand and accept the company's values and expectations.

Of course, there will be other factors in the equation than personnel-related ones; materials supply chains and transportation, competitor position, the nature of the customer base and extent of government subsidy and support will all be key determinants of the siting of a new operation. However, the importance of the human resources input should not be underestimated. This situation provides a clear example of how human resources strategy can support a business strategy, particularly when implementing change process.

The relocating of an existing manufacturing operation to a new European site is a much more complex task than deciding where to set up a 'greenfield' operation. It is likely therefore, only to be a feasible operation for a relatively small number of labour intensive organisations, where moving parts of the operation to Member States such as Greece and Portugal where labour costs are relatively low may be seen as cost-effective in the long run. There is little evidence to date to suggest that this is happening on even a moderate scale.

The threat of 'social dumping' may, therefore, have been exaggerated and, in any case, when is social dumping not social dumping? The European Commission is prepared to award substantial grants to companies creating employment in regions within the Community where the economy is in poor shape and unemployment high. Would, therefore, a company relocating its manufacturing base to Southern Italy, and thereby taking advantage of lower employment costs, be, in the eyes of the Commission, a hero or a villain? The dividing line between exploitation and economic regeneration can, at times, be hard to define.

All that can be said is that the reorganisation of businesses to take advantage of lower employment costs or investment subsidies may grow, these factors are just two among many that will cause employers to evaluate the ways in which they conduct their business, and to realign themselves better to meet their particular market demands within the Single Market. An IDS Focus published in June 1989 gives two examples of companies that have 'taken the plunge':

'In April (1989) for example, the German engineering firm Robert Bosch announced, to considerable publicity, that it had selected South Wales for its new alternator plant, citing a 15 to 20 per cent cost advantage over West Germany. The plant is expected to employ 1,200 people. Rather more discreetly the UK group,

Yale and Valor, recently disclosed that it had shut its Southampton factory, with 600 employees, and moved production of electric blankets to a new assembly operation in Portugal employing about 300 people. Manufacturing costs according to the company will be about 20 per cent lower than in the UK and about 40 per cent of the investment is covered by grants.'

Part four
The challenge in practice

11 The response in practice: ICL and Hitachi Data Systems

In this chapter, the first of three in which case studies illustrating the responses of different companies to the European challenge are presented, my aim is to compare the approach taken by two companies operating in the Information Technology (IT) field: ICL and Hitachi Data Systems. Though their markets are linked, in terms of size, structure and background they are very different, and this is reflected in their varying approach to a number of issues. The IT sector as a whole is a good place to begin a study of individual company responses, as the nature of its products means that it has for many years had to regard the whole of Europe, rather than individual countries, as a market-place in its own right.

ICL: communication and a clear focus on 1992

ICL is the information systems subsidiary of STC plc, the UK-based worldwide communications corporation whose other interests are in the fields of telecommunications, microwave and optical systems, submarine, international marine and defence communication. As part of a group whose financial strength includes revenues in excess of $4 billion, ICL is a major player in its field, its main business rivals being other big multinational IT suppliers such as IBM and Olivetti. It showed a substantial increase in profits of 13 per cent in the year to December 1989, an outstanding performance in a difficult year, largely as a result of sound business analysis and a shift in emphasis from hardware to software services. Specifically, its most important markets are:

- International retail: ICL is the number one supplier of systems to French hypermarkets, and also has substantial interests in North

America. Overall it is the third largest in-store retail systems business in the world.

- Local government and public services: community charge legislation in the UK will be handled by over half the 430 local authorities in England and Wales on a system devised by ICL. The order for a networked system from Yorkshire Electricity Board was, at the time, the largest taken by a non-government public service in Europe.

- Financial services: Nationwide Anglia Building Society's multi-million pound order for a national network system was won on the strength of the expertise of ICL and its acquisition Northern Telecom Data Systems.

- Defence: clients in Europe include the MOD's Corporate Headquarters Office and the Royal Dutch Navy.

ICL's attitude to 1992

ICL responded swiftly to the publication of Lord Cockfield's 1985 Single Market white paper by the setting up of a top level advisory panel to advise the ICL Board on what needed to be done in the run-up to 1992. Containing external representatives with European Commission experience in addition to ICL directors, the panel was revised as the European Strategy Board under Sir Michael Butler in 1988. A top level commitment to Europe was therefore established very early on.

Also in 1988, the Information Systems activities outside the UK were split into two groups, ICL Europe and ICL International, to provide a stronger management focus on the needs of the European market. ICL Europe has since increased the size of its operations by the acquisition of Northern Telecom Data Systems, which has added substantially to the client base in the Netherlands and Italy, and through joint ventures and acquisitions in Spain and Denmark respectively. The company's UNIX-based departmental systems and international office system, "Officepower" (available in all major European languages) have proved to be particularly successful throughout Europe.

ICL's European business strategy is based on detailed research into market trends, consumer preferences and likely social, political and business developments over the next five years. Thus, a '1992 Sectoral Analysis Report' attempts to set the scene for 1992, detailing pan-European economic prospects and the likely impact of EC legislation by 1992 in the different sectors of Retailing, Manufacturing, Financial Services and the

Public Sector. A 'Scenario Model of 1995' has also been produced and is updated on a regular basis, painting a highly detailed picture of what the commercial environment of Europe may be like in 1995. . . 'by which time the Internal Market changes will be in force. The objective of the model is to provide a "best guess" stable platform to allow strategic planning to be undertaken with some degree of confidence'. In particular, business planning has identified trends in Western Europe IT expenditures during this decade, which in broad terms predict that the market for software services and hardware maintenance will expand whereas that for hardware itself will contract, and that PC and small systems will grow at the expense of medium-to-large systems with a purchase and installation cost of $1 million or more.

A business strategy for ICL Europe

On the basis of this and other analytical work, a six-point business strategy for ICL Europe has been drawn up:

- Expertise: which means among other things investing in people, seeking added value to the business from people, and a commitment to change and to quality.
- Integrated solutions: making best use of a multi-vendor environment and in-house manufacturing and logistics capability to provide customers with application, service, training, integration skills and consultancy services.
- A market strategy that recognises a European home base and the international scale of investment and expansion opportunity. Four 'vertical' market segments have been identified; Retail (worldwide market), Manufacturing and Financial Services (both European market) and Public Services (UK market).
- An open framework for products, enabling interworking with other systems and the development of de facto standards.
- Collaborative ventures, to gain access to other sources of technology and skills and a wider customer base, extend research and support vertical markets with appropriate systems and software houses.
- An organisation structure that is market-oriented, business management-focused, and responsive to change.

ICL's European communications programme

One of the most impressive aspects of ICL's preparation for the impact of the Single Market is its communication programme, co-ordinated by the company's 'Europe 1992 Group' based at head office in Putney. This group, which reports directly to the European Strategy Board, also carries out the bulk of the European research work and business strategy development, and is therefore well-placed to disseminate information throughout the organisation. Most important, ICL has drawn up a policy of advising its staff at all levels of European events and developments, both of a general nature and as they affect the company, its markets and the staff themselves. Inherent in this is a determined attempt to make staff 'think European', promulgate awareness of the company's operations and of different national cultures, and create opportunities for staff based in different countries to communicate directly with each other, both on a formal and an informal basis.

At one level, strategic and business planning information is prepared and distributed to senior managers throughout ICL and, in some cases, throughout the STC Group as a whole. The 1992 Sectoral Analysis Report is, for example, a major strategic review containing a mass of detailed information, and setting out projections which evaluate the likely effects of EC legislation and other developments on specific companies and industry sectors. The 'Scenario Model of 1995', regularly updated to take account of latest trends and developments, gives key pointers to success in the changing environment that are of direct relevance to the way managers carry out their jobs. The Europe 1992 Group has some staff based in Brussels and Luxembourg, who produce a regular 'letter from Brussels' which is complementary to the 1995 Scenario Model Document. This gives up to date information on the progress of Single Market legislation at the European Commission, with special emphasis on anything that affects STC's products, markets and structures.

At a broader level, the Europe 1992 Group disseminates regular information on Europe to all STC employees, mainly through the organ of its quarterly magazine 'Europe Sans Frontières'. Professionally published and issued in English, French and German, these magazines contain a variety of articles in order to present a wide perspective:

- Leading articles with titles such as 'A Citizen's Europe', and 'The New Commission', outlining the purposes behind the Single Market Programme, and latest events.

- Company information, concerning such issues as collaborative ventures, and the company's participation in EC research and development programmes. For example, an article entitled 'How ICL's Product Operations is meeting the European Challenge' gives details of ICL's involvement with competitors in the European Computer Research Centre in Munich, and in the EC's ESPRIT research and development initiative.

- Articles concerning 'people' policy, emphasising commitment in such areas as student placements, international career placements and the acquisition of linguistic skills.

- Personal interest items, many of which seek the involvement of staff: for example, family holiday exchanges (staff and customers) and penfriend schemes, children's competitions (e.g. match the 12 car number plates to the 12 different EC Member states!) and articles on schooling or living conditions in different parts of Europe.

- Country profiles, which over time will cover all the Member States within the EC.

These quarterly magazines clearly go a long way to creating an awareness and an interest among the staff in general European affairs, and the company's own strategy regarding the Single Market. Published information is reinforced by talks and seminars given to new and existing groups of staff throughout Europe, which place emphasis on participation and co-operation between people living in different countries, both in their employment and their private lives. In many cases these identify specific skills or abilities, knowledge of foreign languages, for example, which might otherwise remain hidden and unchannelled. In addition to its overall purpose, the approach by ICL and its parent group towards communication has brought to light much information of value in putting together its European human resources systems. In 1990, in addition to the communication initiatives a special management seminar will be launched to provide all managers with an understanding of the new Europe, and ICL's business strategy within it.

Human resources initiatives

Although ICL has been operating in Europe for many years, it was only in the mid-1980s that the potential of the Single Market was fully recognised.

A major issue has been to recognise the differences between operations in 12 different European countries (not all within the EC) all with their own local infrastructures; and at the same time build an overall ICL Europe business culture. The European personnel function has therefore had a delicate task in defining the extent of its responsibility within this framework.

Building a European corporate culture

Broadly speaking, ICL has tried to strike a balance between the *laissez-faire* approach towards European subsidiaries typical of UK companies, and the much more hands-on approach adopted by many US conglomerates. The relationship between European headquarters and subsidiary operations is however being strengthened by eliminating intermediate infrastructures in order to gain greater cross-border benefits.

ICL's European communication programme has been of great benefit in this context. A number of other significant initiatives have been taken, however:

- A recognition of common language blocs (Nordic countries, Benelux, Germany, Southern Europe) has emerged, which is being developed to corporate benefit. Within each bloc a 'lead' country is appointed to co-ordinate activities, share cross-border expertise and break down cultural barriers within the bloc.

- ICL's corporate values handbook, 'The ICL Way' has been relaunched in all languages, to refocus on key messages. This is regarded as 'an anchor on which to benchmark future initiatives'.

- The company-wide Quality programme reaches all employees, material being available in all languages. In 1989 the company's Management Handbook, *Investing in People*, which describes ICL's major people management processes was launched, and is being applied in a consistent way across all countries for the first time. Included are objective-setting, appraisal systems, people development programmes, recruitment and selection and manpower planning. Supporting material is again being published in all languages. The company's intention to develop a common philosophy of "Managing For Performance" in all operations is a key issue here.

- Although English will continue to be recognised as the official business language of the company, the ability to operate in other languages will be increasingly valued as an important skill.

- An opinion survey is used regularly with all staff throughout Europe, to assess the understanding and feelings of staff on both their own operation and the wider European scene.

Remuneration and benefits

Regarding pay levels, ICL's policy is to establish a common approach across European operations as far as possible, while recognising that considerable variations in levels exist between different locations. A very close watch is kept on pay movements in relevant fields throughout Europe, both by professional staff within the personnel function who carry out individual research and participate in sectoral 'salary clubs', and by subscription to a number of specialist surveys and databases. A major objective is to establish a common grading system across Europe, for technical and specialist staff as well as managers. A common policy already exists regarding executive bonus plans and share option schemes, but ICL would like to extend employee financial participation further throughout Europe, while recognising the considerable difficulties that exist in introducing schemes to some European countries.

Resourcing and development

This is a major area of personnel activity. ICL has implemented a number of systems both to recruit new and develop existing staff for a European future.

European base management programmes

A major initiative has been the development of common European base management training programmes. These involve bringing staff from across Europe to be trained together on courses, thus reinforcing both vocational commonality and the development of contacts throughout the organisation. This is a deliberate policy: a common training methodology is applied, in areas such as sales and servicing, to all staff trained, ensuring common standards and procedures throughout Europe.

Eurograduate programme

ICL's Eurograduate Programme is seen as of fundamental importance to the development of a pan-European corporate culture. It is recognised that young people coming into employment for the first time are the most highly motivated towards Europe, and that the first contacts they make within the company will be the longest lasting. Selected European graduates are therefore brought to the UK for ten months' intensive training, during which time they will meet both peers from other parts of Europe and managerial/professional staff within their chosen function. This training is funded centrally, and therefore does not affect local training budgets.

Advertising for recruits to the Eurograduate Programme takes place in several different countries, a measure of its success is the number of applicants who come forward, for example over 200 in both Spain and Portugal during 1989. All recruits are fluent in English, and are put through a programme of induction and technical/specialist training alongside UK graduates. They also attend a 'Welcome to Britain and Cultural Awareness Workshop' run by Employment Conditions Abroad, in which they learn about social and working life in Britain, compare this with life in their home country and discuss problems encountered. Their progress is monitored by the line manager in the home country in liaison with the line manager in the UK; they are set work-related objectives and are formally appraised on completion of their assignment. At the end of the period graduates are sent back to their home countries, having undergone extensive technical training and, most important, having established a wide range of contacts throughout the organisation.

ICL's approach towards European graduates is clearly spelled out in 'Europe Sans Frontiers':

'The true Europeans of the 1990s will be those who have trained and worked with colleagues from many different countries. The winners will be those who understand the opportunities and use their imagination, energy and education to build careers on a stage that transcends national boundaries.'

Language skills, though regarded as important, are less significant attributes in new recruits than an understanding of different cultures and business practices, gained preferably by living and learning outside the home country.

The company is keen to take advantage of the EC's ERASMUS scheme to encourage students to study in countries other than their own; training being partly provided in specially selected universities and polytechnics offering courses in electronics, electrical engineering, business studies and computer studies with languages. Such students are often employed on short term 'industrial traineeships'. ICL also participates in the COMETT programme, the EC-funded scheme to encourage a network of training partnerships between industry and the academic world. The Ashton Manufacturing Operations subsidiary in Manchester has joined a consortium of institutions spanning a number of EC countries; students from countries as diverse as Eire, Italy and West Germany have been given placements of between three and ten months. The programme has proved to be a good recruiting ground for high calibre graduates, and, what is more important, is seen as a means of spreading the image, culture and name of ICL throughout Europe.

The company has for several years been recruiting MBA graduates from INSEAD to increase international representation, bringing them in to responsible positions which will utilise their MBA and their previous experience. The company is becoming increasingly dedicated to boosting the number of foreign nationals based in the UK operation; again, graduates are seen as the key to this. A target has been set that ten per cent of the graduate intake to the UK should come from Europe, many of whom may be transferred back to their home countries at a later stage during their careers. Partly driven by the well-known demographic shortages, this initiative is designed to facilitate the development of a European mobility culture and to 'Europeanise' the company's home base where the majority of product development and manufacturing takes place. Young people, graduates in particular with around two years' experience, are seen as the most freely mobile group, and, as the managers of the future, the group that will create a growing mobility culture within ICL in future years. Those with specific skills and a second language have, in particular, been identified as suitable to be sent abroad on short secondments of up to a year; although all high potential staff are likely to be considered for transfer as part of a managed European career development programme. In most cases the funding for such transfer is provided centrally, so that the budgets of individual managers regarding the extra costs involved are not penalised.

The attitude towards European transfers

In terms of the expatriate packages provided, European transfers are currently regarded as inherently no different from transfers elsewhere in the world. However, the company wants to move increasingly to a mentality that regards Europe as 'home'. Thus, although packages need to be adjusted to reflect local market rates, financial incentives should not be as important as the career development benefits. ICL keeps very close watch on pay and benefits movements throughout Europe, through survey participation and regular exchange of information with other pan-European companies. A problem identified to date is that the majority of transfers take place between the UK and the rest of Europe, rather than between other European countries; and in some locations (e.g. Southern Germany) persuading people to move at all is extremely difficult. Here too it is hoped to bring about change through the young people being recruited to ICL, who are altogether more willing and less expensive to relocate. A hopeful sign is that ICL's mobility policy is itself proving a big attraction to new graduate recruits, who wish to buy in to a mobility culture with the rewards and opportunities it can bring.

Language training

Language training for staff features prominently among the initiatives taken by ICL in responding to the Single Market. A considerable amount of encouragement, both moral and financial, is given; a policy of slow, steady tuition is adopted in all cases except where the staff member is being transferred abroad; here, there is an insistence that both the staff member and his/her spouse must learn the second language, and a more intensive programme is therefore provided. In future, it is likely that all graduate entrants will receive language training during the first 18 months as part of the induction programme.

In the main, tuition is provided by external tutors who come into ICL offices to hold classes. However, as much use as possible is made of existing staff skills, and this has led to some interesting 'self-help' developments taking place, within the company. An example is given in 'Europe Sans Frontiers' of a French-born secretary working in the UK starting up French language classes for colleagues, which have proved to be extremely successful. Not surprisingly, ICL has provided sponsorship and support for this initiative, and the staff have responded by giving up their own free time to prepare for and receive tuition. This is perhaps symptomatic of the level of interest and involvement in European affairs that ICL has managed to generate amongst its staff, since it began its 'Europe 1992 programme'!

Mergers and acquisitions strategy

ICL has effected several mergers in Europe, that with the Danish company Regnecentralen being one of the most significant. In all cases there has been the need to absorb new foreign nationals into the company with all the attendant cultural, contractual and legislative issues this involves. The acquired wisdom of the personnel function in coping with these issues has resulted in the production of a detailed Mergers and Acquisitions Handbook, which sets out all the steps that must be taken to ensure full integration in the first two years from the merger date.

Mergers and acquisitions issues can be ranged under three orders of priority:

- first, those things that have to be done legally;
- second, those things that it will be highly beneficial to combine;
- third, those things that would be desirable to change or combine, but that are not priority.

The Danish acquisition provides a useful case study of the sort of issues dealt with in this priority order. Under the first phase came such things as drawing up new contracts of employment and organisation structures, and instigating a major communication programme from top to bottom throughout the organisation. Under the second phase came the drawing up and implementing of common personnel systems in such areas as staff appraisal and bonus schemes. Items to be dealt with under the third phase have been more diverse, and the implementation programme is still continuing.

ICL's comprehensive strategy for the Single Market is worthy of study by any company extending its products or services into Europe. The programmes of staff communication and involvement, the degree of support given to staff in training for and working within a pan-European environment, provide clear examples of effective means of responding to the changes to the Single Market will bring.

Hitachi Data Systems: flexibility is the key

The business of Hitachi Data Systems (HDS) is, in the words of its president, to provide 'state of the art industry-standard mainframe computers, peripheral equipment and customer support'. It does so to customers in more than 30 countries worldwide, covering most industry sectors including aerospace, banking and manufacturing. The company's history is an interesting one; formerly a subsidiary of National Semiconductor, from the late 1970s its main business focus became the sale of mainframe Hitachi systems, big mainframes and storage devices, to corporate customers. Sold to a joint venture company owned by Hitachi (80 per cent) and EDS (20 per cent), the company became Hitachi Data Systems on 23 October 1989, with almost $900 million turnover worldwide.

In terms of structure, HDS is organised into six geographical regions: three in the USA, the other three being respectively, Europe, Canada and the Pacific Rim including Australia, the Far East and Latin America. Each region has a high degree of autonomy and is headed up by a General Manager. Regional Head Offices (in the case of Europe, based at Isleworth, Middlesex) contain functional departments such as Finance, Human Resources and Marketing, while sales and service organisations exist at country level. HDS Europe operates in 13 different countries, mostly within the EC; there are approximately 750 staff in total, mostly local nationals although an international flavour exists at Head Office, where a number of foreign nationals have been appointed who may, ultimately, move on to third or fourth countries as part of their career development.

The coming of the Single Market is not seen as having a big impact on Hitachi Data Systems, as the company has operated across Europe for many years and therefore already has well-developed policies and procedures. However, it is recognised that 1992 and beyond will be a catalyst to general change, and therefore appropriate responses to this new external environment will need to be drawn up.

Remuneration and benefits

The general approach of HDS Europe towards pay and benefits is to decentralise to local level as far as possible, while retaining central control over many of the general payment systems. In this way a high degree of flexibility is maintained, while new systems to support the overall business plan can be introduced without difficulty.

Base pay is market-driven rather than linked to salary scales; there is therefore no common job evaluation system, as formal job evaluation is seen as inappropriate to a system of reward that is related to skills shortages and market rates. Regarding both pay and benefits the policy is to stay in the upper quartile within each locality. A considerable amount of information on local trends is collected centrally through networks and surveys, particularly information relating to the specific sector within the IT industry in which HDS operates. This ensures that, when action to make adjustments becomes necessary, it can be carried out quickly and to maximum effect. Local salary budgets and headcounts are monitored centrally; some of the 'long-term' benefits such as life assurance are commonly applied, as is the company's formal staff appraisal scheme. This is benchmarked against different job levels and measurement of performance is based on key competences with each job. HDS Europe has no plans to harmonise pensions between operations in different countries. Substantial change to local practices regarding social security or retirement benefit plans is regarded as impractical until such time as harmonisation takes place across Europe at national level, and this is rightly seen as unlikely in the short term. In the meantime, HDS maintains its policy of remaining competitive locally in this item as in other aspects of total pay and benefits.

The company's executive bonus scheme, which is administered centrally and applied on a worldwide basis, is highly flexible to ensure its relevance to different managerial levels and create the right balance between local and company-wide targets. Broadly speaking, it operates at three levels:

- For jobs with a pan-European focus, the main part of the bonus payment relates to European targets with a minority related to worldwide targets.
- For a general manager of a local operation, the main part of the bonus payment relates to local targets with a minority related to pan-European targets.
- For other management jobs within a local operation, the main part of the bonus relates to key functional objectives that are common to the same job in different countries.

The key attributes of the scheme are that it is applied to a common methodology throughout HDS worldwide, and that the objectives set within it can be adjusted to reflect differing functional responsibilities or job purposes at different levels, as well as changing strategic objectives for individuals or whole regions.

Expatriate policy

In this area again, HDS Europe is highly flexible. A variety of arrangements exist; at one extreme the contract will be retained with the home country operation, at the other it will be transferred and the staff member becomes, in effect, a local national. The main determinants are how long the staff member will remain in the host country and whether or not relocation thereafter will be back to home base or to a third or fourth destination. People are moved on an assignment basis, to carry out specific projects; although the international career development opportunities to be gained clearly add value to the growth of the pan-European business.

Despite this, the company is trying to encourage staff to transfer from their home countries and believes the Single Market may be of help in this as awareness of cross-cultural career opportunity grows. The company's multinational customer base means that, already, significant numbers of staff are required to operate across national boundaries. This is particularly true of some of the product managers, service/support sales and strategic accounts staff; in some cases customers are dealt with in a cross-border way, or the product range is handled across the whole of Europe or on a 'country groupings' basis. Staff with either sales/marketing or technical skills combined with language skills are therefore at a premium.

Training and development

Considerable efforts are made to train staff and keep them motivated in their careers with Hitachi Data Systems. This is partly because the right people are hard to find, and partly because it is necessary to keep pace with rapid technological change. The focus is turning increasingly towards management as well as technical training, including, where appropriate, the acquisition of language skills.

The aim of European Human Resources is to ensure that local staff are developed as necessary for their careers and the company's needs, and that a good skills base is maintained in the different countries. The frequency of inter-country transfers is likely to increase and with the length of time spent on each assignment decreasing this will facilitate the movement of staff on a joint project/career development basis. It is also likely that more staff will be given jobs that cut across national boundaries, thus developing cultural awareness and sensitivity skills. The provision of language training is increasing, with total immersion being the most frequently used technique for those requiring to pick up skills rapidly following transfer to a different country.

Recruitment

The recruitment of local staff to fill vacancies in Europe is largely carried out at local level. Within certain parameters, it is regarded as the responsibility of line managers/personnel officers to select and appoint the right calibre of entrant.

However, European Human Resources is responsible for the co-ordination of recruitment activity. A European head count plan is administered centrally, staff numbers being allocated to the operations in different countries according to business need. European Human Resources also acts in a consultancy role to the local operations; specifically, a number of services are provided:

- connecting local operations with internal candidates in other countries who are suitable for transfer, when opportunities exist;
- providing specialist support where necessary (e.g. in the many European operations where no local personnel function exists) using local norms;
- developing a corporate recruitment advertising style to be used by the company across the whole of Europe;
- setting the standards across Europe for the kind of recruits sought, according to defined competences for benchmark jobs. These standards in terms of skill and career development potential are regarded as generic rather than dependent on local cultural norms, particularly for some technical jobs such as technical marketing specialists. It is important that local operations understand this, and therefore seek out and appoint candidates who match the company's overall requirements.

For some more senior or highly specialised positions, HDS call upon the services of international search and selection consultancies to make the appointment. This is particularly true when seeking European nationals to take up positions in the UK. It is regarded as particularly important to deal with consultancies that have subsidiaries rather than just affiliates in different European countries, as the former are more capable of carrying out an effective Europe-wide search campaign, and are aware of the problems and complexities of relocating foreign nationals.

Internal communication

The nature of the central Human Resources function, in particular its role of a co-ordinating/monitoring/consultancy service-provider to local operations, means that regular and effective communication with those operations is imperative. Fortunately, as an advanced IT company, HDS has unlimited computer time available for its internal departments and has its own highly sophisticated electronic mail systems and other electronic communications devices. Some of these devices can also be built in to customer packages to ensure continued communication following sale and installation.

Other means of communication include standard systems such as fax, telex and telephone; all systems are suitable for open communication in English, which is the standard company language. For more personal, private or location-specific information, translation is required. Senior staff spend a lot of time travelling throughout Europe in order to ensure face to face communication with managers in subsidiaries. The company adopts a cascade process for the passing on of information generally, and therefore verbal information is as important as written. Senior managers in European countries are brought together for a two-day management meeting every month (usually held in London) to discuss topical developments and ideas, as well as review recent business performance.

Hitachi Data Systems provides a good example of a smaller company operating throughout Europe that has devised a highly flexible approach to the running of its local operations. In terms of overall management style, HDS is not a 'process-driven' company; a deliberate policy has been adopted to limit bureaucracy to minimum level. An important spin-off from this for the European Human Resources function is that high quality recruits are often attracted to join HDS from bigger rivals that have more structured, inflexible operating styles.

The job of Director of Human Resources, Europe was described to me by the present job holder, Derek Manuel, as being a 'cultural filter' – assessing what will work on a pan-European scale, and what must be left to local level. The cultural complexity of Europe, compared with many other overseas locations, is regarded as a major challenge in the job; it is clearly vital to achieve the right balance between local autonomy and central support concerning human resources issues if the company is to develop its European market to its full potential.

12 The response in practice: NatWest Group, Stephenson Harwood, and a leisure services company

The organisations I have chosen as case studies in this chapter all operate in what may loosely be described as the service sector, although the differences between the kind of services they offer are, quite clearly, very wide indeed. In one way or another they are all focusing attention on the European Market, having identified opportunities which will be accelerated by the Single Market Programme.

Overall, their approach is different in nature from that of manufacturing companies, or the IT companies I reviewed in the previous chapter. This is due to the nature of their markets; services offered frequently need to be tailored to the demands of specific local or national markets, and there is limited scope for standardisation to the extent that is frequently possible in the manufacturing sector. As a result there is greater reliance on local specialist staff rather than expatriate internationalists, and the degree of autonomy afforded to operations in different European countries is, correspondingly, greater.

NatWest Group: careful assessment of business needs

The NatWest Group employs some 113,000 staff throughout its financial services operations, of whom just 17,000 are based outside the UK. Most of these staff work in subsidiary operations; in addition to a major operation in the USA, NatWest has units in France, West Germany, Spain, Switzerland, Greece and Belgium as well as stakes in Dutch and Italian banks. There is therefore a European network which enables provision of services to local markets to take place, according to circumstances, either through the national unit or direct from the UK. The Group is continually looking for suitable market openings, and it is likely therefore that the network will be developed further during the 1990s. NatWest's approach to European business strategy has two main characteristics: first, the recognition that as a retail service industry rigidly-controlled central policies would be inappropriate, as there are wide differences between the markets for financial services in the different states; and second, the predominant goals of the organisation are to maximise shareholder value and to provide the highest quality of customer service.

Languages and language training

The vast majority of NatWest staff employed in Europe are local nationals (in Spain, for example, there are only nine UK expatriates in an operation employing 1,450 staff) and this is likely to continue as local staff are the most capable of understanding the complexities of market preferences and business practices. English is recognised as the international business language of the group, but although many overseas employees have some command of English the value of this to the organisation has not yet been fully assessed. Business transactions invariably take place in the local language between people of the same nationality, but it is being increasingly believed that for many transactions and for Group conferences there may be benefits in having more staff who speak fluent English. The provision of English language training for foreign staff is, therefore, being given consideration.

NatWest's general approach towards language training is business-driven, with an insistence that there has to be a clear need of a second language for an employee before training is provided. Otherwise, it is felt that motivation will be low and the opportunity to practice and become truly fluent limited. The policy regarding language training is being kept under continuous review, particularly with regard to the strategies of other organisations operating in Europe and the need to create a pan-European management cadre.

European graduate recruitment

NatWest has recently begun a European graduate recruitment campaign, co-ordinated jointly between the UK Group Head Office and local subsidiaries. Programmes have so far taken place in France and West Germany; the role of Head Office being to provide specialist graduate recruitment experience and advice, while the subsidiary operation has the knowledge required of local recruitment norms and standards to apply this in practice. Graduates are taken on to work in the home country, although it is understood that they may be sent to the UK or to other countries at points in their careers. The recruitment of European graduates to fill vacancies in the UK is also now starting to take place, and is seen as both a means of meeting the shortfall in numbers of good language graduates coming through our education system, and of beginning the process of 'internationalising' the UK staff. Here, the recruitment process is carried out by Head Office, although the local organisations provide a vital co-ordinating role in identifying suitable sources of supply and establishing liaison.

For both categories of recruit, is is recognised that it is important to offer new staff attractive career opportunity including transfers between operations in different countries. This is seen as particularly vital for those employed initially in their home countries, who might otherwise become too established in the practices and procedures of the subsidiary. International career opportunity is seen as developing a broader approach, and has proved to be a major attractant to high-calibre, well-motivated graduate recruits.

Mobility policy and packages

NatWest tends to have about 200 staff on transfer from the UK to other countries at any one time, mostly to carry out specific work tasks although there is an important element of career development in expatriations. Expatriates usually return to the UK on completion of the period of service abroad.

Being relatively late starters in the international mobility field, NatWest has been able to identify and apply current best practices in order to provide highly-competitive packages to staff transferred abroad. The guiding principle is maintenance of home country standard of living in all cases; basic terms and conditions of employment therefore remain unchanged, but various allowances are added to reflect any differences in cost of living. The same standards are applied to 'inpatriates' – i.e. foreign nationals transferred into the UK for periods of service. Details of the packages offered include assistance with property letting (staff are encouraged to maintain their original homes rather than sell and buy), and financial assistance for travel home and boarding or other school fees.

Personnel management of subsidiaries

A broad overview is maintained of individual subsidiaries' personnel systems within the NatWest Group; this is as true for units within the UK as in Europe or elsewhere. Most subsidiaries look after their own pay and conditions, and neither job evaluation nor appraisal systems are harmonised, but Group Personnel tends to provide a consultancy service to subsidiary operations. All this is a reflection of the differences that exist culturally and in a business sense; it simply would not be appropriate to adopt a blanket approach to a variety of businesses that operate to good effect in their own individual markets. An executive profit share scheme is however controlled centrally, underlining the emphasis NatWest is beginning to place on its senior managers working together as a team.

Views concerning the Social Charter

The European Commission's Social Charter has not as yet been a big issue for NatWest, as is indeed the case for most UK employers. Nevertheless, its progress through various European Summit Meetings has been watched closely. NatWest has had some experience of employee participation in its French and German subsidiaries, and has not found this difficult to cope with. There is a general belief however that communication should be a natural, two-way process rather than an imposition, if it is to be of relevance to employees at all levels.

This case study of the NatWest Group presents a clear example of a service sector organisation that, for sound business reasons, does not wish to interfere too closely with the ways of doing things of its units in the various European countries. However, it is recognised that at senior level there is a need for a cadre of managers who are sensitive to different business and cultural norms and can understand the markets of the different subsidiaries. The European graduate recruitment programme and other steps being taken are a recognition that the strategy for the business as a whole will need to have an increasingly international focus.

Stephenson Harwood: developing a European network

Stephenson Harwood is a medium-sized legal firm based in London, with approximately 60 partners and employing about 430 staff. It is a 'full service' practice providing advice in all areas of legal services, particularly banking, IT, property and general corporate law. The firm's mission is to continue to provide a high-quality service to all clients, and expand the business without merger.

The firm has developed a three-year strategy towards diversification into Europe. By the end of 1992, the intention is to have forged close associations with like-minded legal practices in each of the 12 Member States, one in each initially although perhaps extending the network further in the future to cover several firms in some countries. This route into Europe has been chosen by the firm in preference to setting up its own offices, as it presents the better opportunity to provide a full legal service from the outset to clients in different countries. It is recognised that the provision of a genuinely international service would take many years to build up if it were being developed in-house. Stage One of the European strategy has been to identify suitable European firms, and work with them to establish good mutual understanding and joint-venture relationships.

Exchanges of professional staff

Exchanges of personnel between these firms is seen as an important and cost-effective way of developing both cultural awareness among staff, and an understanding of the business structures of legal practices in different countries which will in time become joint venture partners. Stephenson Harwood has recently taken professional staff from countries as diverse as Italy and Belgium on three to six months secondments, and sees benefits from this arising for the secondee, the host country practice and the home country practice alike. Not only is considerable technical knowledge gained by the secondee, but the staff in the host-country practice gain an insight into his/her cultural norms, and the way the legal profession works in the home country. Most secondees are young, fairly newly qualified lawyers, and there is little doubt that they are thoroughly debriefed by their partners on return to normal duties!

A steady number of applications for secondment are reviewed by Stephenson Harwood from young foreign lawyers with no direct connections with associated firms. Although these are given lower priority, they are still considered on merits and in some cases applicants are taken on, again for periods of up to six months. The informal contacts to be developed between young lawyers of different nationalities, as well as the cultural awareness to be gained by staff of all levels – many of whom are not foreign-minded – are seen as the main benefits.

In addition to taking staff from associated European Firms, Stephenson Harwood sends selected young professional staff of its own abroad as part of the exchange programme. At present, for example, two lawyers are on secondment in Madrid, and a third in Milan. The selection of candidates for such postings is carried out carefully; some language ability is required, but just as important are the qualities of diligence and presentation which, allied to sound technical skills, will make the candidate a good ambassador for the firm whilst on secondment and a valuable source of information on return. Regular contact is maintained with secondees while they are abroad, to ensure they have settled down in their new surroundings and help with any domestic problems encountered. Six months is seen as the minimum period required for a worthwhile degree of familiarity with the ways of the foreign practice to be gained.

Stephenson Harwood is an active supporter of the European Law Students' Association (ELSA), whose activities I described in Chapter 9. Financial support is given towards organised events and young lawyers employed by the firm are encouraged to participate in its conferences and seminars.

Language training

Language training within Stephenson Harwood began with the provision of relatively intensive courses only to staff singled out for foreign secondment. Such training continues for those being transferred abroad, weekly tuition on a one-to-one basis prior to departure being the preferred method. This is clearly essential, as it is unlikely that English will be spoken by any foreign nationals in their own workplace.

This approach to language training is changing, however, due to the degrees of interest that has been shown by staff of all levels in acquiring skills. The provision of courses to those not being transferred abroad is now seen as a cost-effective way of building on awareness of different cultures, which will become increasingly important as the business of legal services becomes more international in flavour. It is also seen as increasing job satisfaction, given the high proportion of staff who have expressed an interest.

Initial courses have been in French, and are provided by the Institut Français, which carries out a lot of language training in the City. Although so far aimed solely at lawyers, it is likely that the course programme will be extended to cover support staff as well at some time in the future. Features of the current programme are:

- tuition is carried out at the workplace by qualified, native French speakers, once a week between 8.00 a.m. and 10.00 a.m. A certain amount of homework is also required. The time commitment is therefore split almost equally between the firm and course participants;
- each series of courses lasts ten weeks;
- the costs are met in full by Stephenson Harwood;
- the course material covers details of the French economy and civil law system as well as basic language training.

The intention is to provide no more than fairly basic skills and knowledge, but it is hoped that some course participants many develop a greater interest and be encouraged to take things further. Such staff may indeed be looked upon in future to build up inter-firm contacts and client relationships in France, and many therefore be put through a more intensive and work-specific programme by Stephenson Harwood.

A possible future development is the provision of similar training in German, the Goethe Institute having been identified as a potential course provider. German is particularly favoured because of the big investment opportunities being opened up in Eastern Europe. Other European languages such as Italian, Spanish and Greek are regarded as of secondary importance, and training in these will almost certainly be limited to secondees who will spend periods of service in these countries.

The human resources initiatives being taken by Stephenson Harwood regarding Europe are highly specific and clearly reflect the firm's perception of its future position in the market for legal services. Stephenson Harwood provides a good example of the sort of issues that may become important to smaller sized organisations diversifying within Europe and the ways in which these can be addressed.

A leisure services company: local markets in a pan-European business

This company has operations in countries throughout Europe; many of these are very small sales outlets only, and the main EC Market States are seen as the core to European Business. Having been in Europe for a long time, the company believes it has a big advantage over other companies that are setting up operations for the first time; however it is recognised that there has been some complacency in the past, and that best advantage has not always been made of acquired skills and experience.

More recently the company has adopted a highly-commercial consumer service approach to its business, which means on the one hand that costs are closely examined and on the other hand that more market-driven attitudes exist throughout the company. It is anticipated that the Single Market Programme will have a considerable impact on the business, and at top level a determination exists to make use of this and turn it into competitive advantage over market rivals in the UK and elsewhere in Europe that have been slower to respond to change. In order to take best advantage of changing market conditions, the company has recently established a European Task Force to examine strengths, weaknesses, threats and opportunities. The focus is very much on marketing and technical issues, and there is no direct human resources input; however several of the new initiatives likely to result have substantial human resources implications. For example, changing sales techniques and styles will require that sales forces undergo considerable training in new areas; in other respects new staff with different skills and attitudes will be needed. The central personnel function is aware of all this, and is beginning to take steps to ensure its voice is heard and appropriate measures are implemented at the earliest opportunity. This is particularly important as outlets in most European countries are small, carry out purely sales/customer service functions and have no professional personnel resources of their own.

Differing staff profiles

The company categorises its European staff either as career expatriates or local nationals. For each category the employment pressures and priorities are different, necessitating their being treated in rather different ways.

Career expatriates, relatively small in number, are mostly-British nationals transferred to a different European country for a relatively short period of time in the interests of their own career development. Some difficulties are experienced in finding staff of the right calibre for such assignments, and in reintegrating them back into the UK organisation on completion of the period of foreign service. To some extent, these are factors of the cultural complexity of the European marketplace. Whereas in the past, African or Asian expatriates were seen by UK employers as an elite group, it is being found that their skills are not so transferable to Europe, where considerably more appreciation of the details of cultural norms and business practices is required. It is the European expatriates who are now becoming the foreign service elite, making it more difficult to transfer new staff into the tight-knit circle of those who have already gained pan-European experience.

Also in this category is a small group of mainland Europeans employed in European countries other than their own or the UK, usually to carry out some specific management or professional task in conjunction with career development. Resistance from local nationals is often a problem encountered, experience having shown that local staff find it easier to accept a British manager employed by a UK company than one from a third European country. Remuneration packages for third-country nationals can cause additional difficulties, particularly regarding taxation and pension provision, which are compounded as many third-country nationals will move on to fourth or fifth countries during the course of their careers with the company.

Local nationals, mostly grouped into fairly small working units, make up the bulk of the European workforce. Such staff are employed on local contracts and receive levels of pay and benefits that reflect those of the local economy; as market rates are maintained competitively, recruitment has never been a major problem. Retention is however seen as a growing problem, as more and more international companies move in to different local markets to compete directly for high-calibre staff. There is a particular demand for well-trained, English-speaking professional staff who are familiar with British management styles and practices; the high level of customer service training given to staff employed throughout Europe makes them attractive targets for companies such as Disneyland for its new venture outside Paris, or USSR companies undertaking joint-venture projects with the UK Government.

Human resources solutions

Historically, the approach to European human resources management has been limited to day-to-day issues, but this is changing rapidly as the company's commitment to Europe increases. Now, with a growing number and diversity of staff in many different locations and realignment of the European market taking place, even the most straightforward of issues may have strategic implications.

Recruitment, for example, has become a much more complex and challenging task in recent years. The need for regular communication between different European operations allied to the cultural subtleties within different countries means that a much more co-ordinated approach has become necessary; it is important to select the right people on the basis of their ability to accept the company's common values and to communicate with colleagues from very different backgrounds. As a result, the unit based in Luxembourg has been given special responsibility for co-ordination of a pan-European recruitment campaign, and has been allocated specialist external consultancy support to facilitate the recruitment of staff in different countries at appropriate rates of pay.

Some key features of this recruitment campaign are as follows:

- It is mainly targeted towards sales staff, although certain specialist posts in Regional Offices have been identified.
- The skills required for various jobs have been more carefully defined and established.
- An international recruitment consultancy has been appointed to carry out the selection process. Psychometric testing forms part of the selection procedure; the consultancy being used has experience of applying tests that are culture-sensitive and therefore can be used to test applicants of different nationalities.
- A separate consultancy has been appointed to carry out research into appropriate levels of pay and benefits for different jobs at different locations. As indicated above, the company's policy is to apply competitive local market rates to all jobs as far as possible. This has caused a re-examination of expatriate policy to take place; in particular the traditional practice of paying a salary supplement to European expatriates is being questioned. Arguments concerning expatriate packages that have continued for years are now being resolved, as principles are established based around the 'local market rates' philosophy.

No attempt is made to harmonise the pay and grading structures for local nationals employed in different European operations. This is a deliberate policy, as the differences between national bargaining structures are considered to be so great as to make harmonisation not worthwhile. Performance-related pay for European managers has been considered, but rejected as impractical within the current environment. Most European states, including France and West Germany, place great emphasis on collective agreements in determining pay increases, which means that profit shares or performance pay can only be allocated on an equal percentage basis. In any case, the principles and philosophies behind performance-related pay are little understood in many parts of Europe. Particular problems identified include the difficulty of keeping track with incremental pay progression across Europe (at present there is no link between local pay records systems and the central system), no effective means of dealing with poor performance, and difficulties in training local staff to manage systems to common standards. It is possible that a reappraisal of European pay policy may take place as business circumstances change in the future, and as the practice of European secondment becomes more frequent during the 1990s.

Language training is being taken increasingly seriously, and a study has been carried out to assess both language requirements and existing skills amongst staff. This is a response to a growing likelihood that, in the future, the European market will become more homogeneous requiring a higher level of contact between staff and customers in different countries.

International career development: creating a 'fast track' team

The Single Market Programme is seen above all as a catalyst to change, requiring staff to come to terms with a different culture and alternative ways of doing things. Two key questions have been raised:

- First, how to cope with the widely-differing social and business norms that prevail in the different Member States. In particular, social practices in some countries are at variance with quality or customer care standards that form a major part of staff training. The use of first names towards customers or even some colleagues, for example, would be regarded as impolite in French business society. The company must ensure that it is aware of all such variances from its declared customer service standards, and tailor training and quality programmes accordingly.

- Second, it is seen as particularly important not to build walls between different country blocs throughout Europe, or create systems and structures that are at variance with the growth of a wider market.

An early response to these questions has been to bring together lower and middle-management staff employed in different European countries for seminars and conferences, in order to discuss issues and learn about the differences and similarities between their customs and practices. From this may develop a more co-ordinated approach to culture training, built perhaps on the ground-base of high quality service standard training given to all employees. The incidence of foreign transfers or short-term secondments to different European locations is already showing an increase; young graduates in particular have been identified as a key target for career assignments abroad. Even at this level, however, problems such as spouse's career can be a considerable bar on mobility. Central personnel is trying to overcome this by offering counselling and career placement help to expatriates' spouses, and services of this nature may increase as more detailed analysis of career mobility patterns and constraints is carried out throughout the organisation. The possibility of introducing short-term European secondments of up to one month's duration for some staff is being explored as a means of developing awareness of the nature of the business in different European locations.

At more senior level, the company is anxious to develop new routes to top management for a selected group of staff, and international experience is seen as the key component of this career development programme. It is also seen as important that the 'elite group', probably of not more than 50 managers, should be drawn from all operations across Europe and not just from the UK.

Discussions have therefore taken place with all the European outlets with a view to identifying staff suitable to be considered for a fast-track programme. It is recognised that there are immense cultural problems in drawing up valid selection criteria and measurement techniques, and that the temptation to standardise to some 'base' criteria must be resisted. It is likely that assessment centres, carefully developed and applied by independent experts with experience of working in a multi-cultural environment, will form a major part of the selection process. The development programme itself will probably involve career moves to operations in different countries, spells of study at international business schools, and assessment/developmental 'events' in which participants from different countries and cultural backgrounds work together and are given feedback by professional facilitators.

Why is there seen to be a need for such a programme? There is a growing awareness that, while the local outlets will need, to some extent, to retain their individual characteristics there will be a growing need for co-ordination of the pan-European business from the top. A multinational senior executive team, fully aware of the cultural and business differences and able to operate comfortably in different environments is seen as essential, and a development programme of this nature as a more cost-effective way of developing such talent than buying it in from outside. Candidates for senior executive positions will also need to gain a broader range of experience, and this can only be accomplished by switching them into different environments and functional areas to develop their general management skills. Career moves in different countries is an ideal means of providing as much scope as possible and of creating a network of contacts between managers at senior level.

13 The response in practice: Eurotunnel and Duracell Europe

This final chapter sets out as case studies two companies that could hardly be more different in terms of industry sector, market orientation, character and stage of development. Eurotunnel is a newly-established organisation, with clearly defined timescales, targets and accountabilities. The opening of the Channel Tunnel is of critical importance to economic growth in the UK and the forging of trade and cultural links with Europe, and the progress of the Eurotunnel project is, therefore, very firmly in the public eye. Duracell is a classic example of a manufacturing company with operations and outlets in many countries, and a product that is standardised on a worldwide basis. Unlike Eurotunnel, it has a well-established market and is therefore dedicated to efficiency/quality improvement regarding production, sales, marketing and distribution of its existing branded products.

These differences will be clearly apparent in the way each company has developed its personnel strategies to support the overall business strategy for the 1990s.

Eurotunnel: towards opening in 1993

The two key tasks of Eurotunnel plc are, first, to oversee the construction of the Channel Tunnel, and then to manage it as a transport link between France and the UK from its targeted opening date in 1993. The company's development to date in successive phases reflects this changing business focus:

- The project was announced in February 1986, with the awarding of the contract to the ten construction companies which with five banks made up the initial consortium. The recruitment of staff for the embryonic project management organisation, Eurotunnel, began at the end of 1986.

- Three major hurdles were overcome in 1987; the parliamentary process confirming government support for the project in both France and the UK was completed: negotiation took place between Eurotunnel and British Rail and its French equivalent, the SNCF, who together will be joint users of 50 per cent of the capacity of the Channel Tunnel; and funds were raised for flotation. Eurotunnel became a public limited company at the end of 1987.

- In 1988, staff numbers grew from 20 to 200 as a management structure was established. Eurotunnel was formally divorced from the construction companies (organised as Trans Manche Link) and this required the establishment of new contractual relationships between the two companies.

- By the end of 1989 staff numbers were approximately 300, one third of whom were French and two thirds UK nationals. The future operational company started to take shape and key managers were recruited.

At present, the company is run jointly from offices in London and Paris; during the next few years operational sites will be established at the terminals near Folkestone and Calais, and the majority of the staff will be located there. The company's non-executive Board members are drawn from major UK and French banking and industrial enterprises while the two joint Executive Chairmen, are, respectively, French and British. There are four mainstream operational activities:

- the *Project Division*, made up by secondees as well as employees, exists to oversee the work of contractors and provide project management engineering expertise. This function will wind down considerably on completion of the Tunnel's construction;

- the *Operations Division* will operate the Tunnel from 1993. The 20 or so current staff, who work closely with contractors, will be increased to about 2,000 by 1993;

- the *Commercial and Marketing Division*, which will also grow considerably in size from about 30 to 150, by the time the Tunnel opens;

- other functions that are grouped together include Personnel, Legal, Accounts and Administration. The Personnel function is headed by a

Human Resources Director based in London, with two Personnel Managers, one in France and one in the UK, reporting in directly.

Eurotunnel makes a particularly interesting case study, partly because it is such a new company and partly because its focus is the development of links specifically between the UK and France rather than the whole of Europe. In terms of Human Resources initiatives, there is a massive task to be undertaken in planning the recruitment, training and motivation of a new workforce, with main in-take to occur in 1992. There is a need also to identify the precise differences in attitudes between French and British employees, to be responsive to these but at the same time to mould a strong and cohesive company culture. The nature of Eurotunnel's future business means that it simply cannot afford to let schism develop between those operating the link from either side of the English Channel.

At present, the staff based in Paris are all native French, engaged on French contracts and local conditions of employment. The London office is largely staffed by UK nationals, although key French employees have been seconded in on expatriate terms and conditions. As staff numbers increase, it is likely that a greater commonality will develop, and the Human Resources function clearly has a major part to play in this. Although the HR strategy is still very much at an early stage of development, it will be seen that a comprehensive set of initiatives is planned for the next two and a half years to ensure that, by 1993, the whole organisation can work together and make the business a commercial success.

Initiatives taken to date

The work carried out so far by the Human Resources function has been in direct response to the key question: 'What are the most urgent steps that must be taken to develop a strong culture for the new company?'

Language training

Effective communication is seen as of crucial importance, and as a result a large budget has been allocated to language tuition. This is mostly to develop French language skills in UK employees, although some French staff seconded to the London office have received English language training. An initial step has been to grade the necessity for different levels of fluency in different jobs, from total fluency to occasional need. Alongside this, every staff member is given a test to establish his/her degree of knowledge. From these two separate analytical exercises it is possible to identify the training need for every individual, and tailor courses accordingly.

Details of the training programme are as follows:

- tuition is given to staff in groups of five of equivalent levels of ability;
- all tuition takes place at Eurotunnel's own premises;
- about two hours training per week is given, in addition to which a certain amount of homework is required of course participants;
- the training is all externally supplied by Chantal Munro Associates, a professional language teaching company. All tutors are native French speakers.

The results of this initiative have been highly encouraging; not only do most staff want to receive training, but the practical effects have been significant. The majority of Eurotunnel staff understand both languages to conversation level, and meetings are frequently conducted on a multilingual basis.

Personnel systems

In a number of specific areas, Eurotunnel has made attempts to harmonise its personnel systems as far as possible. At one level, this is achieved simply by printing documentation – attendance sheets, or performance appraisal forms, for example – in both French and English. At a second level, however, agreements have been reached between the two Personnel Managers in Paris and London which are of direct impact on the terms and conditions applied to staff.

A good example is provided by the company's end-of-year salary review. Here, the Personnel Managers worked together to design a system which is applied on a similar basis to staff on both sides of the Channel, while recognising key differences between the two groups. The methodology behind the review is identical; therefore the same documentation is used, and the same principles are applied in determining the level of pay award. The actual allocation of pay, however, takes account of local factors, such as differences between cost of living increases between the two countries. In 1989, for instance, the budget for French-employed staff was proportionately lower than for those in the UK, due mainly to France's much lower RPI index.

A further example is the performance review and appraisal scheme. Here, identical processes are applied to both sets of staff, and the scheme documentation is issued in French and English. The scheme covers many aspects of performance and development, including achievements in current job, key attributes and competences, and career planning; a rating scale is used, and self-appraisal takes place prior to the formal annual interview. The information is used as a major determinant of performance-related pay. Overall, to have designed a common system for the two different cultures, and to have applied it successfully, represents a significant achievement towards the development of a common culture for Eurotunnel. Staff are not only evaluated in the same way, but the scheme provides a ground-base for the equitable application of training and development, career progression and merit pay systems.

Planned future initiatives

The examples given above are just the first of a series of Human Resources initiatives that Eurotunnel will take in the run-up to opening in 1993. A detailed and comprehensive agenda has been drawn up, listing all the issues that must be resolved, and taking as its guiding principle the need to develop a corporate culture for the whole organisation. In seeking to resolve the issues, the aim will be to establish commonality in practices, terms and conditions as far as is possible. It is recognised however that differences in these areas will continue to exist, and that such differences must be recognised and accepted within the framework of the personnel system as a whole.

A small project team will be assigned to investigate each issue, and report back findings, with recommendations. The issues are being dealt with in priority order, and in this systematic way will all have been addressed by 1993. The accepted solutions will be built into a comprehensive Personnel Manual, to be made available to all staff employed by Eurotunnel.

Pay and payment systems

It is projected that by 1993, average pay and benefits levels in France and the UK will be very similar, and that the scope for harmonisation is likely to be considerable. Eurotunnel already has a common grading structure with very wide salary bands, allowing jobs of similar level at the different locations to be placed in the same grade. This also allows national differences in the rates of pay progression to be recognised; in France, for example, it is common practice to provide accelerated pay increases for managers (cadres) below the age of 30, but to slow these down as the job holders become older. Eurotunnel's intention is, however, to evolve its own common methods of pay progression during the next few years, so that managers come to accept the company's own practices and standards rather than those prevailing elsewhere in the national economies.

Pensions provision is one area where Eurotunnel is seeking to draw up a common practice for all staff, which will almost certainly be based on the standard UK practice of the funded, investment-based pension scheme. Specialist consultants have been brought in to carry out detailed analysis, including costings of the 'best of both' from respectively, the French and British systems if these were applied. From this, a series of models for a company scheme will be drawn up balancing costs against different levels of benefit, leading to implementation of the preferred option.

A further specific area is company car policy. As the tax advantages of company car provision in the UK diminish, and the awarding of cars to staff at middle-management level increases in France, it is hoped that at some time in the future a middle ground will be reached, at which point cars can be provided to both French and British managers at the same grade level. The situation continues to be monitored carefully, with a view to drawing up and implementing a common policy at a suitable moment in time.

Training

Thinking on training is at a relatively early stage, as nothing substantial can be done until the bulk of the company's staff have been recruited in 1992/93. The limited amount of training being carried out at present is mostly vocational, although plans for management training and development and culture-building programmes from 1993 will be drawn up. Initial issues to be resolved are the size of the training budget, and how and where the training will be carried out.

Recruitment policy

A declared aim of Eurotunnel is 'to recruit Europeans of any nationality', particularly for management positions. Language skills are seen as important as has already been explained, but of secondary importance, as these can be taught. What is more important in new staff is cultural awareness of France, absence of chauvinism and the willingness to work with people from different cultures and backgrounds. High level management skills – particularly people management – are sought in addition to technical skills. By 1993, the aim is to have in place a multinational team of managers sharing common attitudes and views, and able to work in an environment in which reporting relationships may be blurred and the ability to take a wide perspective essential.

Recruitment methods themselves have to be developed to take account of the different business cultural norms between France and the UK. In interviewing, for example, there must be recognition of the different manager/subordinate styles that prevail in the two countries, with questioning being varied accordingly. A good understanding has to be developed of the relative qualifications and education systems of the two countries.

At this early stage in Eurotunnel's development as an organisation, much thought is being given to the complex problem of accommodating the very different French and British management styles into a common culture for the organisation. These differences become apparent in unexpected ways; for example the greater formality between manager and subordinate (or boss and secretary!) prevalent in France has thrown up some tensions that have had to be recognised and understood very rapidly. The personnel function has a key role to play in developing systems that can cope with these differences while ensuring that they do not stand in the way of the company's business objectives as it mobilises for 1993.

Duracell Europe: the management of organisational change

Duracell Europe is part of the US-owned Duracell Inc., a private, independent corporation whose business is the manufacture, sales and marketing of disposable power systems: mostly the well known 'copper and black battery cell' at the premium end of the disposable battery market. The company has one main brand name worldwide. Its business objective is to become the leading battery producer in the world; at present it comes second only to Union Carbide, though occupying the number one position in the alkaline/premium battery area.

The European subsidiary employs some 2,700 staff in a range of locations from Finland to Italy, the biggest numbers being in Belgium

(1,100) and the UK (750). The European Head Office, where 90 staff are employed, is based at Crawley, Sussex. Duracell Europe's organisation chart presents a classic example of a structure designed to meet the needs of a pan-European marketplace. A range of service functions operate on a pan-European basis; these include Personnel, Legal Services, Quality Assurance, Finance, Manufacturing and Technical Development, Marketing (including, interestingly enough, the post of Enviromental Services Manager) and Logistics/Information Systems. Separate from this are three geographical zones, each headed by managers reporting directly to the company's president. The zones, representing logical European country groupings, are respectively Northern Europe (Finland, Norway, Sweden, Denmark), a 'Western' zone comprising France, Benelux, Portugal, Spain and Switzerland, and a 'middle' zone of Austria, Germany, Italy and the Eastern bloc.

The European Management Team is a genuinely multinational group, of which several individuals have had experience of working away from their home countries. The current president, for example, is a Yugoslav and a genuine internationalist, having worked in a number of different locations and being fluent in several European languages. Although the majority of managers are 'home country nationals', there are several others instances of third country nationals in place; a West German and an American in specialist positions at Head Office, for example, while the managing director of the Italian operation is Dutch and the UK Zone MD spent five years in Scandinavia. To some extent this is a factor of Duracell's policy of promoting managers from within, and being prepared to move staff internationally in order both to develop their careers and ensure that the right people are placed in the right jobs.

Organisation change in the 1990s

In terms of business development a number of initiatives are being taken by Duracell Europe to ensure that growth continues in the 1990s. These include customer service and product quality improvement programmes, measures to improve productivity and environmental sensitivity. The environmental services manager, as indicated above, has the key task of liaising with the European Commission and individual governments of Member States, and representing Duracell on 'Europile', the European Battery Committee whose role is to agree common standards regarding environmental and related issues. Increased regionalisation is also likely to take place during the 1990s, in order to reduce unnecessary costs and administrative procedures. Two particular issues are of significance to this:

- First, pricing policy: at present some output is sold to wholesalers who sell on in different marketplaces throughout Europe, sometimes at prices that undercut Duracell's own for the product. This is a problem associated with worldwide branding; a product manufactured in Germany will be instantly recognisable on UK retailers' shelves, even though the words on the packaging may be in German. Various solutions are being considered, which include the levelling out of prices across Europe.

- Second, warehousing and distribution: as aspects of the Single Market Programme take hold, it will be more economic to have regional distribution centres supplying perhaps three or four countries each rather than having distribution centres in all 14 European locations. The relaxation of intra-European border controls may, in particular, facilitate moves in this direction.

Though neither of these issues is directly personnel-related, there will be considerable implications for Duracell's overall personnel strategy. In particular, the organisational profile of the company will need to be examined, as well as the degree to which it is to be regarded either as a collection of individual operating units each with its own cultural flavour, or as a cohesive organisation. The management of culture change is something that the European personnel department is familiar with, having been through restructuring in the past including the selling off or closure of several manufacturing sites. A particular concern with regard to future change is to retain management and staff flexibility. Some senior managers will become the MDs of purely sales and marketing operations as distribution centres are shut down, requiring them to think and act differently than in the past. Duracell is keen to retain such managers and ensure that they are properly trained and motivated to cope with the changing business focus.

Human resources initiatives

The human resources strategy of Duracell Europe provides a clear example of how the personnel function can support an organisation's developing business strategy. This will be apparent in several of the individual areas of activity.

Career planning, training and development

In the past, a lot of work has been done in these areas on an informal basis. This is a reflection of the way in which roles on the European Management Team have grown organically, as the business has developed and staff have transferred to different parts of the organisation to carry out specific duties. A main concern for the future is to formalise the career development and training processes, to ensure consistency across the whole European operation.

Management training is a good example of this changing perspective. While a lot of training continues to be given at local level, central programmes are being established which will provide consistent delivery to staff of different nationalities and employed at different locations. Initial programmes are likely to focus on decision-making skills. Other training given in this area is a straight derivative of business issues, for example customer care, quality and technology. Management information systems training takes up a major part of the overall budget, and is clearly seen as of key importance in an organisation with a network of operations across the whole of Europe.

Cultural awareness training is a further area recognised to be of growing importance. A difficulty here however is that, although at senior and middle management levels linguistic ability is high, below these levels it is relatively limited. The provision of culture sensitivity programmes to all levels is therefore hampered, and will remain so until knowledge of foreign languages – particularly English – becomes more widespread.

The corollary of this is that there is an increasing interest in language training. Duracell first introduced courses in 1989, concentrating on those staff who need to speak foreign languages in carrying out their work. Four separate programmes are available, three at different levels in French and one in Italian; the courses last six months and are in 15-module blocs. Fully funded by Duracell, tuition time is split 50:50 between worktime and the participants' own, with additional homework being required. It is hoped to build on this initial training programme by launching language circles in which those who have undergone tuition build on their existing skills.

Careful investigation took place into the suitability of different language training providers before a selection was made. The language department of a local technical college was the eventual choice, partly because it is local but also due to its up to date facilities including a fully equipped language laboratory, and the commitment given by the Head of Languages who has supplied good, native-speaking tutors for courses.

Technical, vocational and other training within Duracell frequently takes place on a pan-European basis. Examples of courses include:

- Induction/company familiarity training. Here, groups of newly-appointed staff from across Europe are brought to Head Office and are put through a programme which includes learning about the roles of specific functions and of Head Office as a whole, and allows them to share experiences. The programme has proved to be popular with the European subsidiaries, building as it does both company knowledge and a network of contacts throughout the organisation. Courses are run every six months, so that over time a steady build-up in acquired knowledge will take place as more and more new staff are put through the programme. They are also tailored towards staff in specific functions, the format being different for staff from, for example, finance or marketing, who are brought together for different programmes as pan-European functional groups.

- A 'battery technology' course is being designed for European sales and marketing staff in subsidiaries. These are to give such staff a technical sales edge, in addition to developing problem-solving and decision-making skills.

- A cash management training course for subsidiary finance managers. Again conducted on a Europe-wide basis, a major objective is to instruct participants in the ways they can contribute to improving cash flow.

- A course aimed at training staff across Europe in how to use the company's performance appraisal system.

The range and variety of these courses demonstrates quite clearly the extent to which Duracell is keen to achieve common thinking in staff across all its European operations, develop teamworking and, above all, ensure that individuals are aware of the business objectives of the company during the 1990s.

Communication

This is an area in which effective pan-European systems are being developed rapidly by Head Office Personnel, to supplement the local systems that are in place within subsidiaries. Again, this is seen as essential to build corporate unity, understanding of business objectives and European networks. A major initiative has been the issue in 1990 of the company's first Employee Report, to all staff throughout Europe.

Recruitment and retention of staff

There is a growing perception that, as a mobility culture develops across Europe and as more companies set up international management groups, the recruitment and retention of staff will become more difficult. This is particularly so in countries such as the UK, Holland and Ireland where, due in part to the practice of leaving home to attend university, mobility patterns are established at an early age. One response to this problem being taken up by Duracell is to use its European network as much as possible to advertise and fill vacancies.

Salaries and benefits

Flexibility is the key word here. Duracell aims to remain competitive in its total remuneration package, and sees this as of growing importance as a mixing of cultures and closer comparisons between practices in different countries takes place. Salary levels throughout Europe are monitored carefully through a combination of 'salary clubs' and surveys; Duracell has increased its level of participation in pan-European surveys, and recognises that it is never possible to have too much information on salaries and benefits.

   The extent to which a balance is maintained between central control and local flexibility is clearly illustrated by looking at, respectively, the grading/salary structure and the company's appraisal system:

- A common grading structure is applied throughout the European subsidiaries and Head Office functions. Based on whole job ranking rather than any more intricate method of evaluation, this ensures that jobs can be defined broadly enough to be compared with others of similar level in different operating environments. Regarding salaries, these are determined largely by local market forces, and different salary scales therefore apply in different subsidiaries. However, salary levels throughout the organisation are monitored at Head Office, usually on the basis of proposals submitted by the different subsidiaries. All salaries are based on performance-related pay and those paid to the 'top third' of the organisation are more closely controlled centrally.

- An appraisal system for Duracell Europe was introduced to the UK in 1987, and to the rest of Europe from 1988. This was developed at Head Office to be an integral part of the overall salary system, particularly the link with performance-related pay; two separate schemes exist for, respectively, managerial/professional and non-managerial staff. Most subsidiaries have adopted it without amendment, although in some cases some modification has been required to fit local circumstances, for example in Belgium where the two schemes for the different levels have, effectively, been combined. As with the grading and salary structure, the system is monitored centrally although subsidiaries are largely left to apply and administer it within their own operations.

Benefits allocation to reflect both company policy and local market norms is a difficult area, due to the limited amount of data available. The company strives to maintain appropriate practices, however, by keeping in touch both with compensation and benefits consultants in different countries, and with managers of subsidiaries. It is frequently the case that the latter approach Head Office Personnel for advice on specific issues, particularly concerning tax efficiency and benefits packages. This has reinforced the internal consultancy and monitoring role that has evolved for Head Office Personnel.

The overall policy, therefore, is to stay competitive in the local market, and take advantage of any tax concessions that may be allowable in the national economy. The provision of company cars more widely throughout Europe has, for example, been investigated, and though for the time being the fiscal burdens in most countries continue to be punishing, it is believed that convergency in tax treatment may occur during the 1990s. Profit sharing is another option that has been investigated and turned down, although the top 70/80 managers in Europe do participate in a form of stock option plan.

Duracell's policy regarding international transfers is to treat staff either as expatriates based on home country terms and conditions in cases when the transfer is to carry out a specific job function, or as 'career transfers' with the remuneration package being based on local market norms. Most staff return to the home country on completion of periods abroad typically of three to four years' duration. A particular problem is finding suitable career opportunities for such staff on return; a significant number of staff leave simply because there are an insufficient number of challenging positions for them to fill.

Reorganisation

Duracell Europe has some considerable experience in this area, having closed plants in Germany and the UK, and sold others in Italy and Greece. The human resources issues associated with this were, in all cases, dealt with at local level, with referral to Head Office at each stage. Three main lessons are to be learned from the process handling:

- Although trade union resistance to closures has the potential to be a major issue, good communications and a fair and reasonable redundancy policy including outplacement consultancy has ensured a satisfactory conclusion under difficult circumstances. There is little evidence that unions are prepared to get together to form a European power-base.

- Good forward planning has been a major factor to the success of each exercise. This has included an outward-looking PR stance, good communications at all times, and, as indicated above, good severance packages and the use of out-placement consultants.

- Decentralisation of the process to local level has also been a major success factor. Consultation with staff and unions to explain the reasons for the changes has been particularly well-received, for example in the case of the West Germany closure, Works Council members were brought to the UK in order to be given a detailed rationale. The open, participative management style of Duracell Europe has, in general, succeeded in creating a receptive atmosphere.

Duracell Europe is an example of a company that has adopted a balanced approach towards the management of European subsidiaries, providing direction and support from Head Office where this is appropriate, but not interfering too closely with the day-to-day running of local operations. This, allied with the company's open management style, has ensured that the ongoing process of change can be dealt with smoothly and in such a way as not to interfere with the delivery of business objectives.

Index

New Work Patterns

Putting Policy Into Practice

Patricia Leighton
Reader in Law, The Anglia Higher Education College and currently Visiting Research Fellow, Institute of Manpower Studies &
Michel Syrett
Director of the Price Waterhouse/Cranfield Project, an international centre conducting research into European employment policy and practice.

An essential book for personnel and senior managers due to the growth in part-time, temporary, contract, agency, freelance and job-sharing working practices. 'Flexible' workers now account for between one third and one half of the total UK workforce. In the first section of the book, the authors quesion the current use of the new flexible workforce in organisations. They argue that in the future such staff should and can be used not only on the periphery of an organisation but, with the correct management, in the core activities of the business.
Building on their experience in both the private and the public sectors, the authors go on to provide the manager with a practical handbook on how to implement such a policy, with case studies, model contracts and documentation and clear guidance on the legal implications of each category of worker. This bcok challenges many of the current assumptions surrounding the employment of 'flexible' workers and offers organisations the opportunity to introduce a more flexible approach to their staffing decisions.

Contents:
New work patterns: concept and reality/Assessing employment needs/Preparing for different work patterns/Redeployment and recruitment: the management of change/Employment law and work contracts/Management and development/Pay, pensions, and benefits/The work environment/Industrial relations/Disputes and termination of contracts/Appendix/Index.

'This book serves as a healthy reminder to us all of the scope of our responsibilities to both the individuals and the organisations we serve' — *Personnel Management*

1989   256 pp   Cased   0 273 02864 2

Corporate Personnel Management

Bryan Livy, IPM Course Tutor at the City University Business School, London.
Contributions by
Greville Janner QC, Len Peach, Paul Roots, Baroness Seear

This major text discusses the corporate functions and principles of personnel management. It elaborates on the 'what?', 'how?' and 'why?' of the subject so that the reader may understand general principles and apply the exemplary applications in the book to real situations.

The authors, viewing personnel managers as professional members of the management team, suggest that they occupy a mediative role between employers and employees in managing human resources. For this reason they draw, when necessary, on other disciplines such as behavioural science and industrial relations that affect workers in organisations.

' . . . . very readable, ... a great deal of good advice and practical value - useful addition to the practitioner's bookshelf.' – Personnel Management

Readership:
Corporate Personnel Management is intended for personnel specialists, whether practitioners or students. The material may be used for courses leading to the IPM qualifications. It will be crucial to students on BA Business Studies, DMS, MSc and MBA programmes.

1988 496 pp Paper 0 273 01950 3

M & E Handbook

Human Resources Management *6th edition*

H T Graham, formerly Principal Lecturer in Personnel Management, Croydon College
Revised by **R Bennett**, Management Consultant and part-time Lecturer in Management Studies at London polytechnics

Now in its sixth edition, **Human Resources Management** retains its very popular appeal as an introduction to personnel management for business studies students.
The structure of the previous edition is maintained, while sections of the book dealing with current employment legislation, computerisation, leadership, stress management and creativity, to name only a few areas, have been amended or added. A selection of recent questions from the main examining bodies consolidates the book's position as the most up to date and accessible text for human resources management for students and lecturers alike.

1989 352 pp Paper 0 7121 0833 5

Selection and Assessment:

A New Appraisal

Mike Smith
Senior Lecturer in Industrial Psychology, School of Management, UMIST
Mike Gregg,
Director of Occupational Psychologists, Craig, Gregg, Russell Ltd &
Dick Andrews,
Group Personnel Manager for Dixons

This book reviews new developments in the theory and practice of selection and assessment of personnel. New techniques and trends such as self-assessment and the use of assessment centres are examined in detail as well as approaches to traditional methods such as interviews. Advice on how to avoid the pitfalls and maximise the opportunities of selection is given in the last part of this book. Practical examples and cases are featured throughout.

Contents:
New horizons in selection and assessment/ Recent strides in analysing jobs and attracting candidates/Criteria for selection/ New light on an old friend: the interview/Newer methods in selection and assessment: Biodata, assessment centres and development centres/Recent advances in psychometric testing/More controversial methods: graphology, astrology, lie detectors etc/Bias in selection/ Calculating the cash benefits of selection/Issues from a practitioner's standpoint/ Deselection and outplacement.

'A useful guide for personnel managers and students.' Personnel Today

1989 160 pp Paper 0 273 03114 7

Managing Employee Absence for a Competitive Edge

Andrzej Huczynski,
Senior Lecturer, Management Studies, Glasgow University &
Michael Fitzpatrick,
Senior Financial Manager, major multinational manufacturing company

Millions of pounds are lost in industry and commerce each year through employee absence. The cost includes not only sick pay and overtime expenses but additional, consequential costs such as unnecessarily high manning levels, lost production and orders, disruptions and shutdown of sections and low morale among company employees. Clearly, understanding, controlling and reducing absence offers major opportunities to improve productivity, quality and service. This book is designed as a starting point for all managers keen to increase profits by effetive control of employee absence.

Drawing on international research, statistics and case studies, the authors begin by defining absence and uncovering the multitude of problems it creates. Next, the book addresses the diverse causes of absence and shows how managers can isolate absence problems in their own companies and develop an effective control programme. At each stage practical checklists and management review questions help managers identify and correct weaknesses in their own personnel practices. The final chapter demonstrates how the systematic approaches to absence that the book recommends have been implemented successfully in a large manufacturing company.

'*The approach is very clearly presented, and will help managers wanting a thorough way of taking the issue.*' – *Personnel Management*

1989 288 pp Paper 0 273 02850 2

Managing Employee Absence for a Competitive Edge